"The respectful tone in this book is as important as its brilliant contents. Because when you take knowledge and add humility, you get wisdom. And then when you take such wisdom and add it to compassion, you get love. And such love is at the heart of life . . . God is love. And so, I hope many will not only learn a great deal from what is said but also from how it has been presented."

—ROBERT J. WICKS
Author of Heartstorming: Creating a Place God Can Call Home

"In times of significant change like the present, people usually turn to religion to make meaning of what is happening. Yet Americans are increasingly turning away from religion. Rodgerson turns a sympathetic yet critical eye and ear toward the Nones in this carefully researched, compelling account of their growth and what it means for the future of church and society."

—CURTIS RAMSEY-LUCAS
Editor, The Christian Citizen

"In an age of religious tumult and opportunity, Rodgerson employs the ancient technique of overhearing dialogue to introduce new ways of considering the Nones and the Christian traditions. This prophetic guide, solidly grounded in research and compassion, evidences how we can embrace religious difference and stand at the threshold of a new era to create a way for all to 'drink at the well of essential nurture, of personal worth, of personal meaning, of love.'"

—JILL L. SNODGRASS
Associate Professor of Theology, Loyola University Maryland

"Tom Rodgerson asks us to consider: 'What is the shelf life of canned religion?' It is a question of perennial quality; people of faith, and of no particular faith, must answer this question at some point. Rodgerson artfully, intellectually, and spiritually provides us with wise guidance to discover together the relevance of the Christian tradition to today's spiritual seekers—inviting us to delve deeply, through dialogue, into the core of our potential for spiritual vitality."

SE FOX
Jniversity

Overhearing a Christian Apology to the Nones

In the Spirit
of Acts 17 —

Tom

Overhearing a Christian Apology to the Nones

Revealing Still Hidden Truths in Dialogue

Thomas E. Rodgerson

RESOURCE *Publications* · Eugene, Oregon

OVERHEARING A CHRISTIAN APOLOGY TO THE NONES
Revealing Still Hidden Truths in Dialogue

Resource Publications
An Imprint of Wipf and Stock Publishers
199 W. 8th Ave., Suite 3
Eugene, OR 97401

www.wipfandstock.com

PAPERBACK ISBN: 978-1-6667-1619-1
HARDCOVER ISBN: 978-1-6667-1620-7
EBOOK ISBN: 978-1-6667-1621-4

10/18/21

To my parents, who provided the foundation
of faith and the freedom to pursue it.

Contents

Acknowlegments

I AM INDEBTED TO the students and faculty of the Pastoral Counseling Department of Loyola University Maryland for the privilege of dialogue over many years where the meaning-making potential of the religious, the spiritual, and the "nothing in particular" could be empathetically evaluated through integrated ways of knowing and an openness to not knowing. I am equally indebted to the innumerable counseling clients who permitted me to join them in the most sacred portion of their lives where stories are discovered and creation continues, and to the many churches who in the overhearing of the spoken word heard more than I had imagined and helped me to see more clearly. I am grateful for technical support and encouragement from Dr. Jill Snodgrass, who made possible the connection with Rennae Wigton and her careful attention to bibliographic detail. This book would have never materialized without the constant encouragement to write from Dr. Robert J. Wicks and his expertise in navigating the world of publishing—all of this in addition to being a longtime teacher, mentor, colleague, and friend. And, finally, I am very grateful to my wife for her valuable critique, invaluable editing, amazing attention to detail, and unfailing support.

Prologue

I am invisible; and I will overhear their conference.

—SHAKESPEARE[1]

THE ACT OF OVERHEARING is a well-known theatrical ploy used to increase intrigue, advance a plot, and reveal levels of meaning that have remained beneath the surface for characters in the play and for the audience who is watching. There can be many levels to the overhearing, as seen in a line from the bard of England, "I stole into a neighbour thicket by, and overheard what you shall overhear,"[2] where the audience also willingly and knowingly participates in the overhearing once they have become engaged in the thickening plot.

Overhearing is not just a theatrical ploy. Any good storyteller places the listener in a position of overhearing with opening lines like "Once upon a time . . ." and by sometimes purposely avoiding eye contact while simultaneously engaged in another activity such as whittling. Spiritual leaders will often convey truth to listeners who overhear a story. Jesus' favorite method of instruction was using parables by which the listener overhears the story of another and is invited to see life in a new way. Much of the Christian Scriptures are in the form of letters written by the Apostle Paul to a small community of believers. Anyone else reading these letters is essentially overhearing a private correspondence that took place in the first century between the Apostle Paul and early believers, but also between the Apostle Paul and God. Other religious traditions

1. Shakespeare, *Midsummer-Night's Dream*, 2.1.187.
2. Shakespeare, *Love's Labour's Lost*, 5.2.95.

1

employ even greater forms of indirect communication such as the use of Koans in Buddhism.

Even nonreligious persons interested in advancing personal change in the lives of individuals will use the technique of overhearing. I did some postgraduate work with Dr. John Money, who was a sexologist conducting research in the Psycho-hormonal Research Unit of Johns Hopkins University in Baltimore, Maryland. He was avidly nonreligious, and so it was a great surprise to me, when discussing a difficult therapeutic case in our group case conference, that he said, "Just *tell them a parable* using material that you have found helpful in other cases." His point was that a general story told about help for others, when interjected appropriately into the therapy, created a seed for change in the overhearing.

Fred Craddock understands "overhearing" as a form of indirect communication consisting of two elements: distance and participation. *Distance* provides the listener with "room in which to reflect, accept, reject, decide. As a listener, I must have that freedom, all the more so if the matter before me is of ultimate importance."[3] He goes on to say, about the other element of *participation*, that it is

> free participation on the part of the hearer in the issues, the crises, the decisions, the judgment, and the promise of the message. Participation means the listener overcomes the distance, not because the speaker "applied" everything, but because the listener identified with experiences and thoughts related to the message that were analogous to his own. The fundamental presupposition operative here is the general similarity of human experiences.[4]

Perhaps every book is an exercise in overhearing, in which the reader is allowed distance and free participation, but this book, which is addressed to Nones (those who claim no religious affiliation) *and* to Christians (sometimes called "Somes" along with those from other faith traditions), overtly employs this approach for two reasons. Firstly, indirect communication is increasingly the norm in our culture, especially for those in a younger demographic (including many of the Nones) or when the topic of conversation is more personal, political, or spiritual. Email, texting, and forms of social media are the cultural defaults for communication and preferred by many when the topic of conversation gets difficult. As Sherry Turkle[5]

---

3. Craddock, *Overhearing the Gospel*, 122.

4. Craddock, *Overhearing the Gospel*, 123.

5. Turkle, *Reclaiming Conversation*.

has documented, this avoidance of face-to-face conversation is connected to a loss of relational empathy in our culture and the inability to have the civil discourse necessary to maintain a healthy democracy. This form of indirect communication also seems to encourage a pseudo-form of direct communication which can easily turn into an assault on those with different opinions and a retreat to tribalism where our Facebook feeds simply reinforce our chosen prejudices. For those who have grown accustomed to forms of indirect communication, this book encourages a healthier form of *indirect* communication in the overhearing of a conversation between someone who might identify as a None and someone who might identify as a Christian, and it is in reality a stepping-stone to a healthier form of *direct* communication seen in true dialogue.

Secondly, overhearing and indirect communication may be the only way to break the cultural standoff between Nones and Somes (and, perhaps, religion and science), which comes from living in a "Christian America" where it is assumed that the basic identity of all citizens will be Christian and that we all know what being Christian means. Fred Craddock raises this point by building on the work of Søren Kierkegaard (1813–55), who said, "There is no lack of information in a Christian land; something else is lacking, and this is something which the one man cannot directly communicate to the other."[6] As we will see later in this book, the flood of information in our culture may be part of the problem, diverting us from that which is less visible, more inward, and only capable of being transmitted tacitly. That which the Nones may be communicating in their resistance to a Christian America and what some Christians may be communicating in their preference for a Christian America cannot be heard, much less understood, through sociological surveys of religious preference or though aggressive advocacy for or against plans of salvation. Beyond this is the cultural accommodation Christianity must make in a Christian America that can easily distort the essence of Christianity. Kierkegaard saw this as a significant problem in the Danish Christian culture in which he lived, blocking those who identified as Christian from the true transformational work of the faith. He said, "In brief, it is easier to become a Christian when I am not a Christian than to become a Christian when I am one."[7] Because of this, Kierkegaard advocated for an indirect form of communication, which he

---

6. As quoted in Craddock, *Overhearing the Gospel*, 9.

7. Kierkegaard, *Concluding Unscientific Postscript*, 327.

borrowed from Socrates (c. 470–399 BC), namely, the *"maieutic* method" (coming from the Greek, which refers to the actions of a midwife) in which one helps to bring forth the latent ideas, memories, and inward truths of others through Socratic questioning or dialogue, circumventing what is culturally and defensively known.[8] Perhaps in the overhearing of a dialogue between a Christian and a None, both Christians and Nones can find, in the interplay of distance and participation, the freedom to step out of their identified ways of "knowing" into an "unknowing" that offers the possibility of "giving birth" to new meaning which is so badly needed in this time of great change and great divisiveness. In a culture that sees itself as majority Christian, the threat of losing that position of privilege and power (a threat symbolized in the Nones) may now provide an opportunity for Christians to step into an unknown reality and learn what it means to be Christian for the first time. Nones who choose to join them in that unknown reality by way of dialogue may also see a different Christianity than the one they have imagined and gain additional data for their unique meaning-making quest on what it means to be fully human, whether religious or not.

This book, then, intentionally invites the reader into an overhearing, but it is also intentionally an *overhearing of a dialogue* between a Christian and a None for three reasons. Firstly, this follows the frequent use of dialogue between characters in any novel or play to advance a story line or reveal a plot. As well, the use of dialogue is a frequent method used by writers to advance theoretical, philosophical, or theological meaning. For instance, all of what we know about Socrates comes through Plato's *Dialogues*, in which we overhear Socrates' own dialogues with his students and are introduced to his teachings. Of course, in writing this way, Plato, who was a student of Socrates, was also advancing his own philosophical understanding of the world. In the eleventh century, Anselm advanced a key doctrine of the church about atonement by way of a dialogue between himself and his student, Bono, who was questioning the faith. Spiritual teachers from all faith traditions often advance their understanding of what it means to live fully in a world of suffering by means of questions and answers with students or naysayers, often recorded by others for later generations to overhear. Likewise, the dialogue observed in this book between a Christian and a None is intended to advance possible new ways of understanding.

8. Craddock, *Overhearing the Gospel*, 91.

Secondly, this book intentionally advocates for a form of dialogue that is a healthy form of direct communication, which allows for a "dignity of difference"[9] and for a deep understanding of others as opposed to simply taking a stand on entrenched beliefs and opinions. It is solely this dialogue that will allow for the "revealing of still hidden truths"[10] and allow us to *stand* together in the place where those truths emerge without participating in *standoffs* so prevalent in our divisive culture.

Thirdly, the dialogue elucidated in this book is uniquely between a Christian and a None primarily because I identify as a Christian, and it is the only position from which I can write and from which I can enter the dialogue. Those from other faith traditions are not meant to be excluded. The process of dialogue could equally be applied to those from other faith traditions and the Nones, as well as between other faith traditions and Christianity. Those from non-Christian faith traditions may find themselves entering a higher level of overhearing as they read this book, participating with and distancing from both Nones and Christian Somes as necessary.

Let me also say that the dialogue observed in this book is fictional in the sense that the roles of the Nones and the Christian Somes are representative of those who might populate these categories. However, the dialogue is rooted in the nonfictional conversations documented in a decade of sociological research in which interviews employing deep listening techniques have been conducted with a wide variety of persons who might identify as a None. This book considers those interviews as the first step in a dialogical process and, based on that data, begins to imagine how a dialogue might proceed between a None and a Christian, focused less on the actual words of the conversation and more on the complex, underlying themes that need to be acknowledged for the dialogue to move forward and for "hidden realities" to emerge from within us, between us, and beyond us in midwife-like fashion. In this imagined dialogue, it is also assumed, based on what has already been documented in the lives of Nones, that Christians could help advance the dialogue by taking an apologetic position and, perhaps, on the basis of reading this book, find a nonfictional model for conversations of deep understanding with neighbors, coworkers, spouses, children, etc., who have legitimate differences when it comes to spirituality and religion.

9. Sacks, *Dignity of Difference*, 45.
10. Polanyi, *Science, Faith, and Society*, 17.

Finally, I would admit that the reader of this book may be overhearing nothing more than an internal dialogue of one person who has a genuine interest in the meaning that Nones are bringing to American culture and in the unique, sometimes peculiar, role that Christianity has played, and is playing, in that same culture. What one may be overhearing is nothing more than an internal dialogue between myself and God, between myself and culture, and between the part of me that identifies as a Christian and the part of me that identifies with a mysterious "nothingness." The reader is invited to observe and to overhear, assuming whatever position they choose on the continuum of participation and distance in the inner and outer dialogue where new stories emerge.

Introduction

IF YOU ARE A None, I need your help. Now I know that calling anyone a None is unfortunate, and although I will have plenty more to say about this in chapter 1, including some advantages for the nomenclature, let me offer an apology now for calling anyone a None. I did not create the title. Perhaps we can blame the researchers, but it just evolved from those sociological surveys where people are asked about their religious affiliation. At some point it became apparent that to capture appropriate data on religious affiliation one needed more categories than Catholic, Protestant, or Jew, and one of the options given was "None," or "None of the above," or "Nothing in particular." This was not a major scientific breakthrough, and very few even noticed until the numbers in that category began to increase with percentages in the general population rising to "5 percent in 1972, 7 percent in 1975, 8 percent in 1990, 14 percent in 2000, 18 percent in 2010, and at least 20 percent in 2012."[1] The Pew Research Center indicated that the numbers of the Nones in North America continued to rise, stating that "the religiously unaffiliated share of the population, consisting of people who describe their religious identity as atheist, agnostic, or 'nothing in particular,' now stands at 26 percent, up from 17 percent in 2009,"[2] and while this trend holds true across all age groups, "In stark contrast, only half of millennials (born 1981–96) (49 percent) describe themselves as Christians; four-in-ten are religious 'Nones,' and one-in-ten millennials identify with non-Christian faiths."[3] That trend caught the curious eye of researchers and, as you can imagine, generated some anxious handwringing by those who have a vested interest in religious organizations.

1. Mercadante, *Belief without Borders*, 2.
2. Pew Forum, "Decline of Christianity," 3.
3. Pew Forum, "Decline of Christianity," 8.

Some of those anxious responses are a bit puzzling to me, and that begins to get at why I need your help. For instance, I was talking with a colleague of mine who relayed to me a painful story about his daughter and her attempts to participate in the life of the church where she grew up. Now in her late twenties, his daughter had earned a PhD in clinical psychology and was developing a clinical practice. She had recently married, and her husband, who had considerable musical talents, was helping to bring a new style of music and life to a church that over the past decades had experienced a steady decline in membership. In an attempt to live out her own Christian faith, my colleague's daughter had taken a leadership role in the church. After a recent leadership meeting in which critical comments were made about her husband and his music by the longtime, aging organist of the church and other long-standing members, and in which key initiatives for change to attract younger persons were "shot down," she ended up in the church parking lot in tears. As he relayed the story, my colleague was shaking his head in disbelief not only over the insensitivity to his daughter and her husband, but also over the lack of awareness by the church leaders on how their actions and attitudes were contradictory to their stated goals of trying to rebuild the church and attract young people to their mission. This led us to a further discussion in which we had to admit that in our decades-long counseling work with clergy and consultation work with churches, there were times in which we questioned the appeal of a particular church to any person, young or not.

I figured that you, as a None, would understand and that I could talk with you about this. Do you think my colleague's daughter will now become a None? Does this relate in any way to your own decision to become a None? I know there are many unique reasons for moving into the category of a None, and I want to explore more of those reasons with you in the next chapter, but can you identify with her struggle? If so, you might be a key resource in helping me understand the struggle she is going through as she decides whether to leave the church or not.

I would not be surprised if she left the church, or even if it pushed her into becoming a None. Given the conflicts I have seen in churches, I am also not surprised at the increasing number of Nones in the general population, although I realize that church conflict is only one possible variable in the rise of the Nones. I tend to agree with Kaya Oakes when she says, "When the Pew Forum released the results of its multi-year study of religious life in 2012, the news that up to one-third of people in their twenties, thirties, and forties describe themselves as having 'no religion' was about as shocking as discovering that we really like iPhones."[4]

What does surprise me in this story about my colleague's daughter is the response of the aging organist and the long-standing members. At a minimum, I figure that you would understand if I vented about my confusion and irritation over their contradictory messages. From the perspective of a None, what do you think is happening? Here are some of my initial thoughts for our potential dialogue.

An Age of "Shattered Carapaces"

It is helpful for me to place the responses of the church members in a larger context. For example, we can think about this broadly in terms of cosmic or global change. Jason Kelly, following the three-fold schematic of consciousness (simple, self, and cosmic) developed by Canadian psychiatrist R. M. Bucke, posits that understanding the spiritual-but-not-religious (SBNR, one category of Nones) might be framed in terms of a developing cosmic consciousness, saying, "I suggest that a deeper understanding of cosmic consciousness, which I characterize as the experiential awareness of one's connection to or unity with the cosmos, can provide a solid historical context to ground ecological theorizing about the future direction of the SBNR."[5] Rory McEntee and Adam Bucko, building on the work of theologian Ewert Cousins, see the change as an entering into a Second Axial Age that integrates the tribal aspects of the pre-Axial Age and the individual consciousness of the First Axial Age (800–200 BCE), saying, "The Second Axial Age is an age of integration . . . We need both our individuality, the development of our uniqueness in higher and higher degrees, *and* an understanding of our intrinsic belonging within a vast Kosmos."[6] Phyllis Tickle indicated that what is happening now is a "great emergence" and is part of something that can be documented as happening every five hundred years in the life of the church. She calls upon the wit and wisdom of the Anglican Bishop, The Right Reverend Mark Dyer, who gives a visual image of what is happening to twenty-first century Christians in America when he says, "About every five hundred years the church feels compelled to hold a giant rummage sale . . . About

4. Oakes, *The Nones Are Alright*, 4.

5. Kelly, "Rogue Mystics," 182.

6. McEntee and Bucko, *New Monasticism*, 50.

every five hundred years the empowered structures of institutionalized Christianity . . . become an intolerable carapace that must be shattered in order that renewal and new growth may occur."[7]

It is one thing to think intellectually and theoretically about cosmic shifts in consciousness or the transition from age to age, but it is quite another thing to experience the "shattering of a carapace" at a personal or emotional level, especially if that "shattering" affects our core meaning-making systems tied to spiritual or religious beliefs. A "carapace" is the shell or bone-like covering of the turtle, armadillo, crab, etc., which gives shape to the animal, protects the animal, and allows the animal to navigate with some safety in an unpredictable and, at times, unsafe world. Yet, if the carapace does not change, grow, or even shed completely, the animal will die. Think of the carapace in the church in the opening vignette of this chapter as having to do with the way the church is organized, those who have power or not, the kind of music that is played and sung, the way in which the Bible is interpreted, the way in which the life of Jesus is understood, the ways of understanding and coping with suffering and death, the ways of interacting with one's neighbor or behaving in the world, etc. The obvious inference from the analogy would be that the carapace must change, or the church will die. But this begs the questions, "What is the carapace, and what is the body that must be kept alive?" The obvious inference also ignores the core experience of the "shattering," which is one of profound vulnerability and anxiety for the individuals involved, not only because it affects an institution which is, for them, a beloved institution, but also because it has to do with the very personal ways in which each person has come to understand the world, create identity, and navigate their own unpredictable and, at times, unsafe world.

Maybe this is what is going on at some level for the aging church members in the vignette that I shared. I imagined that you might understand some of the "shattering experience" as you have wrestled with your own core beliefs and identity issues as a None living in an overtly religious culture. Or, as Kaya Oakes says, "Between the emotive faith of . . . young evangelicals and the decisive self-severing of atheists from the possibilities of belief is a space of doubt and tension. It is where millions of Americans dwell."[8]

---

7. Tickle, *Great Emergence*, 16.

8. Oakes, *The Nones Are Alright*, 4.

You see, I can understand how the rise of the Nones and the calls for change by younger people might create enough anxiety for church members so that their fight-flight response kicks in and they respond defensively. It is one way to deal with the vulnerability and anxiety in that five-hundred-year cycle which is bringing about the "shattering of our carapaces." However, it seems to me that there is a better way; a way by which we engage the vulnerability, engage the other, engage the unknown, and live out the idea of community (ironically suggested for the scientific community) proffered by Michael Polanyi who says, "The creative life of such a community rests on a belief in the ever continuing possibility of revealing still hidden truths . . . which, being real, will bear surprising fruit indefinitely. To-day [sic] I should prefer to call it a belief in the reality of emergent meaning and truth."[9] Essentially this book suggests that the process of engagement needed is a *process of dialogue*, a process which might take us to the threshold of possibility where there will be the "revealing of still hidden truths which will bear fruit indefinitely." I was hoping that you might be willing to join in that process of dialogue.

If we were to have such a dialogue, we would be joining a process that has already emerged in the twenty-first century with regard to the Nones. For instance, the process of straightforward data collection and the process of grounded theory research have elicited valuable insights into the demographics, differences, beliefs, practices, and experiences of the Nones.[10] But the emergence of these data and data trends has created a corresponding emergence of cultural and sub-cultural anxiety as Edwin Friedman predicted it would. He goes even further to name the over-focus on data as a form of cultural addiction that creates a form of chronic anxiety as more data emerges. Interestingly, Friedman compares the current state of cultural chronic anxiety to the anxiety in Europe five hundred years ago when the Western population was attempting to move from an understanding of the world as flat to a world that is round. The equator at that time was representative of "the mythical, anxiety-provoking end of the world,"[11] and those adventurers who sailed off to the edge of the world were bound to fall off the edge of a flat earth. Could it be that the increasing data on the rise of the Nones are pushing us to the edge of the religious world as we know it in America and to the corresponding

9. Polanyi, *Science, Faith, and Society*, 17.

10. See Drescher, *Choosing Our Religion*; Mercadante, *Belief without Borders*; Oakes, *The Nones Are Alright*; Pew Forum, "Decline of Christianity."

11. Friedman, *Failure of Nerve*, 23.

anxiety that in some way we might "fall off the edge"? If so, the process that is needed now is not a process of collecting more data, but a process of understanding how best to engage our anxiety and the emotional processes involved.

One way of describing the process of engaging our vulnerabilities and anxieties is to name it as a *process of dialogue*. Kaya Oakes comments on the very diverse expression of beliefs and ideas presented by students in Sproul Plaza at the University of California, Berkeley, saying, "On Sproul Plaza students may encounter dozens of evangelicals actively trying to recruit them, but there is little dialogue between people of faith and nonbelievers, unless it involves shouting or turning away from an outthrust flyer."[12] Could it be that Sproul Plaza is saying something about the lack of effective dialogue in our wider culture on many topics, but especially between the religiously affiliated and the religiously unaffiliated? Again, this is not to say that the structured interviews of grounded theory research have not already begun a process of dialogue with the Nones. But would it be possible to extend this process of effective listening to a wider audience, both the religiously affiliated and religiously unaffiliated? And would it be possible to extend the process of dialogue to a new level of understanding, accompanied by a sensitive response, that might build an experience of community where there will be the "revealing of still hidden truths . . . which . . . will bear fruit indefinitely"?[13] This is the process that I think is a better response, and a process with which I need your help. But before you agree, perhaps I should say more about the process of dialogue.

The Process of Dialogue

In theory, the process of dialogue is simple and elegant. For instance, David Augsburger says,

> Dialogue usually proceeds through three states. The first is a discovery and dispelling of misinformation and faulty assumptions as we come to know each other as we are. The second is seeing values in the other's tradition and wishing to appropriate them

---

12. Oakes, *The Nones Are Alright*, 124.

13. Polanyi, *Science, Faith, and Society*, 17.

for our own. Third comes the discovery of new areas of reality and meaning we were not aware of before.[14]

The elegant movement, then, begins in an awareness of our own cultural, spiritual, or religious location, proceeds with a willingness to truly enter into the cultural, spiritual, or religious world of another by "passing over" into that world, and continues by "coming back" to our own (renewed) location. In reality, "to 'pass over' is to enter a new world; to 'come back' is to return a different person."[15] Rory McEntee and Adam Bucko call this a "dialogical dialogue" and say, "Dialogical dialogue is a way of relating to one another, such that we allow ourselves to be changed in the light of the wisdom of the other. It is a dialogue that is always an exploration."[16]

Of course, the simple elegance of this movement belies the necessary inner awareness and critical examination of the self that happens in at least three ways. Firstly, one must be willing to step back and evaluate one's own cultural, spiritual, or religious location. Citing a Malay proverb, David Augsburger suggests that we usually begin this process with an encapsulated worldview in which we are "like the frog under the coconut shell" (the "coconut shell" being similar to the "carapaces" mentioned above).[17] In the context of the opening vignette in this chapter, for the long-standing church members to enter into the process of dialogue they would need to take a step back from their way of understanding worship, or their preferences for music, or their way of interpreting Scripture. This would be like the "frog coming out from under the coconut shell" who not only sees the rest of the world, but also sees the coconut shell for the first time and begins to evaluate the strengths and limitations of that place called "home." It is hard to underestimate the degree of anxiety created in the process of stepping out from under the coconut shell. How that anxiety is managed will determine whether the young clinical psychologist and her husband bringing new ideas will be seen as dialogue partners who are extending an important invitation to evaluate the coconut shell, or whether they will be pushed away as careless adventurers who are about to cause us to fall off the edge of the earth. It becomes clear, then, that the process of stepping back to evaluate the coconut shell would not

---

14. Augsburger, *Pastoral Counseling*, 42.

15. Augsburger, *Pastoral Counseling*, 37.

16. McEntee and Bucko, *New Monasticism*, 77.

17. Augsburger, *Pastoral Counseling*, 22.

primarily be a process of collecting data about the coconut shell, but a process that brings to light the emotional dynamics involved in stepping out from under the coconut shell and seeing it for the "first time" from another perspective. If this anxiety management is difficult when engaging new ideas from someone still inside the church, how much more difficult it must be to understand the outside perspective brought by you as a None—even if it is the perspective that is needed!

Secondly, the process of dialogue in which one "passes over" and "comes back" requires a certain acceptance of and awareness of the "boundary" that exists between one's location and that of another. David Augsburger says it this way: "Disidentification of the self from old cultural identifications leads to rediscovery of the self in at least three contexts—one's own culture, a second culture, and that unique third culture that always forms on the boundary between the two."[18] On the one hand, this is a very creative place, alive with new beginnings, but it is also a very "messy" place. Gary Gunderson, in his work on boundary leaders, likens this boundary space to the vast lowland tidal marshes in Georgia where the tides are often seven to nine feet, extending the wetland marshes miles inland. He says, "This verdant muck cradles a significant fraction of sea and bird life. Where does earth end and sea begin? The question obscures the answer: the 'boundary' moves in a tide of constant change that is the engine of life."[19]

Part of the "muck" that exists on the boundary between one culture and another, between one religious perspective and another, might be labeled as our "boundary issues." These would be our "automatic instinctive responses"[20] that cause us to see the worst of the other perspective, the abuses of the other perspective, the irrationality of the other perspective, or the theological incorrectness of the other perspective. In turn, this has the potential for creating an angry, dismissive, or judgmental response to the other (inwardly or outwardly) and creating a certain blindness to the inconsistencies, irrationalities, or incorrectness of one's own position. How one engages the "muck" on the boundary is crucial to the process of dialogue. Is this the place where we find the "engine of life," or is it a messiness from which we run? Think of the space between the Nones and the evangelical Christians in Sproul Plaza on the UC Berkeley campus, or of

18. Augsburger, *Pastoral Counseling*, 13.

19. Gunderson, *Boundary Leaders*, 12.

20. Augsburger, *Pastoral Counseling*, 39.

the space between the young clinical psychologist and the aging organist in the opening vignette. Having more data to define the differences will only go so far. How we engage our emotional processes on the boundary between one spiritual or religious location and the other is crucial.

Thirdly, the process of dialogue requires a unique listening presence. By combining the words "inter," "cultural," and "empathy," David Augsburger comes up with a new word for this listening presence, "interpathy," which he defines as "an intentional cognitive and affective envisioning of another's thoughts and feelings from another culture, worldview, epistemology. In interpathy, the process of knowing and 'feeling with' requires that one temporarily believe what the other believes, see as the other sees, value what the other values."[21] In another place, he says, "In interpathic 'feeling with,' empathy is extended beyond known borders to offer grace that draws no lines, refuses limits, claims universal humanness as sufficient foundation for joining another in a unique world of experience."[22] "Feeling with" another human being in the "muck" of our differences while experiencing a certain "shattering of our carapaces" opens us to a threshold of possibility wherein lies the "engine of life" and "the revealing of hidden truths which will bear fruit indefinitely." It seems to me that it would be of interest to the Nones, to Christian Somes, or to those from any other worldview to understand and find the power by which we might stand non-anxiously in that "muck."

My invitation to you as a None would be to join a process of dialogue that has already begun in many informal ways throughout American culture, but also in formal ways through data collection, the process of grounded theory research, and structured interviews—all of which have demonstrated a form of deep listening and all of which have brought to light the many and complex identities, beliefs, and practices of Nones. In all fairness, I must say that my invitation to join that process of dialogue comes from a particular location. What that means is that I am entering the dialogue as a religiously affiliated person from a Christian tradition. To say that one is joining a dialogue process from a "Christian tradition" begs the question of exactly which Christian tradition is being represented. The Christian tradition itself is astoundingly complex in its identities, beliefs, and practices. While trying to accurately represent the essence of the Christian tradition in this book, it is only fair to say that I

---

21. Augsburger, *Pastoral Counseling*, 31.

22. Augsburber, *Pastoral Counseling*, 31.

join the process of dialogue with you as a None from a particular location that is influenced by my experience as a Protestant minister trained in a European seminary and as one who has served in parish ministry, directed a pastoral counseling center, and trained professional counselors and educators at the graduate level in a university over the last forty-five years. While the process of dialogue to which I am inviting you is a dialogue between you as a None and me as a religiously affiliated person from a particular Christian perspective, the process of dialogue itself, as outlined above, could just as easily be entered into as a dialogue between different Christian groups, between other faith traditions and Nones, or between one faith tradition and another faith tradition, acknowledging that those inter-religious, intra-religious, inter-faith, and inter-spiritual dialogues have been in process for well over a hundred years.

Beginning with an Apology

Before you accept my invitation to dialogue, let me reiterate that I am requesting your help, but also that I am extending the invitation with an attitude of *apology*. The word "apology" has multiple meanings. It essentially means to "speak from" with roots in the Greek word *apolégein* (*apo* = "from" and *légein* = "to tell or speak") with connotations of either giving a full account of oneself with the implication of regret or with the implication of a defense and a full justification for oneself.[23] Part I of this book relies upon the first meaning of the word "apology" and suggests that, as a Christian, I need to enter into the process of dialogue with anyone who identifies as a None, validating the implied and overt critiques they are raising about Christianity and admitting that in many ways their critiques are correct. Chapter 1 of this book attempts to unravel the historical and cultural roots connected to the rise of the Nones in American culture and to name some of the beliefs, practices, and experiences now associated with the Nones. Gratitude is offered for their contribution to the new story that is now emerging in the spiritual and religious landscape of America, and curiosity is encouraged as we look for a clearer understanding of what the story is going to be. Chapter 2 continues with an admission that *when* the Christian church loses touch with its original animating energy and descends into debates about various beliefs, it produces a religion that can be fairly toxic and bypasses the individual

---

23. Barnhart, *Dictionary of Etymology*, 42.

spiritual work called for by the founders of the faith. For this fall from faith to religion, an apology is needed. In chapter 3, there is an admission that *when* the Christian church fails to identify ways in which it has become entangled with the overarching cultural paradigm of the market economy, it shifts to become an institution more interested in transactions than in transformation. In that case, not only is an apology needed when we push hollow transactional religious rituals onto the Nones (or anyone else), but also an apology is needed when we shift our market-share anxieties onto the Nones, whose growth in numbers raises serious and unavoidable concerns about the trend of religious decline.

Part II of this book is influenced by the other meaning of the word "apology" and has overtones of the more classical understanding of Christian apologetics in which a defense of the faith is given. "Defense" in this case must be distinguished from "defensiveness," just as "dialogue" must be distinguished from "debate." There comes a point in the process of dialogue after one has listened deeply, after one has "passed over" and "come back," and after one has identified and come to terms with one's own boundary issues, when one must then try to "speak from" one's own (renewed) understanding of one's spiritual/religious location in a language that might have some level of appeal. Chapter 4 invites the reader to consider the various "technologies" that underlie the beliefs in any religion and even underlie the beliefs advocated by the Nones. In this case, the word "technology" is understood not as a machine-like operation, but more like "grammar" that is operating in any meaning-making language. This lays the foundation for chapter 5, which will offer a Christian "spiritual technology of freedom" as a way of "speaking from" the experiential reality of the Christian faith with clear implications for understanding the process for, and the intended direction toward, becoming fully human. This will lead into chapter 6, where the implications of a "spiritual technology of freedom" will go beyond the individual to consideration of a restorative justice for all of creation. In this there will be an invitation to hear the "groaning" of creation, to enter into the suffering of the world, and to find a power coming from a liminal position by which empires and systems are rendered powerless over us. Finally, in the Epilogue, we will see how this pivotal moment in history is a time of "something is happening" where we find ourselves on the threshold of possibility in the creation of new stories. It is the process of dialogue suggested throughout the chapters that allows this threshold to emerge as we empty ourselves of our ego-defensive stories and risk standing together in a "nothingness" that opens to the Infinity of "everything." Interestingly, this way of being on the threshold may resonate positively with you as a None (just as it does with the more "apophatic" Christian traditions) and, with our combined efforts, may lead us to a unique threshold of possibility where there is an opening for the revealing of still hidden truths.

A Marketplace Invitation

The discerning critics among you, having read the above material, may be reminded of the comment attributed to Alfred North Whitehead that the total history of Western thought is no more than "footnotes to Plato."[24] I would be foolish to discount the debt to Plato and the importance in Greek philosophy of a dialogue process (*diá-logos*) that would ultimately lead through pure thought to the true Idea (*logos*). Such philosophical dialogues would take place in the city marketplace. A notable example of this from the Christian Scriptures is that of the Apostle Paul in his visit to Athens where, it says, "So he argued (*dielégeto*) in the synagogue with the Jews and devout persons, and also in the marketplace every day with those who happened to be there. Also some Epicurean and Stoic philosophers debated with him" (Acts 17:17–18).[25] Again, the discerning critic might point out that Paul seems to be more interested in "apologetics" than offering any kind of "apology" where one attempts to validate the position of another as noted in the dialogue process mentioned above. However, this would not be totally accurate, as later in the story Paul gives evidence that he has read key philosophical documents from the others' spiritual location and quotes one of those documents (Epimenides; Aratus, *Phaenomena*, 5) as a way of building a bridge with the other, saying, "For 'In him we live and move and have our being'; as even some of your own poets have said, 'For we too are his offspring'" (Acts 17:28). As N. T. Wright points out, the Apostle Paul was greatly influenced by the Greek Stoic philosophers in his theology and "expected that there might be points of overlap, of congruence."[26] He says that Paul did not reject all the wisdom, understanding, and insight of the pagan world, but there is "an *epistemological* revolution at the heart of Paul's worldview and theology. It isn't just that he now knows things he did not before; it is, rather, that

24. Pevateaux, "Being Spiritual," 241.
25. All verses cited are NRSV.
26. Wright, *Paul*, 236.

the act of knowing has itself been transformed."[27] And, therefore, Paul will use words and ideas in a way that has "multiple resonance,"[28] reverberating with the meaning-making of the Greek, Jewish, and Roman cultures, but with new meaning brought into the mix from Paul's own profound spiritual experience.

Realize, then, that in this book and its invitation to dialogue, there is a "multiple resonance" with Greek philosophy that goes back to the beginning of Christianity. Realize also that what looks like similar language can have meaning which is connected to other ways of knowing. For instance, the process of dialogue suggested in this book can look very similar to the marketplace discussions of Greek philosophy, or even look like the subsequent dialectical process suggested by Marx and Hegel based upon that Greek philosophy. But while there is a resonance in that way, there is also a "multiple resonance" coming from Paul's reinvention of Stoic philosophy and using words like "We are his offspring" in new ways. Further, while the Greek word *diálogos* never actually occurs in the Christian Scriptures, it has multiple resonance in its derivatives that do occur in those Scriptures, such as *dialégomai* (meaning "to dispute, reason, or discuss") or *dialogízomai* (meaning "to reckon, consider, or ponder"). When Mary, the mother of Jesus, is faced with a spiritual experience that she cannot understand from her current frame of reference (for example, the angel Gabriel speaking to her and, later, the shepherds visiting her and reporting their own angelic visitation), it says that she "pondered what sort of greeting this may be" (Luke 1:29) and "pondered them in her heart" (Luke 2:19). Likewise, in this book, to enter into a process of dialogue will be an invitation not only into a marketplace discussion, but also into a "pondering in the heart" where one pays attention to the emotional processes and the internal back-and-forth-ness that may lead to the revealing of still hidden truths.

Even to say that one is being invited into a "marketplace discussion" has multiple resonance. Such a phrase has resonance with the Greek philosophers, and it has resonance with the Apostle Paul in Athens, but it also has a different kind of resonance with those living in America where a predominant cultural paradigm is that of the marketplace economy. In reading this book (produced and sold in the marketplace) and accepting my invitation to dialogue, you as a None will enter all of those possible

27. Wright, *Paul*, 1356.
28. Wright, *Paul*, 1379.

meanings of "marketplace"—and more. And the "more" would be an invitation into a "public" forum for dialogue that reminds us, firstly, of the Greek marketplace where the philosophers discussed their philosophies; secondly, of the Christian-cultural dialogues of the first century; and, thirdly, of the internal dialogue accompanying any spiritual experience.

Indeed, if you accept the invitation to dialogue by reading this book, there will be many other resonances that emerge between you as a None and me as a Christian Some. Beyond that is the possibility of a ripple effect as you begin to dialogue with others in the culture, whether religiously affiliated or religiously unaffiliated. While reading this book, I encourage you to listen for the "resonances" and the "ponderings." Note when you agree, when you disagree, when you have "aha" moments, when you are angry, when you shut the book, when you want to (or don't want to) recommend the book to others. Note when you are participating in the dialogue and when you need distance. Note when you have "boundary issues" and when you can or cannot pass over and come back. Write in the margins, keep a journal, or in your own way make space for the revealing of still hidden truths.

After five years of researching the religious experiences of Christian teenagers with the conclusion that their faith could be described as "almost Christian" or as a form of "moral therapeutic deism," Kenda Creasy Dean says, "For the first time in twenty years of ministry, I had to admit that I often have trouble seeing Christ in church. And yet—the church is where Christ found me, and . . . continues to call me to serve. Where is the problem? In the church? Or (the likely answer) in me?"[29] Or, in the beginning of her book, she "cuts to the chase" and says that American young people are fine with religious faith, but it does not concern them too much and it is not durable. Then she adds: "One more thing: we're responsible."[30]

I resonate with both of Dean's positions. On the one hand, I resonate with the feeling that it is sometimes hard to see Christ in the church and hard to understand the decisions made and the actions taken by Christians. Perhaps there are other Christians who will read this book, overhear the dialogue, and have similar feelings. On the other hand, I resonate with Dean's other position—namely, "we're responsible." Perhaps other Christians will join me. I can only speak as one Christian when I admit some responsibility for the way the church is and for creating the

29. Dean, *Almost Christian*, 186.

30. Dean, *Almost Christian*, 3.

conditions which may have led to the decline of the church and the rise of the Nones. But, mostly, I take responsibility for the nature of our dialogue and for interpathic listening that might open us to new possibilities, new shared stories, and the revealing of still hidden truths. And, so, I begin with an apology of admission.

Part I

Apology as Admission

I don't attend (church) altogether for religious reasons. I feel more religious, in fact, here beside this corrupt and holy stream. I am not sectarian or evangelical . . . I am, maybe, the ultimate Protestant, the man at the end of the Protestant road, for as I read the Gospels over the years, the belief has grown in me that Christ did not come to found an organized religion but came instead to found an unorganized one.

—JAYBER CROW

1

None-Sense

Admission as Confession and Invitation

IF AN APOLOGY IS an admission of regret, usually by way of confession, then I must confess that I have ambivalent feelings about calling you a None. Part of me is truly sorry for using the term. I can see how it would be difficult for you to participate in a dialogue if you felt labeled as a None and if you felt the labeling ascribed to you a pejorative identity, or even a lack of identity, as someone who is a "nothing." If you are a "nothing," then there is the implication that you have no beliefs or values, or that you have not thought about your current decision to be unaffiliated with a religious tradition. Worse yet, if you are a "nothing," then there is the (unspoken) implication that you are not fully human, and we know what happens in this country when someone is not considered to be fully human. You become a target: a target for negative labels (sinner, heathen, pagan, infidel, etc.), a target for conversion, a target for research, or a target for the anxious projections of others. In a so-called Christian nation, you become the outsider, the leper, in a story that is all too often reduced to those who are "us" and those who are "not us." What follows from this usually is not helpful and might be labeled as "nonsense."

You would be right to accuse me, as a white Christian male, of having no idea what that nonsense feels like. I can only wonder out loud in our dialogue if it is in any way similar to the feeling I get when other Christians put me in the "not us" category and angrily label me as "not saved" because of supposedly errant theological views. I imagine that some Christians reading this book right now might be having such

25

thoughts. For instance, I was introducing a friend who identifies as a Baptist (a Protestant Christian) to speak at a retreat where the audience was a mixture of believers from various religious traditions. In his opening remarks, he felt compelled to say, "I am a Baptist. But not *that* kind of a Baptist!" Of course, he was resisting being identified with a certain way of being Christian which has been popularized in the media.

If I am to own my boundary issues in this dialogue, I would have to confess to my own internal reactivity when I get "put into a box" because of my Christian beliefs. This is true when other Christians label me, but also, if I am honest, I must catch my own internal reactivity when someone speaking from the position of a None makes assumptions about the nature of my religious affiliation, such as a statement by Cristel Manning when she is highlighting the importance of *choice* for those who are Nones and states, "Organized religion is rejected in part because it fails to allow individuals that choice."[1] Really?! My religious forefathers and mothers literally were put to death in the colonial period of this country for emphasizing religious choice. These were people who helped write the Bill of Rights in this country and who believed in freedom of religion and freedom from religion. Choice is something that we still highly value in my organized religious tradition. I wonder if my reactive feeling is similar to what you feel when someone labels you as a None, with the implication that you are a "nothing" or have no identified values or beliefs.

With some level of empathy, or even interpathy, I admit that an apology is needed for labeling you as a None. But, of course, you can see that I am still using the term. I am obviously ambivalent about labeling anyone as a None. If the term is limiting and demeaning, then it is not helpful. However, I want to be sensitive to the fact that sometimes the label of None seems to be a "badge of honor" for some of you or a central component of your chosen identity. Cristel Manning comments that especially in very religious parts of the country, Nones are choosing to identify as outsiders, saying, "Nones hold very diverse worldviews and are unified only by their rejection of organized religion. By claiming the outsider narrative, Nones here gain a clear sense of identity, of boundaries, which are otherwise absent."[2] Linda Mercadante points out that being against certain religious beliefs "allows for a common enemy and thus a crucial measure of agreement in a diverse group often thought to be

1. Manning, *Losing Our Religion*, 49.

2. Manning, *Losing Our Religion*, 99.

highly eclectic and transitory."[3] For that reason, I am hesitant to give up the terminology of None if, in fact, it is central to your identity.

I also see some advantage in using the label of None if it is a term that opens us to complexity rather than a term that is used to stereotype and target you as an outsider. In fact, what started out as a simple sociological category of "none of the above" in the collection of data about religious affiliation has blossomed into very rich research that teases out who the Nones are and what their very existence is telling us about religion and spirituality in America. One example of this research is by Chaeyoon Lim, who sought to distinguish between "stable Nones" and "unstable Nones."[4] The latter, over a period of time, might change their response on questionnaires about having no religious preference. They are best categorized not as "unchurched" or "seekers," but as "liminal Nones" who are often "betwixt and between" in their religious preference. This is only one example of how the term "None" has provided an opportunity for scientific categorizing that has opened us to complexity. For that reason, I am hesitant to give up the term, and I want you to understand my ambivalence as an invitation to explore complexity.

Beyond Stereotyping

Exploring complexity is really the first of three stages in the process of dialogue described by David Augsburger as "a discovery and dispelling of misinformation and faulty assumptions as we come to know each other as we are."[5] Simple categories like "None" and "Christian" may attract us to, and set the stage for, a marketplace discussion, but our dialogue only begins when we appropriate an attitude of curious discovery about the Other and, in essence, accept an invitation to complexity. Dialogue begins when I move beyond my interest in you as someone who is labeled a None to seeing you as a person who is as unique as a fingerprint and who has a complex history, a special worldview, and an individual way of mentally and emotionally navigating the joys, sorrows, and uncertainties of human existence. This is doubly complex because, at the same time, I must accept the invitation to examine the complexity of my own assumptions about you as a person, generated out of my patterned ways

---

3. Mercadante, *Belief without Borders*, 230.

4. Lim et al., "Secular and Liminal."

5. Augsburger, *Pastoral Counseling*, 42.

of navigating human existence. My patterned ways are prejudicial in the sense that they are my preferred ways of understanding the world, what Hans Gadamer called the "spell of our own fore-meanings" and "the tyranny of hidden prejudices."[6] In the language of The Right Reverend Mark Dyer, read "my prejudiced patterns" as "my carapaces." In language which originated in the printing world, read "my stereotypes" with the image of a one-piece printing plate that figuratively becomes "an unvarying form or pattern . . . having no individuality as though cast from a mold."[7]

Beyond Stereotyping of the Nones

More data is helpful in the dispelling of misinformation, but the additional data must go hand-in-hand with attending to my own complex assumptions about you and with attending to my own emotional processes attached to those assumptions. For instance, James White summarizes the data about Nones and provides the following portrait:

> He's a he. He thinks abortion and same-gender marriage should be legal. He is white. He's young. He's not very religious. He's more likely a westerner. He's liberal or moderate. He's a democrat. He's not necessarily an atheist. He's not necessarily hostile toward religious institutions; he just doesn't want to belong to one.[8]

This is an interesting snapshot (stereotype?) of you as a None which may be the result of early data summaries and White's reliance on the interpretation of that data through a religious news service. But I also wonder if this picture of you as a None is influenced by political, theological, and missional assumptions made clear by White when he says, "Our mission will actually have to target the *Nones*"[9] and also, "A None-targeted climate is just that—targeted on facilitating the process of evangelizing Nones."[10] It is interesting that with a different set of assumptions, the portrait of you as a None appears a lot more complex. Would a different set of assumptions not allow for a deeper dispelling of misinformation and promote a process of dialogue in which you are not a target but a dialogue partner who is helpful in the revealing of still hidden truths?

6. Gadamer, *Truth and Method*, 268, 270.

7. *Webster's Dictionary*, "Stereotype," 1785.

8. White, *Rise of the Nones*, 23.

9. White, *Rise of the Nones*, 77.

10. White, *Rise of the Nones*, 97.

Those doing objective research are not without their assumptions. As Cristel Manning[11] points out, researchers doing quantitative research need to create labels that can be easily measured and compared, and that reflect their interests and the interests of their sponsors. Categories that are given on surveys, as well as when the surveys are administered, shape the information that emerges from those surveys—and sometimes misses information! For example, a Jewish person who does not believe in God would certainly categorize themselves as a Jew on any religious survey, but functionally they could be categorized as a None. As another example, The General Social Survey has only one box for Nones to check ("no religion"), but the Cooperative Congressional Election Study has three options for the religiously unaffiliated: atheist, agnostic, or nothing in particular. As Ryan Burge found, looking at the "nothing in particular" category by itself produced a very different picture of the Nones than what James White describes. He says, "While their gender distribution reflects that of the United States as a whole, they have incredibly low levels of educational attainment, and many of them make below-average incomes. Socially and politically, they are isolated."[12]

As well, the type of statistical analysis used to assess the information also influences results. For instance, Kelley Strawn, using binary logistic regression to examine five decades of General Social Survey data, produces results that differ significantly from the stereotype of a None provided above by James White, who used some of the same social survey data. Interestingly, Strawn refers to her data as "Nones-sense."[13]

Those doing qualitative research come closer to the first stage of dialogue in that they elicit information through sensitive conversations following a consistent protocol with every interviewee. This phenomenological approach to research attempts to "bracket out" any biases the research might have. However, as you might imagine, the very construction of the questions for the interview and the follow-up collating of, and interpretation of, the emerging information is unavoidably influenced by the assumptive world of the researcher. Again, Hans Gadamer, in his study of how we interpret truth, refers to this as the "tyranny of hidden prejudices."[14]

---

11. Manning, *Losing Our Religion*.
12. Burge, *The Nones*, 122.
13. Strawn, "What's Behind the 'Nones-sense'?"
14. Gadamer, *Truth and Method*, 270.

Despite these limitations, such research does help to dispel misinformation and move us beyond stereotypes. You might find yourself surprised by the complexity of trying to define those who mutually identify with you as a None. Elizabeth Drescher found in her interview of those who self-identified as religiously unaffiliated that they used the following terms to label themselves: Atheist, Weak Agnostic, Strong Agnostic, Secular Humanist, Humanist, Secular, Spiritual, Spiritual but Not Religious, Neopagan, Wiccan, Nothing-in-Particular, All of the Above, or None of the Above.[15] Drescher's approach to summarizing and interpreting the complex stories she heard from her interviewees was to categorize those stories in terms of the spiritual practices of Nones (not spiritual beliefs). Making the point that the religiously unaffiliated *do* affiliate, she says that when she spoke with Nones about who and what inspired them in their spiritual lives, "what emerged were influences shared across local, distributed, and digitally integrated social networks and communities that could be characterized as a form of unaffiliated affiliation."[16] These affiliations were formed around spiritually meaningful practices that included physical activity, nature, art, and music. But the top four spiritually meaningful practices were as follows: enjoying time with family, enjoying time with pets or other animals, enjoying time with friends, and preparing or sharing food. Drescher came to call these "the Four F's of Contemporary American Spirituality: Family, Fido, Friends, and Food."[17] Notably, prayer came in as number five in her list of spiritual practices. While some Nones only see prayer as begging and as a waste of time, others see prayer as facilitating "spiritual being and becoming in relationship with other beings and the natural world, and . . . with a supernatural being or force. Prayer connects Nones to the concerns of others and connects them to their own religious past and to the religious contexts of the lives of people who are important to them."[18] Would any of this ring true for you as a None?

Linda Mercadante prefers to summarize the complex stories she heard from Nones around spiritual beliefs (not spiritual practices). She says, "Instead of a desertion of belief, we hear the formation of a new set of principles to guide practice and action. A sea change in belief and an

15. Drescher, *Choosing Our Religion*, 28–29.

16. Drescher, *Choosing Our Religion*, 90.

17. Drescher, *Choosing Our Religion*, 44.

18. Drescher, *Choosing Our Religion*, 181.

emerging set of core principles is discovered when we listen carefully."[19]
Acknowledging that she is looking more narrowly at those who identify
as Spiritual but Not Religious, she says they can be further subdivided
into Dissenters, Casuals, Explorers, Seekers, and Immigrants with unique
beliefs cataloged around themes of Transcendence, Human Nature,
Community, and the Afterlife. Mercadante summarizes the new ethos
she was hearing by stating,

> This ethos includes an impersonalization of transcendence,
> a sacralization of the self, a focus on therapeutic rather than
> civic goals, and a self-needs orientation to community and
> commitment. To do this, concepts borrowed from non-Western
> religions (such as monism and reincarnation) or those bor-
> rowed from psychology, science, or alternative philosophies
> (such as positive thinking, "cellular" knowledge, energies, self-
> realization) are equally simplified, homogenized, or altered, and
> then brought in as alternatives. The end-product is distinctively
> American and it is widespread. For, as we have seen, a portion
> of this rhetoric, as well as some of its particulars, can be found
> inside as well as outside religion.[20]

Alternatively, the organizing theme that Cristel Manning brings to
the complex stories of the Nones is that of choice. Her particular focus
is on parents who are raising their children as Nones, whom she sub-
categorizes into Unchurched Believers, Seeker Spirituality, Philosophical
Secularists, and Indifferents. What unifies these groups is their strong
emphasis on choice for themselves and for their children. She says that
as diverse as Nones are, "they are unified by more than just a refusal to
identify with organized religion. This book has argued that Nones, although not a coherent movement, share a deep commitment to personal
worldview choice that distinguishes them from many of their churched
counterparts."[21] Interestingly, the Nones she interviewed saw "church
people" as "inheriting" their religion as opposed to their strategic decision to construct their own spiritual beliefs and to maximize their children's options. Of course, you might hear a stereotyping of Christians in
those opinions.

---

19. Mercadante, *Belief without Borders*, 9.
20. Mercadante, *Belief without Borders*, 231.
21. Manning, *Losing Our Religion*, 184.

Beyond Stereotyping Christians

If, in the first stage of our dialogue, we are attempting to dispel misinformation and faulty assumptions as we come to know each other as we are, what emerges from formal and informal interviews with Nones across the country are complex and sacred stories cataloged through the interpretive lenses of researchers, but as unique as a fingerprint for each person. These stories need to be heard in all their complexity without stereotypes. Is it helpful for you to be heard in this way? Were you surprised by the complexity of those who, like you, have some identification as a None?

What seems less complex in these stories, however, is an understanding of Christianity. In her interviews of Nones, Linda Mercadante notes, "Many interviewees homogenized and simplified core theological themes labeled as characteristic of Western religion—Christianity in particular—and then rejected or radically altered them."[22] Although I will have more to say about this in the second half of this book, I wonder if it would be helpful at this stage of our dialogue to invite you beyond stereotypes into some of the complexity of Christianity since we are attempting to know each other as we are.

The complexity of Christianity is truly overwhelming (and we are talking about just one of the complex religions in which the religiously affiliated participate). I wonder if that complexity becomes a part of your disinclination toward religion, not just that you want to be "anti-" something. Quite frankly, many Christians do not understand the complexity of their own religion, which may contribute to their tendency to strongly identify with only certain aspects and beliefs in Christianity as a means of reducing complexity. I taught a class for over twenty years in which I attempted to train professional counselors to listen deeply to someone from a different faith tradition. We practiced deep listening first by listening to differences within the class. Ironically, it was often students from different Christian traditions who had a hard time listening to each other. This seemed harder than listening to someone from a completely different religion. Differences between "camps" in their own Christian religion seemed more of a challenge to their personal religious identity than differences with other faith traditions, or even someone without a faith tradition.

Part of the complexity of Christianity is the formation of "camps" which developed in the broadest sense with the "rummage sales" held by

22. Mercadante, *Belief without Borders*, 230.

the church every five hundred years. In the eleventh century, the church in the East (often referred to as the Eastern Orthodox Church) split with the church in the West (often referred to as the Roman Catholic Church). Five hundred years later in the sixteenth century, what became known as the Protestant Church split from the Roman Catholic Church with further divisions occurring around doctrine, beliefs, and practices. We are currently in the midst of another "rummage sale" in the five-hundred-year cycle of change with the "cleaning out of our basements" and the "shattering of our carapaces." From a distance, these divisions and differences seem very trivial, but to those who self-define with a certain religious expression, these differences are very important.

I can understand why you may want nothing to do with these complex differences. I can also understand that it is easy to be critical of the institutions who are invested in maintaining these differences and those individuals who choose to self-identify (often strongly) with denominational, cultural, and sub-cultural manifestations of the faith. You might be surprised at how many of the religiously affiliated Christian Somes share your concerns about religious institutions and have some of the same questions about Scripture, church teaching, and theological explanations for the meaning of life. Some of these may even be clergy. Wendell Berry gives us a glimpse into the inner world of such a "Some" in the fictional character of Jayber Crow, who at one point feels a call to preach and goes to a Christian college. He gets into trouble when he questions some of the Christian doctrines and, in particular, the truth of every word of Scripture. He decides to leave Pigeonville College and become a barber (from 1937 to 1969) in the small Kentucky town of Port William; a barber who listens deeply to the stories of people's lives; a barber who is also a part-time janitor for the local church. When he leaves Pigeonville College, he says, "I assumed that since I didn't have the religion of Pigeonville College I didn't have any religion at all. That seemed a big load off my mind. I felt as light as a kite."[23] But with the cultural expectations of a small town, and as the church janitor, he stays connected to the church, often reflecting on the nature of the young seminary pastors who came to preach sermons that were over-focused on hell. He says, "I did not believe it. They made me see how cut off I was. Even when I was sitting in the church, I was a

23. Berry, *Jayber Crow*, 68.

man outside."[24] Reflecting on the men who sat in his barber's chair and who also sat with him in church, he says,

> The church, I would guess, meant little enough to many of the men of Port William, who (if they went) were not comfortable in it and whose chief preoccupation with respect to it was to keep the preacher from finding out how they really talked and thought and lived. Like, I think, most of the people of Port William, Roy lived too hard up against mystery to be without religion. But like many of the men, he was without church religion.[25]

Jayber Crow is a fictional character, but in Elizabeth Drescher's research of the Nones, she often came across non-fictional Christian Somes who were operating like Nones, such as the church music director who said, "I've been around church for long enough to know that most of it is a lot of crap. I don't believe very much of it. But I like to sing . . . I'm probably a None. A Lutheran None. So, I keep quiet."[26] Or, the forty-year-old Presbyterian minister who said, "If I'm really honest and ask myself if I'd go to church regularly if I weren't clergy, I have to say, 'No.' It just doesn't always feed me spiritually."[27]

Even those who are deeply committed to the spiritual path of their religion can have ambivalent feelings about church, such as the Franciscan priest, Richard Rohr, who talks about the importance of finding the divine Presence in the universal Christ, saying that when you find that Presence, "church, temple, and mosque will become totally boring and unnecessary."[28] Similarly, the anonymous nineteenth-century Russian pilgrim, who gives an account of his spiritual journey as he attempts to find a way to "pray without ceasing" and always be mindful of the Jesus Prayer, says that he began his inquiry in churches and listening to sermons on prayer, but then, "inasmuch as listening to public sermons had not given me any satisfaction, I stopped attending them and decided, with the grace of God, to look for an experienced and learned person who would satisfy my ardent desire and explain ceaseless prayer to me."[29] Still further, Paul Smith, who has been a Christian pastor for almost half

---

24. Berry, *Jayber Crow*, 161.

25. Berry, *Jayber Crow*, 152.

26. Drescher, *Choosing Our Religion*, 13.

27. Drescher, *Choosing Our Religion*, 13.

28. Rohr, *Universal Christ*, 53.

29. *Way of a Pilgrim*, 4.

a century, says, "I love God. I love Jesus. I love the church . . . However, I have a life-long lover's quarrel with the church."[30] He argues that there needs to be a different kind of church for those who are at different stages of consciousness and a map for understanding how that movement from stage to stage occurs. It would be natural, then, for one to outgrow one's religion at a particular stage. He says,

> What do you do when you have outgrown your religion? Some become agnostics and atheists. Others keep going to temple, mosque, or church by checking their minds at the door and getting some nostalgia and comfort inside. An increasing number search out other religions or try a cafeteria-style, "I'm spiritual but not religious" assortment. Many leave their religion but hang on to God. However, there is another option. Move to a higher stage of your own religion![31]

Again, I offer this as an invitation to complexity in the first stage of our dialogue as we attempt to dispel misinformation and faulty assumptions. Just as it is easy for Christians to stereotype Nones, it is easy for Nones to stereotype Christians, taking a strategy that is "a 'language game' or 'straw-man,' which allows for a common enemy."[32] As Nancy Ammerman says as she makes the point that fully 80 percent of American adults claim to be religious *and* spiritual, "those who see religion as an enemy are likely to be fairly inarticulate about what religion actually is. The 'religion' being rejected turns out to be quite unlike the religion being practiced and described by those affiliated with religious institutions."[33]

As we move together in our dialogue beyond stereotypes, you might add to your wonderment that early Christians were considered to be religiously unaffiliated (Nones!?). N. T. Wright makes the point that early Christianity may have been seen as a philosophy, but "the word 'religion' only gradually came to be used, in the ancient world, in relation to Christianity, and the idea that there might then be different 'religions' was an innovation of the late sixteenth and early seventeenth centuries."[34] In fact, early Christians were seen as atheists by the religious people of their day

---

30. Smith, *Integral Christianity*, xix.

31. Smith, *Integral Christianity*, 219.

32. Mercadante, *Belief without Borders*, 230.

33. Ammerman, "Spiritual but Not Religious," 275.

34. Wright, *Paul*, 249.

because they did not believe in the rituals, auguries, sacred books, or gods of the local culture. As Wright says,

> Earliest Christianity, including that of Paul, was in first-century terms not a "religion." That verdict was shared by their contemporaries, who saw them as "atheists"—a term which now, to some, indicates a tough-minded resolve not to be taken in by religious superstition, but which then carried a profound anti-social stigma. "Atheists" were, by definition, people who were not playing their part in keeping the gods and the city together, in sustaining the multi-faceted social and civic harmony upon which all else depended. They posed an implicit threat to social stability and security.[35]

It would be ironic indeed if you as a None were considered by the religious in our day to be a threat to social stability and security. Perhaps you as a None have something in common with the earliest Christians!

The Nature of Our Entanglement

As we move beyond stereotypes in our first stage of dialogue, we get a hint of later stages of dialogue where we discover "new areas of reality and meaning we were not aware of before."[36] Without sacrificing the unique differences and identities that each of us share, dialogue begins to reveal a new reality between Christians and Nones where, at times, Somes and Nones have similar questions and concerns where categories of "us" and "not us" are not so starkly delineated. In reality, when we look at our common culture and recent history, we are quite entangled.

In her investigation of spirituality and the American religious imagination, sociologist Cortney Bender takes the advice of John Dewey and his recommendation in approaching topics to "begin with things in their complex entanglements rather than with simplifications made for the purpose of effective judgment and action."[37] For those who claim to be spiritual but not religious (and for the very understanding of spirituality itself in American culture), she sees complex entanglements with questions of history, with understanding of the secular, with the nature of religious experience, and with attempts to integrate scholarship/science

---

35. Wright, *Paul*, 1331.

36. Augsburger, *Pastoral Counseling*, 42.

37. Bender, *New Metaphysicals*, 44.

and spirituality. New realities emerge when we begin to dialogue about these complex entanglements.

Broadly speaking, we are entangled in culture. Robert Fuller and William Parsons document cultural stands that have come together to make the rise of the Nones possible. "These include democracy, immigration, globalization, pluralism, the high cultural emphasis on individualism and pragmatism, the rise of a secularized consciousness, the impact of visual and social media, and the pervasive networks that constitute neoliberal capitalism."[38] It is not just the Nones responding to these cultural trends; there are complex entanglements of action and response where Christians (or the religiously affiliated) might take action to survive in a changing culture, and others in the culture (like the Nones) might react. (Of course, this could happen in the reverse.) For example, Robert Putnam and David Campbell use the language of "shock and two aftershocks"[39] to describe religiosity in America. There was a tremendous growth in church attendance after World War II, accompanied by soaring birthrates of the Baby Boomers. Then there was a "shock" in the 1960s of sex, drugs, rock 'n' roll, and "God is dead," followed by the first "aftershock" in the 1970s and 1980s with the rise of religious conservatism. This was followed by the second "aftershock" in the 1990s and 2000s with what they call the "youth disaffection from religion" as "young Americans came to view religion, according to one survey, as judgmental, homophobic, and too political."[40] However, the cultural reactions are not monolithic movements from one generation to the next, as one of Kaya Oakes' interviewees makes clear when he talks about how he relates to God, saying, "a lot of things are products of your raising. You engage with the culture of your parents. My parents are Boomers, and a reason the Nones exist is because a lot of us had nonreligious parents. They wouldn't call themselves atheists or nonbelievers. I grew up in a nonreligious house. When I went to college, I met seriously religious people."[41]

38. Fuller and Parsons, "Spiritual but Not Religious," 15.
39. Putnam and Campbell, *American Grace*, 91.
40. Putnam and Campbell, *American Grace*, 121.
41. Oakes, *The Nones Are Alright*, 163.

Entangled with Individualism

Within these wider cultural actions and reactions there are very interesting and complex themes with which we are entangled. For instance, we are entangled around the theme of individualism. Emphasis on the individual in Western society may go back to the Graeco-Roman philosophers, but certainly the focus on the individual emerges clearly in the Protestant Reformation and Martin Luther's proclamation of salvation by faith alone as well as in the Western Enlightenment with its focus on reason and the thinking man or woman (for example, Descartes's "I think, therefore I am."). As noted above, as a None you seem to place a high degree of importance on individual choice with regard to having religion/spirituality or not. Others of you would describe this in terms of the importance of the Self where the core of spiritual authority is not located theistically or in the church, but in one's own inner voice. "The resulting 'unmediated individualism,' or sacralization of the Self, means that each person is now his or her own spiritual authority."[42] While the issue of authority has some differences, for much of Protestantism there is an emphasis on personal salvation that one must choose, grounded in a personal relationship with Jesus that is mediated by no one. Would this not also be a form of "unmediated individualism"? Perhaps in our dialogue it would be helpful for us to process our common entanglement in Western individualism and, maybe, to dialogue about the balancing role of community.

Entangled with Secularism

And what about the theme of secularism? Some would argue that the increase in those of you who identify as Nones is the direct result of an increasingly secular culture and the loss of religion in the public square. One of Elizabeth Drescher's categories is that of a Secular None, defined as "someone self-described as concerned with the separation of religion from public life."[43] She goes on to say, "Some academics, religious leaders, and members of the general public see growing unaffiliation as evidence of increasing American secularism, not unlike that seen in

---

42. Mercadante, *Belief without Borders,* 73.

43. Drescher, *Choosing Our Religion,* 28.

formerly majority Christian European nations."[44] In America, religious people themselves have been ambivalent about religion in public life with preference at times for a privatized form of religion in order to protect religion from the attacks of scientific reason (for example, in the Scopes trial in 1925 over evolution, in which conservative Christians won the legal case but lost in terms of public opinion and retreated for a time from the public square). At other times, minority religions have kept religion out of public life in order to protect their own form of religion from the dominant religion in the culture (for example, in Colonial America, Roman Catholics were told to keep their religion to themselves to avoid the persecution of dominant Protestants as seen in the seventeen-century instructions of the Second Lord Baltimore to the Catholics whom he allowed to settle in Maryland "to see that they suffer no scandal nor offense to be given to any of the Protestants . . . to worship as privately as may be, and not to discuss religious matters in public."[45]).

Similarly, the idea of the separation of church and state is strongly believed by many religious persons today, and it was an idea Christians in Colonial America fought to get ensconced in the American Constitution. Hence, we have no state church or state religion. However, many of those same religious persons expected to have religious influence in public life to the extent that some would say we had a *de facto* state church of a Protestant and pietistic kind until the 1960s. Since then, there continues the expectation that Christianity will be the national religion. When this ideal is threatened, the cry of secularism can become a rallying cry for legislated values and political influence. Of course, I understand this might create a backlash for some of you who identify as Nones and who would advocate for the exclusion of religion from public life. Interestingly though, some of you would be okay with spirituality in public life, such as yoga and meditation in the workplace or schools. Then, in reaction, some Christians would argue that it seems to be okay with you to have Eastern forms of religion in public life but not Christian forms. We are entangled. Can we dialogue about the role of religion and spirituality in our common, public life?

44. Drescher, *Choosing Our Religion*, 60.
45. Ahlstrom, *Religious History*, 331.

Entangled with Social Science

And what about faith and science, especially social science? Interestingly, it was liberal Protestantism that opened the door to the scientific evaluation of Scripture through forms of biblical and literary criticism in the late nineteenth and early twentieth centuries. They applied scientific reason to Scripture, asking many of the same questions that you as a None might ask today, such as why there appear to be contradictions in Scripture, or different accounts of the same events, or similarities with sacred texts in other religions.

Applying this same method of scientific inquiry, liberal Protestants joined with liberal secularists in the exploration of all world religions, both having an interest in common religious themes found in all faith traditions that could serve to unite people across cultures but also provide some proof as to a common experience of the divine. "These forays into the science of experience were far from purely academic, as American religious liberals embraced science and scientific methods, and both argued and hoped for demonstrations that 'true religion' was 'religion in general' and authentic religious experience and naturalistic theories of religion were not incompatible."[46] It is worth noting that the result of this line of scientific inquiry into world religions finds itself as a bedrock belief for most of you as Nones who have adopted some form of "perennialism" (i.e., the view that all religions at their core teach the same thing) and who have taken this belief to the next level in surmising that no one religion gets it completely right. As Linda Mercadante says of her interviewees, "What they did agree upon and articulate . . . was that because no one religion gets it all right, yet all at base teach certain fundamental principles, there was no need or motivation for them to align with any particular religious group."[47]

Another bedrock perspective for you as a None seems to come from a psychological understanding of the world and human nature. Building on the work of Linda Mercadante and Philip Rieff, Sean Fitzpatrick and William Parsons say about the SBNRs (Spiritual But Not Religious) that "the typical SBNRer surveys the religio-cultural terrain using a psychological lens. The major reason for this . . . is that we live in a cultural soup pervaded by . . . the 'triumph of the therapeutic.'"[48] The therapeutic

---

46. Bender, *New Metaphysics*, 10.

47. Mercadante, *Belief without Borders*, 188.

48. Fitzpatrick and Parsons, "Triumph of the Therapeutic," 30.

"cultural soup" was influenced from the religious side by the same liberal Protestants in the work of someone like Anton Boisen (1865–1965), who in 1925 began to train clergy in the hospital setting to integrate psychology and theology in the understanding of what he called the "living human document." Boisen based his case study method of training on what he learned from Richard C. Cabot, who was in the Harvard Medical School. Boisen felt that all clergy should be trained clinically, and his work still influences the clinical pastoral education (CPE) approach to the training of chaplains.[49]

At the same time, there developed the study of the psychology of religion, originating in America with William James (1842–1910) at Harvard. Someone like G. Stanley Hall (1846–1924), who was a student of James and who taught at Johns Hopkins University and then Clark University, worked intensely to integrate Christianity and psychology. His massive two-volume work, *Jesus, the Christ, in the Light of Psychology*, was published in 1917.[50] "This work better than any other captures the liberal religious effort to renovate Christianity in the light of psychology."[51] Many of the founders of this discipline, "men such as not only Hall but also George Coe, James Leuba, Edwin Starbuck, and James Mark Baldwin, had evangelical childhoods and yet were unable, as adults, to experience conversion or sustain conventional religious faith."[52]

One of the disciplines that emerged from this research was the field of pastoral counseling, or pastoral psychotherapy, with therapists who were trained in theology and psychology. This was not without controversy and not without significant ambivalence over the prospect of not only diagnosing psychological disorders but also diagnosing theological or spiritual disorders.[53] You might resonate with the feeling of one of these pastoral psychotherapists, who was criticized for integrating psychology into his pastoral work when he says,

> One reason Freud and Jung "rescued" theology for the modern age . . . is that they gave us tools to deal with man's true iconic depths, depths that pious and banal moralisms and preaching often missed by a thinly disguised legalism and/or grace

49. Asquith, *Vision*.

50. Hall, *Jesus, The Christ*.

51. Hedstrom, "Buddhist Fulfillment," 63.

52. Hedstrom, "Buddhist Fulfillment," 63.

53. Rodgerson, "To Diagnose or Not to Diagnose."

so generally applied that it resembled a doctor lining up his pneumonic patients and spraying penicillin at them instead of injecting it in their veins. One can scarcely fault the enthusiasms that carried pastoral psychology along when pastors began to discover the "injection methods" depth psychology and pagan doctors introduced to us.[54]

Even though you might not realize it, these movements have influenced the psychological "cultural soup" that is a bedrock to your worldview as a None. Although Buddhism is now the "soup de jour" in scientific attempts to integrate psychology and religion, replacing the role that Protestantism once had,[55] residuals of this integrative work are found in many self-help groups and especially in Alcoholics Anonymous. Linda Mercadante indicated that nearly one-third of the Nones she interviewed had some experience with a twelve-step group. "For many . . . this had been the alternative community that helped them deal with personal problems and where they got introduced to the idea of spirituality without religion."[56] The founder of Alcoholics Anonymous, Bill Wilson, was the first to popularize the phrase "spiritual but not religious," referring to AA as "a spiritual rather than a religious program." "Bill W. had been inspired by the writings of William James to develop a metaphysical rationale for a mode of spirituality that is at once deeply personal, optimistic, and progressivist and is couched in the essentially therapeutic language of self-actualization."[57]

In this complex entanglement, it was actually conservative Christians who rejected this intertwining of faith and the social sciences. From the Catholic perspective, the rejection of the modernist views of the Bible goes back to the nineteenth century. "In *Providentissimus Deus* (1893) Pope Leo had taken a very conservative position on critical studies of the Bible; and in 1907 Pope Pius X condemned 'modernism' in *Pascendi Gregis* and published a comprehensive Syllabus of Errors (*Lamentabili Sane*)."[58] The response of conservative Protestants to modernism was the publishing of ninety essays between 1910 and 1915 under the title of *The Fundamentals: A Testimony of Truth* as a defense of orthodox Protestant beliefs in opposition to such things as higher criticism, modernism,

54. Stein, "Reactions," 22.

55. Hedstrom, "Buddhist Fulfillment."

56. Mercadante, *Belief without Borders*, 173.

57. Fuller and Parsons, "Spiritual but Not Religious," 18.

58. Ahlstrom, *Religious History*, 839n9.

liberal theology, spiritualism, and evolution.[59] Christian Fundamentalism in America as we know it today had its origin here.

What is fascinating in this complex entanglement is that many of you as Nones have inherited much from liberal Protestantism while conservative Christianity has rejected much of liberal Protestantism. When you express an anti-Christian sentiment, it is often an attack on a form of Christianity that is conservative, often unaware that you are living out of many of the tenets argued for and developed by liberal Protestantism (and Vatican II Catholicism). Ironically, while your numbers increase as Nones in the general population, the greatest decline in numbers for the religiously affiliated is with liberal Protestant denominations. Can we dialogue further about our complex entanglement in ideas about faith and social science, and perhaps broaden that discussion to consider how faith and science generally become entangled in the term "spirituality" as a way of bridging the culturally constructed boundaries between science and religion?[60]

Entangled with Religious/Spiritual Experience

When I talk about religious or spiritual experience, I understand that for some of you as Nones this may not be a relevant topic. For instance, those of you in Cristel Manning's category of "Indifferents" mentioned above probably could not care less about such experiences. If that is the case for you, I would simply urge you to overhear the dialogue that might occur around this topic as an exercise in avoiding the stereotyping of either Nones or Somes.

However, what you may resonate with is a theme that emerges in this discussion concerning the importance of having an authentic self, or the importance of having "an internal rather than a transcendent 'locus of authority.'"[61] While this theme has relevance to many topics, it raises questions regarding the issue of religious or spiritual experience, such as who gets to decide the validity of those experiences and, even, who gets to decide what is spiritual. For the Nones, it is not simply a rebellion against authority but a question of relocating that authority. "They relocated it within, relativized it to each person, and detached it from any particular

59. Torrey and Dixon, *Fundamentals*.
60. Ecklund and Di Di, "Global Spirituality Among Scientists."
61. Mercadante, *Belief without Borders*, 74.

spiritual community."[62] For those in the Christian community, this has some resonance, since Jesus seemed to advocate something similar with his call to be in touch with a Spirit that flowed like water out of the heart (John 7:38) or the kingdom of God within (Luke 17:21) as distinct from having the religious or spiritual experience mediated through the external religious authorities of his day.

This desire for direct and unmediated spiritual experiences also seems to be important for many of you as Nones. Cortney Bender found the statement made by one of her interviewees to be relevant in many ways to what Nones were searching for when the interviewee said, "I think that in your research, what you're finding is that all of this is about direct experience."[63] Whether connected to bodily practices, feelings of energy, guided writing, channeling, or nature, there was for Bender's interviewees not only an internal authority but also an "experiential authority"[64] couched in consistent narrative plots that gave validation to the experience.

You, as a None, may not understand that for many Christians the desire for a direct experience with the divine is also important and is often indicative of whether one is a "true" Christian or not. *But the narrative plot is different.* For some Protestants, their conversion experience is often a validation of being "saved" and usually follows the narrative plot of the Apostle Paul's Damascus Road conversion experience in which he directly encounters the risen Jesus in a flash of light and a voice from heaven (Acts 9:1–9). For Roman Catholics there is the direct experience in the Mass of the Real Presence of Christ following the narrative plot of Jesus' last supper and his instilling of new meaning in the bread and wine as his body and his blood (Mark 14:22–25). (Similarly, every other faith tradition has its own narrative plot[s] about direct experience with the divine, but we are speaking only of the Christian religion here since the current dialogue is focused on Nones and Christians.)

The narrative plot for many of you as Nones (especially the Spiritual But Not Religious) is more like that of the nineteenth-century Transcendentalists (associated with the names of Ralph Waldo Emerson, Henry David Thoreau, Margaret Fuller, Louisa May Alcott, Walt Whitman, and others). As Jason Kelly says,

---

62. Mercadante, *Belief without Borders*, 186.

63. Bender, *New Metaphysicals*, 57.

64. Bender, *New Metaphysicals*, 69.

By encouraging self-reliance, liberalism, social reform, and a deep love of nature, the teachings of the transcendentalists presented an unorthodox, if not radical, response to the social and political challenges of their times, leading many of the movement's most prominent figures to question the authority of traditional religion. Ultimately, the transcendentalists called for a new way of *being-in-the-world*, one that valued spiritual experience over religious belief.[65]

Of course, Transcendentalism had ties to the doctrine of the Unitarian Church as taught at Harvard Divinity School at that time and later influenced the nineteenth-century "mental sciences" such as New Thought, Religious Science Unity, and Divine Science.[66] Many of you as Nones have experimented with these "mental sciences," but so have many Christians.

Transcendentalism is sometimes referred to as nature mysticism, and certainly there are connections with mysticism in your desire as a None for direct spiritual experience. While there are clear narrative patterns for mysticism within early Christianity, such as the Apostle Paul's visit to the third heaven (whatever that is!) in an out-of-body experience (2 Cor 12:1–4) or the visionary experience of St. John on the Isle of Patmos that produced the book of Revelation, the institutional church has always been cautious (or even reactive) toward "mystical" religion. For while direct religious experiences of individuals have the power to regenerate religious organizations, "a mysticism that takes shape outside of churchly settings also becomes a rhetorically valuable anti-religion: it is improperly socialized religion."[67] Hence, your desire for direct spiritual experience with an internal locus of authority raises complex entangled issues within the church as well as with you as a None operating outside of "churchly settings." As we continue to find new areas of reality and meaning, can we dialogue about the importance of direct spiritual experience and our different narrative plots that often provide a way of authenticating our internal sense of Self?

65. Kelly, "Rogue Mystics," 182.
66. Wikipedia, "Transcendentalism."
67. Bender, *New Metaphysicals*, 11.

What's the Story Going to Be?

While it is significant in our dialogue to name our different narrative plots as a way of dispelling misinformation and seeing similar values, in our "passing over" and "coming back" between our different worlds we also open up the possibility that we will become different persons. To be different persons, we not only develop the ability to name our narrative plots and to appreciate the narrative plots of others, but we also begin to see new story lines, new characters, new meaning in the same descriptions, or even entirely new plots and subplots in the stories that we tell ourselves about a complex and unpredictable world. As we dialogue around our entanglements, the way you understand individualism, or the secular, or science, or spiritual experience may open my eyes to new ways of understanding the Christian story, even if I keep the same plot of that story. From a Christian point of view, this reenvisioning of the Christian story would be more typical than unique. For instance, in the first century the Apostle Paul as a Jew was intent upon keeping the same plot to the story of a covenantal relationship between God and the people of God, but he reworked that story based upon his direct spiritual experience of a risen Christ and based upon his dialogue with the Greeks, Jews, and Romans of his day. Paul develops "a robust reappropriation of the Jewish beliefs—monotheism, election and eschatology, all rethought around the Messiah and the spirit" and "actually *invents* something we may call 'Christian theology.'"[68] While keeping the same plot, the church periodically (every five hundred years?) "reinvents" the Christian story in dialogue with the events and culture of the day, not unlike the pattern invented by Paul. Much of the Christian story today is still stuck in the deep narratives of Reformation and Counter-reformation from the sixteenth century (the last major reinvention) as well as in deep narratives of privilege and exceptionalism created when those stories were brought to America.[69] Could it be that our dialogue between you as a None and me as a Christian is part of a larger reenvisioning of the Christian story (and other stories) that is now called for in our entangled culture?

I understand that any reenvisioning of the Christian story is probably not a priority from your side of the dialogue as a None. In fact, having the identity of a None more than likely means that you have reworked the deep narratives of your life to remove the Christian plot from your

68. Wright, *Paul*, xvi.

69. Van Gelder and Zscheile, *God's Mission*.

identity narratives. Drawing upon the work of philosopher Paul Ricoeur, Elizabeth Drescher says that our identity is based on the stories we tell about ourselves and is comprised of two elements:

> A *stable self* made up of those parts of our stories that stay much the same over time—our birthdays, genders, personal and family names, and so on—and a more malleable, *reflexive identity* that, like musical notes on the lines of the staff, hum, trill, and harmonize with others to create an ongoing song of the Self. Religious affiliation has for a very long time been understood to be the baseline of the more static, stable self-identity, but it is more and more just one part in a grand self-identity opera with many different spiritual and religious variations.[70]

Or with no spiritual or religious variations at all! Our narrative identities are changing all the time. Identity crises can occur when we change the basic stories about ourselves; or when we move, for example, a religious story about ourselves from being a part of our static, stable self-identity to our malleable reflexive identity; or when we remove the religious story altogether. Many of you as Nones have found that when the religious stories as you know them no longer make sense, you experience an identity crisis which can involve the open rejection of a religious identity, or the faking of a religious identity in order to preserve certain relationships, or a deep wrestling with whether or not to switch to another narrative plot from another religious or spiritual story.

In my opinion, it is important to keep in mind, as we identify, discuss, and reenvision our deep narratives in light of our dialogue, that we are experiencing this in the context of much broader evaluations of our common stories including the (largely academic) discussion of whether or not, according to Postmodernism, there is any truth at all in common stories or meta-narratives (such as religious or cultural narratives). In that approach, there is no truth to larger religious stories about life. Truth resides only in individually constructed narratives as truth for that person only. Truth is relative. But, of course, the story that says there are no meta-narratives is itself a meta-narrative, leading, then, to the position of Metamodernism, which values the oscillation between modern and postmodern, between universal truths and political relativism, between construction and deconstruction, with an emphasis on the

70. Drescher, *Choosing Our Religion*, 38.

"between-ness" and what Linda Ceriello calls fluid identity narratives readily recognizable in the Spiritual But Not Religious.[71]

The broader context also includes current evaluations of our common American story (whether ultimately truthful or not) and the role that religion is to play in that story. In the documentary *God in America*,[72] Randall Balmer reminds us that Americans have always embodied the story that America has a unique role to play in the world as a providential nation and with a destiny ordained by God. In the seventeenth century, that story was articulated in the idea of a "city upon a hill" operating as a beacon to the rest of the world. In the eighteenth century, that story was articulated as the sacred cause of liberty. In the nineteenth century, it was manifest destiny. In the twentieth century, it was making the world safe for democracy. We have not yet developed a common articulation of the story for the twenty-first century. In that same film, Stephen Prothero goes on to say that from the beginning of American life, we have had this notion as a country of having a special relationship with God. Who is included in that special relationship with God has always been up for debate. As the debate has progressed, more and more people and more and more religions have been included in that special relationship. The sacred canopy has grown wider and wider. This moment in American life is about pluralism, and the question now is how important religion will remain. Will we be the most modern country in the world and also remain one of the most religious countries in the world? We have no narrative for this yet. Will we be able to come up with one? What's the story going to be?

I would argue that our dialogue is crucial for the emergence of that story. It is tied inextricably to the emergence of our individual stories, or deep narratives, in a process that will allow for the discovery of new areas of reality and meaning, and the revealing of still hidden truths—and where faith is not tied simply to competing religious stories about God but tied to the *direct experience of the process itself* by which new stories emerge and by which we come to understand the *grammar* that holds these stories together.

In that direct experience of the process itself, there resides a final reason why I would like to hold onto the description of you as a None. There is, in my opinion, significant meaning in the terminology of None

---

71. Ceriello, "Toward a Metamodern Reading," 202.

72. *God in America.*

that I would not want to lose. While I will say more about this in the second half of the book, I will confess at this point to valuing the "nothingness" that you as a None bring to this dialogue. Of course, the term "nothingness" as I am now using it has "multiple resonance." It is not a derogatory term but a term residing at the heart of many spiritual traditions. In some Eastern traditions, there is meaning beyond words in the idea of "emptiness" or "nothingness." Emptiness (*sunyata*) is connected to "non-self" or "not-self" (*anatman*), the experience of which opens us to Reality. Thich Nhat Hanh says, "We cannot talk about it, but we can experience it. We can experience the non-born, non-dying, non-beginning, non-ending because it is reality itself."[73]

In the Christian tradition, there is an approach to understanding, or drawing near to, God that is sometimes referred to as "negative theology" (*apophatic* theology) or the negative path (*via negativa*). This approach suggests that since God is beyond all that we can speak or comprehend; we can only know God by first moving to a state of unknowing where we empty ourselves of our own constructed ideas about God. For instance, in the sixteenth century, John of the Cross wrote about his spiritual journey, described as *The Ascent of Mount Carmel*. He provides a diagram of this journey with these words occurring at the very center: "The path of Mount Carmel the perfect spirit—nothing, nothing, nothing, nothing, nothing, nothing, and even on the Mount, nothing."[74]

In our dialogue, I would invite you to be curious with me about the significance of the "nothingness" that you bring to the dialogue as a None and how this is part of the "None-Sense." Your very presence as a None in this dialogue is a reminder of a way of being religious generally, and of a side to Christianity in particular, that is often lost in Western approaches to spirituality. When this side is lost, Christianity can become simplistic, materialistic, and even imperialistic. I wonder if your very presence as a None in the American culture is a necessary call to rebalance the very way in which we approach religion and spirituality. I even wonder if your identification as a None might have more significance to you than you realize if, in fact, you were to listen deeply to the "nothingness" that you are experiencing. If so, out of our mutual curiosity we might be able to create a narrative together that overcomes the "us" and "not us" stories

73. Hanh, *Living Buddha, Living Christ*, 139.
74. Kavanaugh, *John of the Cross*, 45 (punctuation added).

so prevalent in our culture today and allow for a story to emerge that will reveal still hidden truths.

However, before we can get there, more apologies are in order.

2

What Is the Shelf Life of Canned Religion?

Loss of Energy

ALONG WITH DIRECT EXPERIENCE (around which we are entangled), the word "energy" catches something that is important to many of you as Nones. What this energy is, or is not, is notoriously difficult to define. Sometimes the notion of energy is indirectly present in ideas you express about connection or in meaningful experiences that give feelings of enjoyment and fullness of life such as being in nature, or as reflected in Elizabeth Drescher's "Four F's of Contemporary American Spirituality: Family, Fido, Friends, and Food."[1] At other times, the concept of energy is directly referred to, such as when those of you explaining beliefs about transcendence have said, "I have trouble with the concept of God. But if you talk about a universal presence or a resonating energy at a certain frequency the result of that is quietude or peace, or the harmonics within you are quieted."[2] Or, "I'm having trouble [with the word] because 'sacred' means it's something that I have to detect . . . It's this formless energy that is present in all of life . . . I would call it spiritual energy. It's definitely not a single being."[3] Energy is even more important for those of you with metaphysical leanings, such as the Nones interviewed by Cortney Bender, who reports, "Rather than engage their flesh and blood bodies as the primary site of religious identity, metaphysicals favored language and imagery that highlighted their energetic bodies, manifested by

1. Drescher, *Choosing Our Religion*, 44.
2. Mercadante, *Belief without Borders*, 107.
3. Mercadante, *Belief without Borders*, 119.

particles of energy. '*We are just bits of energy, moving all the time,*' Crystal reminded me repeatedly. Hans echoed: '*We are all like the energies around us, just like the dust in the air.*'[4]

The energy language of "qi" or "prana" centered in the chakra system was often used, and practices such as meditation, yoga, Reiki, acupuncture, etc. "provided ways to find and maintain physical bodies that were open, aligned, or relaxed, and therein properly attuned to the energies that simultaneously coursed through them and constituted them."[5] Of course, as traced by Cortney Bender, these energy practices are seen to be a particularly Americanized version of Eastern religions, mediated through the Transcendentalists (especially the American "mind cure" offshoots of New Thought, Theosophy, and Spiritualism) and psychology (e.g., William James's concern for Americans' mental hygiene for which he offered esoteric Protestant practices in his 1899 address, "The Gospel of Relaxation"), and actualized in the meeting of Swami Vivekananda (who had come to speak at the World's Parliament of Religion in 1893) and William James in the Cambridge, Massachusetts home of Sarah Bull. Bender goes on to say,

> The similarities between William James's and Vivekananda's diagnoses and cures to what ailed tense, bottled-up Americans suggests a fertile mixing and meeting of various Asian and American concepts. The relations and overlap traveled in both directions, suggesting to some that Vivekananda's representation of yoga and the "classical Pedantic tradition" have "far more to do with a psychology born in the context of esoteric Protestantism."[6]

The 1965 publication of Jess Stearn's popular *Yoga, Youth, and Reincarnation* further sealed the connection of the *asanas* (yogi postures) energy attunement practice to American Transcendentalism through the lineage of Stearn's great-grandfather, who was pastor of First Church in Cambridge, Massachusetts, and knew the Transcendentalists personally. "Yoga becomes fundamentally *American*, translated and sprung from its Indian origins."[7]

While there are residuals of the entanglement theme from the last chapter emerging in this material, the point in this chapter has more to

4. Bender, *New Metaphysicals*, 90.

5. Bender, *New Metaphysicals*, 93.

6. Bender, *New Metaphysicals*, 109.

7. Bender, *New Metaphysicals*, 110.

do with the importance of energy for many of you as Nones; how it is understood by you, and how this contributes to your rejection of religious institutions when the experience of this energy is missing or better found somewhere else. The fact that this energy is missing from religious institutions is supported by the very definitions of "religion" and "spirituality" that have been culled from the general population by sociologists and psychologists as they have tried to understand the emerging distinctions between these words. For instance, listen to this definition of "spirituality" coming from counseling research: "The animating force in life, represented by such images as breath, wind, vigor, and courage. Spirituality is the infusion and drawing out of spirit in one's life. It is experienced as an active and passive process. It also is described as a capacity and tendency that is innate and unique to all persons. It moves the individual towards knowledge, love, meaning, hope, transcendence, connectedness, and compassion."[8] Now hear the definition of "religion" from that same research: "Religion refers to a set of beliefs and practices of an organized religious institution. Religion tends to be expressed in ways that are denominational, external, cognitive, behavioral, ritualistic, and public."[9]

Across his research, Robert Wuthnow[10] found these words associated with "spirituality": something that is personal, authentic, real, has to do with a meaningful relationship with God, has to do with a unique experience that impacts one's life, has to do with openness and not with rules and regulations, and is sometimes found in churches but often is not. On the contrary, he found these words associated with "religion": something that is structured, traditional, historical, distant, cold, organized, ritualistic, fear-based, social, limiting to life, not meeting one's needs, and associated with churches and church buildings. Out of such research, there developed the following joke: religion is defined as a person who goes to church and thinks about fishing, and spirituality is defined as a person who goes fishing and thinks about God. In whatever way you might define the concept of energy, it appears almost by definition that it is something harder to find in institutional religion.

This is interesting given the fact that all institutional religions have at their center stories and words that speak to this essential energy of life where biology and spirituality are interwoven. "Breath" and "spirit" are

---

8. Wiggins-Frame, "Spirituality and Religion," 15.

9. Wiggins-Frame, "Spirituality and Religion," 15.

10. Wuthnow, *After Heaven.*

referenced in the same word in most religious traditions. *Prana*, coming from the Hindu tradition, means life-force, vitality, breath, omnipresent and infinite power of the universe, or cosmic energy. *Ruach*, coming from the Jewish tradition, means breath, wind, or spirit. *Pneūma*, coming from the Christian tradition, also means breath, wind, or spirit. The fullness of life was always found in the recognition of an essential energy of life that was beyond biological breathing but intertwined with it. The evidence for the presence of this essential life energy in the life of a person or community (sometimes referred to as "fruit" of the spirit) could be variously described with words like sorrowless joy, happiness, righteousness, justice, compassion, bliss, love, light, peace, patience, kindness, humility, healing, etc. The intricacies of every institutional religion were originally designed to reveal the source of, and a path to, this essential life energy through unique spiritual beliefs and practices, with implications for becoming fully human in this life and the afterlife. I imagine that this same essential life force has something to do with the energy that is important to you as a None. (If you are an Indifferent or an Atheistic None, you may prefer the Bergsonian philosophical concept of the *élan vital* as "the original life force, the creative linking principle in the evolution of all organisms."[11]) What is interesting is the fact that, almost by definition, this essential energy will *not* be found by you in institutional religion and, particularly for our None-Christian dialogue, will *not* be found by you in the beliefs and practices of churches. When this is true, in my opinion, you need to hear an apology from the Christian side of our dialogue acknowledging that we (as Christians) have somehow failed in our core reason for existing as an institution.

For the purposes of our dialogue, you might be interested to know that for Christian Somes there is a real concern about the presence of this life-giving energy in what they do, often resulting in an over-focus (as seen in the disproportionate amount of time, energy, and resources expended) on how this might happen in a church worship service one hour each week. The term "energy" might not be used, but you can hear resonance with the term when worshippers reflect on whether the Spirit was present or not; whether there was a Presence or not; whether one was moved, or felt uplifted, or felt alive or not. Of course, this can get rather complicated because what might bring a sense of aliveness to one person is a spiritual killer to the next. Shall we have a praise band

---

11. *Webster's Dictionary*, "*Élan vital*," 581.

playing contemporary music, or a majestic organ with traditional hymns or classical music? Shall we gather in a simple meeting house, a soaring cathedral, or an amphitheater? Shall we have spontaneous expressions of faith or a solemn ritual that points us to the beyond? In our marketplace culture, people will often sort themselves out for church attendance less by denominations and more by worship style where they can experience an energy or, perhaps as in your case as a None, opt out altogether.

All of this can put a lot of pressure on those who have been tasked with the responsibility to make this energy available to people on a weekly basis—usually the clergy. You can see how this might lead to an over-focus on the clergy and their ability to perform, entertain, or please the majority. It might also create a susceptibility to such things as manipulating the emotions of people, hiding behind the liturgy, blurring the lines between certain feeling states and the Transcendent, or feeling a sense of failure when worship attendance declines.

Further, you can see how this might encourage clergy or denominational leaders to look for ways to minimize the uncertainty in this process by creating packaged ways to replicate the experience of this energy. Craig Van Gelder and Dwight Zscheile speak of many post-World War II Protestant churches as "franchise churches" where denominational Sunday school curricula, hymnbooks, and worship resources were utilized by denominationally trained clergy who became a part of the "machine." "Like interchangeable parts in a machine, they were understood to be capable of serving in any franchise outpost of the denomination. In the postwar suburban-church boom there were even standard architectural designs for church buildings available off the shelf from denominational offices."[12] Along with the "franchise" approach, there was a tendency to institutionalize high-energy experiences such as camp meetings, tent meetings, or revivals; "these movements all too often become institutionalized into standardized programs that rely on technique to continue trying to re-create the experience of what took place originally—for example, the church that schedules an annual revival each year in the third week of August."[13]

This loss of energy through a franchise approach or functional repetition of an earlier experience is not lost on the fictional world. Jayber

---

12. Van Gelder and Zscheile, *God's Mission*, 290.

13. Van Gelder and Zscheile, *God's Mission*, 265.

Crow describes the seminary students who came to pastor the small church in Port William, Kentucky, as

> always young students from the seminary who wore, you might say, the mantle of power but not the mantle of knowledge. They wouldn't stay long enough to know where they were for one thing . . . They were not going to school to learn where they were, let alone the pleasures and pains of being there, or what ought to be said there. You couldn't learn those things in school. They went to school, apparently, to learn to say over and over again, regardless of where they were, what had already been said too often.[14]

Taking a more dystopian approach in describing a fictional, highly controlled, and militantly managed Christian society in North America, Margaret Atwood at one point has one of the Handmaids describe franchise stores known as the Soul Scrolls located in every city center and suburb. In these stores are machines with the disrespectful name of Holy Rollers that

> print out prayers, roll upon roll, prayers going out endlessly . . . There are five different prayers; for health, for wealth, a death, a birth, a sin. You pick the one you want, punch in the number, then punch in your own number so your account will be debited, and punch in the number of times you want the prayer repeated.[15]

While you can see the fictional exaggeration here, it picks up on something that can be all too real. In my own experience of having served for a number of years as a parish pastor, I have heard plenty of prayers that seemed to come out of a machine, whether read out of a prayer book or "spontaneously" offered in a format that was clearly scripted by a unique religious subculture. I have also experienced denominational formatting, or local church customs, that operated like a sacred unwritten law, violated at the risk of losing one's career.

I had a pastor friend during this period of my life who advised young ministers to be cautious about ever pastoring a church with a cemetery next to it. While he obviously overlooked some of the positive aspects of family and community represented in those cemeteries, he warned that those in the graves could still control the church through their

14. Berry, *Jayber Crow*, 160.
15. Atwood, *Handmaid's*, 167.

descendants. In reality, there are "cemeteries" next to any church strongly influencing the current moment. All of this obviously affected me at conscious and unconscious levels at the time because I had a dream, which I still remember with great clarity, in which I am a store clerk stocking shelves with canned goods, and a voice comes out of nowhere and says, "*What is the shelf life of canned religion?*"

It is easy to be critical here. People are often just doing the best they can, and they are simply trying to pass on to others the spiritual energy they have experienced. "Canning" the experience is an attempt to preserve the experience and make it available to others, with an ironic side effect of protecting the "canner" from any new experience. (You see, *new* transforming spiritual experiences can be dangerous and unsettling; they are not all happiness and bliss in the beginning.) Perhaps we need expiration dates on our canned religion. In my opinion, we need to offer you as a None an apology when we offer you a canned religion whose expiration date has long passed; a canned religion that reminds us of where *we were* but misses where *you are*; a canned religion that now may be toxic. It would be helpful to me if we could dialogue about this.

Bound to What?

If there is a lack of spiritual energy in the very cultural definition of religion, with some of the reason for this found in the honest attempt to "can" a once vital experience, it is worth pursuing the problems inherent in the transmission of any spiritual experience and the difficulties inherent in the very meaning of religion as having something to do with "binding" (The word "religion" comes from the Latin noun *religio*, which in turn comes from the Latin verb *religare* meaning "to bind back" or "to bind together.").[16] The very idea of being "bound" to something probably raises a red flag for you as a None since many of you reportedly exercise caution in the commitment or obligation to groups—especially spiritual groups. Linda Mercadante found in her interviews of Nones "the overwhelming agreement among interviewees that their primary spiritual commitment was to themselves and their own growth"[17] and that their ideal group would have "no dogma, no written texts, no labels, no belief systems, no symbols, no pressure, no fixed leadership, and would

16. *Webster's Dictionary,* "Religion," 1527.

17. Mercadante, *Belief without Borders,* 165.

be entirely non-judgmental."[18] It would be natural, then, in our dialogue for you to raise questions around the process of "binding" and to ask, "Bound to what?"

In the first century, when Christianity emerged, religion was defined as a binding process in which humans and the gods were bound together in the *cultus deorum* (cult of the gods) through cultic "obligations" (*religiones*). The cultic obligations were, in fact, "cultural," meaning that not only were individual humans and the gods bound together in these acts, but also there was a binding of the community, the entire culture. The cultic obligations involved ascertaining the will of the gods, the proper public ordering of worship, sacrifice, prayer, etc. N. T. Wright goes on to say:

> All was done, as far as Cicero was concerned . . . in relation to "a political community or body of citizens, one that included both humans and gods." The whole point was to maintain and enhance the *pax deorum*, the "peace of the gods": the Roman people and their divinities had to maintain a harmonious relationship, and anything which went wrong in personal or civic life had to be analyzed, diagnosed, and treated with appropriate "religious" ceremony (sacrifice, prayer, the fulfilling of oaths, or whatever). Much better, though, to get the religious observances right in the first place and thus ensure that all would be well.[19]

Of course (as noted previously), in this sense Christianity was not a religion. But there quickly developed (especially through the writings of the Apostle Paul) resonances of this kind of religion through unique practices of worship inclusive of prayer, baptism, and the Eucharist (Lord's Supper). These were binding exercises or obligations (*religiones*) for binding together the community of God, but *not* for the purpose of appeasing God or keeping one united to the wider culture. These binding exercises were for the purpose of binding the individuals in the spiritual community to one another and to God for the purpose of experiencing (body, mind, and soul) agape-love[20] and transmitting that love in all their relationships.

But the binding process can go awry in at least two ways, both of which are transmission problems where the direct experience of anything

18. Mercadante, *Belief without Borders*, 189.

19. Wright, *Paul*, 253–54.

20. This term as used throughout the book refers to the sacrificial love revealed in Christ as characteristic of God and essential for Christian community, coming from the Greek word *'agápe*.

deeply spiritual (like true agape-love) can be very difficult to transmit to another person or another generation. On the one hand, how do you keep alive or expand in your own life what you might have experienced as mystical oneness, or unspeakable joy, or abiding love, or luminous vastness? On the other hand, how might you share that experience with someone else when, in fact, the experience is beyond words? Many would say that the transmittal of these experiences can only happen without words. (We will come back to this in the second half of this book.) For instance, there is the saying that Christianity can only be caught, not taught.

Michael Polanyi confronted this problem in his exploration of how true knowledge could be transmitted from one generation to the next. He concluded that such knowledge could only be transmitted tacitly. He came to this conclusion by observing master craftsmen and how they would pass on their craft to an apprentice. Polanyi visited tanneries to understand how a master tanner would select hides for leather goods. He observed wine connoisseurs and other experts whose knowledge could not be formulated explicitly in formulae. For instance, he observed that a novice violin maker could produce an instrument that met the exact technical specifications, but when played produced a poor quality of sound. Only in repeatedly working beside a master violin maker, watching the master select the wood and then shape and adjust the instrument to the uniqueness of the wood, did the novice begin to produce a quality instrument.[21] Polanyi says, "All arts are learned by intelligently imitating the way they are practiced by other persons in whom the learner places his confidence . . . The tacit coefficients of speech are transmitted by inarticulate communications, passing from an authoritative person to a trusting pupil, and the power of speech to convey communication depends on the effectiveness of this mimetic transmission."[22]

Understanding and transmitting something that is essentially beyond words and beyond normal human experience is a real problem for craftsmen, artists, theologians, mystics, and even astrophysicists. (For example, Professor S. James Gates Jr. from Brown University, with expertise in supersymmetric particles, fields, and strings, wrote a paper connecting a description of the universe to ancient African adinkra symbols.)[23] Spiritual experiences, spiritual energy (like agape-love), or a vital life

---

21. Rodgerson, "Attending to Hidden Realities."

22. Polanyi, *Personal Knowledge*, 206.

23. Gates, "Symbols of Power."

force of creation are especially difficult to define, discuss, or transmit because words fail us. Out of this difficulty, our human inclination is to *bind* the spiritual experience to something and, in the process, to become religiously *bound* ourselves.

A Type-One Error in the Binding Process

One way in which the binding process goes awry, arising from the difficulty of trying to transmit the essence of a spiritual experience or spiritual energy that is beyond words and primarily transmitted through inarticulate communications, is to become *bound primarily to the religious obligations (religiones) themselves* (i.e., the forms of worship, the rituals, the prayers, the doctrines, the creeds) and mistake this experience for an actual binding to, or connection with, the original spiritual experience or vital spiritual energy. Forms of religious expression such as prayer or worship are natural attempts to remember a profound spiritual experience and to bring it into the present. These forms of religious expression are also natural mechanisms for trying to introduce others to the very life and energy of the original spiritual experience. However, since it is easier to communicate and transmit the forms of religious expression (the obligations or *religiones*) than it is to transmit the unspeakable spiritual experience or energy itself, it is easy to become bound to the forms of religious expression and mistake this for a binding to the actual spiritual energy (like agape-love). In time, the religion loses its ability to "bind" people to anything other than the external religious forms of that religion.

In the language of Michael Polanyi, the religion, then, begins to over-focus on the technical specifications of how to "make the violin," missing the necessary "inarticulate communications."[24] The master craftsman in this case becomes the pious one who knows and carries out these binding obligations or right way to do things. As apprentices, we are taught to bind ourselves to these well documented and technical formulas so that we might experience something but, in the process, miss that which is inarticulate. Using our previous metaphor, we are taught to bind ourselves to the canning process rather than learning the essence of what is worth preserving.

Another image of the binding process going awry came to my attention in visits to places like Jerusalem and Rome. On nearly every

24. Polanyi, *Personal Knowledge*, 206.

site where historical tradition records the occurrence of an important spiritual event, there now stands a basilica. They are often beautiful. They transmit something in their beauty that might be a form of inarticulate communication, but they are often fought over and have the same problems as any church with a cemetery next to it.

This problem was anticipated by Jesus in a high-energy moment with his disciples when he was transfigured before them, having his countenance altered and being seen with Moses and Elijah. Peter immediately wants to build three "booths" on the spot to mark and preserve the experience. Instead, the disciples are instructed not to build anything but to remain in the silence, learning how to preserve the inarticulate communication of the experience (Matt 17:1–8, Mark 9:2–8; Luke 9:28–36). In another way, the author of the First Epistle of John in the Christian Scriptures speaks to the transmission issue, coming at a time when the first generation of those who had directly experienced life with Jesus were passing away—those who had seen and heard and touched the Word of Life and who now wanted to testify to their direct spiritual experience and pass on the vital energy of eternal life (1 John 1:1–4). John proclaims that what they experienced revealed God as light and that the light is transmitted by following only one commandment, the commandment to abide in agape-love, a love that casts out all fear (1 John 4:18). He goes on to say, "Whoever says 'I am in the light,' while hating a brother or sister, is still in the darkness. Whoever loves a brother or a sister lives in the light, and in such a person there is no cause for stumbling" (1 John 2:9–10).

Herein lies the evidence for the existence of a type-one error in the binding process—when one demonstrates a strong adherence to the obligations (*religiones*) of the faith (e.g., prayer, regular worship, daily Mass, Scripture reading) but fails to communicate agape-love; when one overtly transmits the technical formulas of the faith (e.g., what one must do to be "saved" or to not be excommunicated from the church), but tacitly, through inarticulate communications, communicates something very different from agape-love. In that case, one is bound in their religion (*religio*) to the obligations (*religiones*) of the faith but has missed the essentials of the binding process that would "bind" that person to the very energy of agape-love and to relationships of love in the spiritual community.

It is easy to caricature a person who experiences this type-one error, such as the character of Church Lady on *Saturday Night Live* television broadcasts when my children were growing up. We had a neighbor whom they would call "Church Lady." She was probably the most faithful person in the neighborhood to her Pentecostal religion, attending services several times a week, praying faithfully for others, and witnessing to others whom she noticed were not in church on Sundays. But she was experienced by the children as the meanest lady on the block with her scolding words and judgmental attitude, which clearly transmitted something other than agape-love. As a None, you have probably experienced this type of religious person. You may not have realized, however, that this is a type-one error in the binding process of religion where the person becomes bound to the obligations (*religiones*) of the faith without being bound to, or connected to, the vital energy of agape-love.

A Type-Two Error in the Binding Process

The other way in which the binding process goes awry, arising from the difficulty of trying to transmit the essence of an experience of spiritual energy that is beyond words and primarily transmitted through inarticulate communications, is to unwittingly *bind the original spiritual experience to the language and symbols of the culture in which one lives* to the point that the cultural manifestation of the faith is mistaken for the essence of the original spiritual experience. Again, it is natural and necessary to use the language and the cultural forms of expression that we and others know in order to try and communicate our spiritual experiences or perceptions. For instance, the Apostle Paul very clearly uses the language and cultural symbols of Israel, Greece, and Rome to try and convey the essence of his experience of the risen Jesus. But while he might be using the same language and symbols with multiple resonances, he is always pointing clearly to something else.

You can see how this gets confusing by looking at some of the definitions of "religion" and "culture" and noting how both rely on images and symbols to convey what is important in the human experience. For instance, Don Browning, in defining "culture," says, "By culture I mean a system of symbols and norms which guides a society or group by providing general images of the nature of the world, the purpose of life, and... the basic principles by which life should be lived."[25] Compare that with a discussion of "religion" in which Dale Cannon says, "Religion or religious practice involves a system of symbols and symbolic actions for

25. Browning, *Religious Thought*, 5.

drawing near to and coming into right relationship to ultimate reality."[26] It is quite easy to confuse religious symbols and cultural symbols that intend to convey the purpose of life or ultimate reality, especially when those symbols are being used to point to something beyond words. For instance, the Apostle Paul used the ideal image of a good citizen in the Roman Empire (someone who respects authority, pays their taxes, and pays their debts to their neighbors) as the ideal image of what it means to be a good Christian (Rom 13). But when these things are done, informed by the command to "love your neighbor as yourself" and with allegiance to a "Lord" who is not Caesar, these images of being a good citizen take on very different meanings, generating a very different kind of power for the citizen and actually subverting the power of Caesar nonviolently. To be a good citizen in this way, one had to find a way to be bound to the vital spiritual energy of agape-love and not bound primarily to the empire. This became much harder when the Christian religion became the official religion of the Roman Empire in the fourth century, and the possibility arose in which one could live as a good citizen with allegiance to Christian kings and Popes while having lost touch with the nonviolent and subversive power of agape-love.

Similarly, in "Christian America," there can occur a binding process where Christian spirituality is bound fast to and obligated to the surrounding culture itself. When this occurs, it is possible that the direct spiritual experience and vital spiritual energy of the faith gets confused with the "good citizen energy" of patriotism, nationalism, or family and local traditions, mingling with the feel-good emotional experience of favorite hymns, a certain style of preaching, or a comfortable ritual. The very way in which the Christian story is told for the purpose of transmission becomes culturally formulated in a familiar cultural style in which cultural symbols and religious symbols become confused if not completely merged.

For instance, you have only to listen to Christian sermons or homilies around the Fourth of July in the USA to get an idea of the total confusion of, or merger of, Christian symbols of "freedom" with patriotic symbols of "freedom." As the transmission of the original spiritual experience gets bound to the language and symbols of the culture and no longer bound to the vital energy of agape-love, what is lost is the ability to make appropriate distinctions around what "freedom" means. Or, in

26. Cannon, *Six Ways*, 32.

the language of the Apostle Paul, who faced this same type-two error in the early church, "For you were called to freedom, brothers and sisters; only do not use your freedom as an opportunity for self-indulgence, but through love become slaves to one another. For the whole law is summed up in a single commandment, 'You shall love your neighbor as yourself.' If, however, you bite and devour one another, take care that you are not consumed by one another" (Gal 5:1–5).

These errors in the binding process due to transmissions problems can be clearly seen in the research of Kenda Creasy Dean on the religion of American teenagers who, she says (like American adults), "appear positively besotted with religion,"[27] but it is a religion from the Christian point of view that is "Christian-ish" or "almost Christian." Building on the data gathered in the National Study of Youth and Religion (NSYR), this kind of faith is aptly described as Moralistic Therapeutic Deism. "The faith most teenagers exhibit is a loveless version that the NSYR calls Christianity's 'misbegotten stepcousin,' Moralistic Therapeutic Deism, which is 'supplanting Christianity as the dominant religion in American churches'"[28] for which the teens' parents and the congregations in which they participate are responsible, she says. It is a transmission issue where what is being transmitted is "almost Christian" and that calls for a different approach to the "mission" that is in the trans*mission* of the faith.

Such errors in which the Christian experience gets inextricably bound to particular religious forms or to the dominant culture have also prompted calls for a "religionless Christianity." Dietrich Bonhoeffer suggested this idea in his *Letters and Papers from Prison* as he waited for his death in a Nazi prison, contemplating how the Christian church could be so erroneously bound to Hitler's Nazi Germany. He asks, "If religion is only a garment of Christianity—and even this garment has looked very different at times—then what is a religionless Christianity?"[29] Commenting on this trend, Robert Wuthnow noted that Harvey Cox was living in Berlin prior to writing *The Secular City* and "he read Bonhoeffer's works and was deeply influenced by them. Cox argued that 'dereligioning' was a good thing because it freed people from oppressive moralities and made them think hard about their own spirituality."[30] Even the "death-of-God"

27. Dean, *Almost Christian*, 193.

28. Dean, *Almost Christian*, 7.

29. Bonhoeffer, *Letters and Papers*, 280.

30. Wuthnow, *After Heaven*, 73.

controversy in the 1960s, with Thomas J. J. Altizer at the center, was really not so much about the death of God or even the death of religion, but about calls for the death of a Christianity that had become bound to the religious forms and cultural symbols in a way that actually blocked the ability to be bound to the vital spiritual energy of agape-love. Leigh Schmidt, quoting a reflection in the *Christian Century* ten years after the "death-of-God" controversy, says, "To affirm the death of God was to remove the Mosaic-Calvinistic censor from the door of the Holy of Holies and to break open the white, masculine, Protestant world of divinity."[31]

I can only wonder as we continue our dialogue if your decision to become a None, to become religiously unaffiliated, has in some sense been similar to, or influenced by, these trends that have picked up on a type-one or a type-two error in the religious binding process. Intuitively, you may have known that these problems can actually cause any religion to become toxic or, using the metaphor with which we started this chapter, a form of canned religion that is long past its expiration date.

Toxic Side Effects

If, in the binding process of religion (remembering that *religio* comes from *religare*, meaning "to bind" or "to bind together"), we become bound to religious externals or bound to cultural symbols instead of being *bound* to the original spiritual experience and vital spiritual energy of agape-love, at some point the essence of the original spiritual experience and the vital spiritual energy is lost. For example, we may have the words for love, but the actual energy of love to transform any suffering or darkness or negativity is either completely lost or remains in a shadowy mirage of promise and possibility. For a period of time, we can resort to canned religion to preserve and pass on the original spiritual experience or energy, but eventually whatever has been "canned" loses its vitality. It has no energy and no ability to discern between spiritual power and the power of empire. As empty ritual, it operates like a vacuum, drawing to it any passing spiritual fad or charismatic personality.

What happens next is truly remarkable. To some degree, it is a brilliant solution (if you will allow me to play with this metaphor of "canning" a bit further). Since we no longer have any of the original spiritual experience or vital energy to "can," and we still have all of the external Christian

31. Schmidt, "Death-of-God Theology," 50.

labels that tell us what should be in the can, why not fill the cans with something else? In fact, we can fill the cans with whatever is still existing in our lives that has nothing to do with agape-love. We can take our fear, hatred, jealousy, anger, violence, unresolved trauma, etc. and put it in the cans and put the cans on a shelf. That way we do not have to look at these things anymore and, to some extent, these undesired tendencies within us are "taken care of;" they have been "converted" from "seen" to "not seen" in our conversion to the faith. Better yet, others cannot see these things (or so we hope), especially because the cans have a Christian label on them, thus giving us a new image or identity. There is only one problem—since the cans now hold toxic material, they eventually leak.

There is a name for this in the social science research community: *spiritual bypass*. Here is an early definition: "Spiritual bypass refers to the use of spiritual experiences, beliefs, or practices to avoid (or bypass) psychological wounds and other personal and emotional unfinished business, in essence rejecting these experiences."[32] Here is a somewhat refined definition by those who created an instrument (with the two sub-scales of psychological avoidance and spiritualizing) to measure spiritual bypass: "We define spiritual bypass as a defensive psychological posture cultivated by a tendency to privilege or exaggerate spiritual beliefs, emotions, or experiences over and against psychological needs creating a means of avoiding or bypassing difficult emotions or experiences."[33] Here are the negative consequences of spiritual bypass as recorded by these researchers:

> Possible negative consequences of spiritual bypass include the need to control others and self, dichotomous thinking, shame, spiritual obsession, fear, emotional confusion, addiction, high tolerance for inappropriate behavior, codependence, pain, compulsive goodness, narcissism or ego inflation, obsession or addiction, blind belief in charismatic teachers, spiritual materialism (use of spiritual practice for material gain), developmental arrest, and abdication of personal responsibility.[34]

In the language of our current metaphor, we have a can with a Christian label on it that has found a way to get rid of toxic personal material (presumably out of sight and out of mind) and we have put it on a shelf. Now, rather than having a storehouse of agape-love, one has a storehouse

---

32. Cashwell et al., "Using Developmental Counseling," 403.

33. Fox et al., "Opiate of the Masses," 2.

34. Fox et al., "Opiate of the Masses," 2.

of toxic material, and the toxic material always leaks. This is not a new phenomenon. Speaking to the religious leaders of his day, Jesus used the following metaphor: "Woe to you, scribes and Pharisees, hypocrites! For you are like whitewashed tombs, which on the outside look beautiful, but inside they are full of the bones of the dead and all kinds of filth" (Matt 23:27).

Neither is this a phenomenon limited to the Christian religion. With the popularity of Buddhism in America, Wilber labeled this as "Boomeritis Buddhism" where "very quickly Buddhism—known as the 'religion of no-ego'—often became 'the religion of express your ego.'"[35] In this case, one could appear to be avant-garde with one's practice of mindfulness meditation and Eastern externals, while at the same time completely avoiding the inner work of "emptiness." Craig Cashwell also noted how spiritual bypass can happen in twelve-step groups and hamper the recovery process, such as a misstep in Steps One and Three where, in the process of admitting powerlessness and turning one's life over to a higher power, one "wholly abdicates personal responsibility for his or her program of recovery."[36]

A powerful image of this phenomenon from the non-religious world comes from the Marshall Islands where, during the Cold War, the United States dropped nuclear and biological weapons on the islands sixty-seven times for the purposes of testing. Reporting on this, Matthew Gault says, "Once the US finished, it scooped the irradiated and ruined soil from the islands, poured it into a crater left behind from a nuclear detonation, mixed it all with concrete, and covered the whole thing in a concrete dome. They called it 'The Tomb.'"[37] Now with rising sea levels due to climate change, The Tomb is cracking open, leaking its toxic material into the Pacific Ocean.

In all fairness, spiritual bypass as a phenomenon is not totally negative. It may be a necessary step in spiritual development in which negative aspects of our inner selves are contained until we can learn how to transform them by means of agape-love. We must start somewhere. This is especially true for someone coming out of a chaotic world such as that of addiction or violence. Containment may be necessary before

35. Wilber, *Integral Spirituality*, 105.
36. Cashwell et al., "Step by Step," 41.
37. Gault, "Climate Change."

true transformation is possible. Or, spiritual bypass may be a short-term adaptive solution that temporarily relieves depression.

However, if spiritual bypass is used as a long-term solution or contributes to an illusion that one "has arrived" at a spiritual pinnacle (e.g., having been "saved" or having "perfected" some sort of spiritual practice), it always leaks. It leaks in the everyday "meanness" of the Church Lady mentioned above. It leaks in the life of someone like Rev. Ted Haggard, who built a megachurch in Denver, Colorado, and who became president of the National Association of Evangelicals. He preached a gospel of clear morals to the point of supporting Amendment 2, a Colorado referendum nullifying civil protections for gays and lesbians. Then, in November 2006, it came to light that for several years Haggard had a relationship with Mike Jones of Denver, a male prostitute who also sold him sex and methamphetamines.[38] It leaks in the sexual abuse of minors by Catholic priests. It leaks in someone like the powerful Texan judge, Paul Pressler, who was an architect of the Conservative Resurgence that took over the Southern Baptist Convention and then partnered with the Council on National Policy to build a right wing takeover of mid-America media and Republican politics in order to revive "Christian morality" in the country, only to be accused in 2019 of paying hush money to Duane Rollins to cover up sexual activities with him that began when he was only fourteen. This became known as the "worst-kept secret in Houston."[39]

At some point, canned religion that has passed its expiration date, or that has canned that which is not love, becomes a poison that leaks. Just as the Greek word, *pharmakos* (the root of the English word for "pharmacy"), can mean "medicine" or "poison" (think, for instance, of chemotherapy with its potential for healing and for toxic side effects), so can religion be a source of life-giving energy or a deadly toxin. While, in the first century, Ignatius (AD 30–107) could write in his Epistle to the Ephesians that the Eucharist was the "medicine of immortality [*pharmakon athanasias*], and . . . a cleansing remedy driving away evil,"[40] that same act of the Eucharist, taken only as a *pro forma* ritual or as some form of magical protection, can be evidence of a canned poison. (Note that I am *not* saying the Eucharist itself is poison.)

---

38. Vick, "Trial by Fury."

39. Nelson, *Shadow Network*, 266.

40. Roberts and Donaldson, *Ante-Nicene Fathers*, 57.

In her novel *The Poisonwood Bible*, Barbara Kingsolver writes a story told by the wife and four daughters of Rev. Nathan Price, a fierce evangelical Baptist from Georgia who takes his family as missionaries to the Belgian Congo in 1959. They carry with them everything they believe they will need from home, but they soon find that all of it—from garden seeds to Scripture—is calamitously transformed on African soil. Reflecting at the end of their sojourn in the Congo after a complete failure of the mission, Rachel Price says, "You can't just sashay into the jungle aiming to change it all over to the Christian style, without expecting the jungle to change you right back . . . Father's mistake, see, was to try to convert the whole entire shebang over into his exact way of thinking."[41] Like the preachers experienced by Jayber Crow (mentioned above) who didn't go to school to learn where they were, but to say "over and over again regardless of where they were what had already been said too often,"[42] Rev. Nathan Price did not allow the difficulties of the jungle to transform him, but kept pushing a canned religion that did not acknowledge where he was, symbolized in what he said over and over again each Sunday. His daughter Ada Price tells it this way:

> "TATA JESUS IS BANGALA!" declares the Reverend every Sunday at the end of his sermon. More and more, mistrusting his interpreters, he tries to speak in Kikongo. He throws back his head and shouts these words to the sky, while his lambs sit scratching themselves in wonder. *Bangala* means something precious and dear. But the way he pronounces it, it means the poisonwood tree. Praise the Lord, hallelujah, my friends! for Jesus will make you itch like nobody's business.[43]

The words that were intended to be a medicine became a poison.

At least for some of you who identify as a None, this is familiar territory because you have lived it. In their book, *Empty the Pews: Stories of Leaving Church*, Chrissy Stroop and Lauren O'Neal have compiled numerous stories from Nones who experienced the Christian religion not as a healing medicine but as a poison. Deirdre Sugiuchi tells the story of how she grew up in a family that became fundamentalist after her father had a conversion experience and began to apply the teaching of Bill Gothard, the founder of the Institute in Basic Life Principles. These principles

---

41. Kingsolver, *Poisonwood Bible*, 515–16.

42. Berry, *Jayber Crow*, 160.

43. Kingsolver, *Poisonwood Bible*, 276.

included rigid rules about dress, socializing, entertainment, etc. with the father being the head of the household who, in his attitude of not sparing the rod in order to save the child, repeatedly left welts and bruises on her body. The same was true of the discipline she received in a Christian bootcamp in the Dominican Republic where she was sent to overcome her spirit of rebellion. When Deirdre asked her sister about when she thought the family experience started to go wrong, her sister says, "Mom and Dad almost got a divorce and instead of working on their problems, Dad got religion."[44] In the language of our metaphor, the toxicity of the marriage got canned and put on the shelf with a Christian label on it that served to hide the real problems. And it leaked in the scapegoating of the children in the family, as it did with the founder of the Institute in Basic Life Principles. "In 2014, Gothard resigned from his post after being accused of molesting thirty-four teenage interns and staffers."[45]

For those of you as Nones who have experienced this form of Christianity where the inner work of transformation has been bypassed and the vital energy of agape-love coming from the original Christian experience has been lost and replaced by a negligent "canning" process, you need an apology. And, if it would be helpful, I would offer more than an idle apology. I would offer a true dialogue where you can be understood for who you are. From my perspective in this dialogue, I can only say that you are sorely needed because, coming from who you are and where you are, you have the ability to expose the ways in which religion gets canned.

A Loss of Self

If Deirdre Sugiuchi's experience of scapegoating illustrates the way in which canned religion can leak, it also raises an equally important topic regarding the Self. The Institute in Basic Life Principles was originally called the Institute in Basic Youth Conflict. What the institute taught was, in part, a set of principles designed to help parents manage the emergence of the Self in the life of a child (when the child works on individuation or self-differentiation and family conflict can increase) by establishing a clear hierarchical structure in the family and very clear moral guidelines. In principle, this is not necessarily negative. In fact, as my mentor in Scotland, Dr. Winifred Rushforth, said, when raising a child, think

44. Sugiuchi, "Fundamentalist," 119.
45. Sugiuchi, "Fundamentalist," 122.

of the child as being in a room. If the child cannot feel the walls in the room (i.e., does not know where the boundaries or limits are), it creates a tremendous amount of anxiety in the child that complicates their self-development. But she went on to say, if the walls are too tight (i.e., the rules, the boundaries, the family requirements, etc. are too restrictive), the child is crushed and responds either through compliance or rebellion, both of which complicate self-development. In the case of Deirdre, the latter seemed to be the case, with the limitations of canned religion manifesting in severe restrictions on the child's self-development, essentially attempting to put the Self in a (small) can with a Christian label on it.

To diminish the Self, to deny self-expression, or to can the Self in terms of forced choice by institutional standards—especially when it comes to spirituality—seems to be particularly abhorrent to you as a None and gets at the core of the anti-religion sentiment lying behind the term "None." Finding the Self and not losing it seems to be particularly important to you, to the degree that others have accused you (unfairly, as I indicate below) of having a self-spirituality and of being narcissistic. It is interesting to look in the index of a book like Linda Mercadante's[46] to see the number of topics coming from her interviews with you that have to do with the Self: self-development, self-esteem, self-focus, self-fulfillment, self-help, self-improvement, self-interest, self-soothing, and self-spirituality. Commenting on the latter, and building on the work of Paul Heelas, she says:

> Paul Heelas calls the crux of the new thought-world a *"self-spirituality"* and says it is the "essential *lingua franca*" of this movement. It starts with an assertion that the person's life "does not work." However, it is immediately asserted, this situation is fixable. Since the person is held to be essentially spiritual, "to experience the 'Self' itself is to experience 'God.'" This inner realm can then serve as the source for developing the authentic qualities of the perfect life.[47]

With the Spiritual But Not Religious (SBNR) in particular, Jorge Ferrer and William Vickery speak in their research to the problem of narcissism:

> SBNR has many positive attributes . . . but one major problem. *Spiritual narcissism* can be understood in two different but often interrelated ways: (a) the appropriation of spiritual to bolster

---

46. Mercadante, *Belief without Borders*, 319.
47. Mercadante, *Belief without Borders*, 73.

egoic ways of life (i.e., spiritual materialism) and (b) the belief in the universal superiority of one's favored spiritual choice, path, or account of ultimate reality (i.e., sectarianism) . . . But, what is the essential spiritual belief of the SBNR movement? . . . The contemporary "spiritual turn" is characterized by "the idea that the Self is divine and by the immanent conception of the sacred."[48]

On the topic of self-focus to the point of narcissism, there is plenty of finger-pointing to go around for everyone in American culture (not just the Nones). The twentieth century has been labeled by Adam Curtis in his documentary as *The Century of the Self*. American culture has been labeled by Christopher Lasch in his book as *The Culture of Narcissism*. Summarizing Lasch's thesis, Cristel Manning says that he gave a stinging critique of our culture's "glorification of personal choice . . . that . . . not only undermines community but ultimately also leads to pathology . . . Most Americans today have developed a form of narcissism, a preoccupation with self that derives from dependency and weakness of ego and requires continuous external validation."[49] Commenting on the process by which Nones have come to focus on the Self, Robert Wuthnow gives a summary of the trends that we have inherited from the twentieth century:

> This process is not one that individuals simply choose for themselves. It reflects changing understandings of the self in the wider culture. Some of these changes are evident in the ways public debates about the self have been framed. In the 1950s, social observers worried that the rugged, inner-directed individualist of the past was becoming a soft, other-directed suburban bureaucrat who survived by fitting in and by doing whatever he or she was told. The self seemed mostly to be a conformist. The 1960s witnessed widespread rebellion against the other-directed self that observers had identified as the fifties' norm. People went off on a proverbial quest for themselves, tuning out and turning on, and doing their own thing. The 1970s became known as the Me Decade, and the 1980s as the Decade of Greed, both apparently taking the narcissism of the 1960s to its logical extreme. Despite efforts to rediscover and redefine standards of moral discipline, the 1990s came to be known as an era of addictions.[50]

---

48. Ferrer and Vickery, "Transpersonal Psychology," 219, 221.

49. Manning, *Losing Our Religion*, 150.

50. Wuthnow, *After Heaven*, 147.

He goes on to say, that of all the "self" words that appeared in popular discourse (e.g., self-acceptance, self-emancipation, self-esteem, self-fulfillment, self-identity, self-realization), "the term that most aptly characterized the new mood, however, was *self-expression*."[51]

Lillian Daniel, in her tongue-in-cheek way of addressing the Nones, puts you (but not the religious) in the cultural narcissism category, as she grows weary of hearing the Spiritual But Not Religious claim they can find God and their deeper selves in sunsets (as if Christians could not): "Thank you for sharing, spiritual but not religious sunset person. You are now comfortably in the norm for self-centered American culture, right smack in the bland majority of people who find ancient religions dull but find themselves uniquely fascinating."[52] But, in his research, Robert Fuller found, "Empirical research using the Narcissism Personality Inventory (NPI) shows . . . that SBNR and conventionally religious individuals have almost identical NPI measures—with both groups having higher measures than wholly nonreligious individuals."[53] The data seem to show that some of you as Nones would be *less* narcissistic than the rest of the culture and that others of you are no more narcissistic than Christian Somes.

Finger-pointing will get us nowhere in our dialogue. Rather, in my opinion, it would be much more helpful if we could be curious together about the unique and valuable emphasis that you put on understanding the Self and how this unique emphasis is not only telling us something about you as a None, but also telling us something about our religious institutions and wider culture. Perhaps we can be curious together not only about the danger of canned religion that can result in canning the Self, but also curious about larger unresolved issues having to do with the Self that continue to nip at the heels of both religion and culture in America.

Unresolved Ambivalence About the Self

Perhaps we could dialogue about the curious ambivalence concerning the Self that has a long history in our religions and our culture. In a previous work, I noted the long-standing ambivalence in the very meaning of the word "self" pointed out by Roy Baumeister:

51. Wuthnow, *After Heaven*, 148.
52. Daniel, *"Spiritual but Not Religious" is Not Enough*, 128.
53. Fuller, "Minds of Their Own," 95.

The very usage of the word *Self* as seen in the Oxford English Dictionary changed from the Middle Ages to the Romantic era. In the 1680 edition, the usage of the word had the example of "Self is the Anti-Christ and Anti-God in the world," whereas in the 1870 edition offered, "respect to self and its ultimate good pertains to the very nobility of man's nature." Baumeister (1991) says, "Thus in two centuries, *self* went from the ultimate bad to the ultimate good" (p. 112). Beyond this, well into the twentieth century, social morality was defined by what was best for the welfare of the group and usually meant overcoming self-interest condemned as selfishness, greed, or egoism. Virtue meant conquering self-interest. Vice meant putting the self first and acting on desires and impulses of the self counter to the best interest of the community. "Thus, self-interest and moral values created a balance of opposing forces. But in the twentieth century this balance has been destroyed. Morality has become allied with self-interest . . . The modern message is that what is right and good and valuable to do in life is to focus on yourself, to learn what is inside you, to express and cultivate these inner resources to do what is best for yourself, and so forth."[54]

In the core meaning-making activity of the culture there are profound shifts occurring regarding the Self and more than a little ambivalence about the value to be placed on any emphasis on the Self. Edwin Friedman notes that this ambivalence can also be seen in the varied and contradictory ways in which the word "self" is used in the English language:

When "ish" is added to many words (e.g., *bookish, reddish, faddish, Jewish*) it simply means "having the quality of." But when "ish" is added to *self*, it becomes a pejorative term. The word *Self* can be used in a purely reflexive mode (*self-explanatory, self-evident, self-expression*), it can be added to a neutral word and make it negative (*self-centered, self-justified, self-congratulatory*) or it can be added to words indicating a positive quality because of the absence of *Self* (*self-denial, self-sacrifice, self-less*). "How can it be good to be both self-sufficient and self-less, self-made and self-effacing, self-respectful and self-denying . . . ? Actually, the word *self* has trouble retaining its self" (p. 175). Friedman (2007) goes on to say that this ambiguity and ambivalence contributes to a "failure of nerve" by leaders who (when seen from a systems perspective) cannot get the balance right between

---

54. Rodgerson, "Clergy Self-Renewal," 409.

individuality and togetherness . . . He says that to be true leaders, leaders must get past the pathologizing of the self.[55]

By your emphasis on the Self which you bring to our dialogue, you are reminding us of this unresolved ambivalence. It is an ambivalence that resides not only in our culture and the English language, but also in the very words of the Christian Scriptures where, on the one hand, we are called to love one's neighbor as one's self (Lev 19:18; 19:34; Matt 19:19; 22:39)—implying that there is an appropriate love of self—and, on the other hand, to humble the self, hate the self, or crucify the self (Luke 14:11, 26; Gal 2:20). Is there some way that we can stand in that ambivalence together, allowing for new meaning to emerge and the possibility of revealing still hidden truths?

Unresolved Difficulty in Defining the Self

Perhaps there would be less ambivalence about the Self if we could agree upon what it is. H. D. Lewis gives a broad definition—"What differentiates a person or makes one the being one is"[56]—but then goes on to name the wide differences in understanding this simple definition from the point of view of physicalism, materialism, behaviorism, or a spiritualism that connects the Self to something beyond; a timeless pure Self.

Sigmund Freud gave us insights into the Self as related to mental processes defined by a division of the mind into three systems (unconscious, preconscious, conscious) and further defined in his "structural hypothesis" in which "the *id* comprises the psychic representatives of the drives, the *ego* consists of those functions which have to do with the individual's relation to his environment, and the *superego* comprises the moral precepts of our minds as well as our ideal aspirations."[57] To be adequately in touch with reality as a healthy person, one's ego would need to distinguish between stimuli from one's outer world and from one's inner world (i.e., the wishes and impulses of the id) and be able to distinguish what is "self" and what is "not self." Even here we see the confusion of the terms "ego" and "self," or as Charles Brenner says, "to tell whether something is 'self' or 'not self' is obviously a part of the general function of reality testing, a part to which we refer as the establishment of

55. Rodgerson, "Clergy Self-Renewal," 409–10.
56. Lewis, "Self, Philosophy of," 1125.
57. Brenner, *Elementary Textbook*, 35, italics added.

firm ego boundaries. Actually, it would be more accurate to speak of self-boundaries than of ego boundaries."[58]

Building on Freud's work, C. G. Jung saw the Self as partly related to the ego, but bigger than the ego, "consisting of the sum of conscious and unconscious processes."[59] He "suggested calling the total personality which, though present, cannot be fully known, the *Self*. The ego is, by definition, subordinate to the Self and is related to it like a part of the whole,"[60] with other parts of the Self being unconscious and referred to as anima, animus, shadow, and collective unconscious. Christ was seen by Jung as an "*archetype of the Self*,"[61] and the work toward wholeness of the Self involved an integration of conscious and unconscious material in a higher union, a "*coniunctio oppositorum*."[62] Failure to integrate the shadow or unconscious part of the Self with the conscious part of the Self could lead to disaster for individuals or for cultures who would project the shadow onto others (not unlike the leaking of canned religion). He says,

> What our age thinks of as the "shadow" and inferior part of the psyche contains more than something merely negative. The very fact that through self-knowledge, i.e., by exploring our own souls, we come upon the instincts and their world of imagery should throw some light on the powers slumbering in the psyche, of which we are seldom aware so long as all goes well. They are potentialities of the greatest dynamism, and it depends entirely on the preparedness and attitude of the conscious mind whether the irruption of these forces and the images and ideas associated with them will tend towards construction or catastrophe.[63]

With a different understanding, Kegan sees the Self as evolving through developmental stages named as the incorporative, impulsive, imperial, interpersonal, institutional, and interindividual stages. At each developmental stage, there is a unique way in which a person makes sense of what happens *between* subject and object, *between* an event and the reaction to it; a zone of mediation where meaning is made "variously called by personality psychologists the 'ego,' the 'self,' and the 'person.'"[64]

58. Brenner, *Elementary Textbook*, 58.

59. Jung, *Aion*, 189.

60. Jung, *Aion*, 5.

61. Jung, *Aion*, 37.

62. Jung, *Aion*, 31.

63. Jung, *Undiscovered Self*, 119.

64. Kegan, *Evolving Self*, 3.

Hence, the Self changes as one develops. As one sees objects and events in new ways, one is "hatched out—but over and over again"[65] in a process that is a continuous balancing and rebalancing of subject and object, self and other. This activity "is experienced by a dynamically maintained 'Self,' the rhythms and labors of the struggle to make meaning, to have meaning, to protect meaning, to enhance meaning, to lose meaning, and to lose the 'Self' along the way."[66] In other words, in order to grow as a Self, one must *lose the Self* from one stage before coming to rest in the *new Self* of another stage.

With your emphasis on the Self which you bring to our dialogue, you are reminding us of this unresolved difficulty in defining the Self. The definitions mentioned above are only examples, coming from a psychological framework; a framework we have noted in the previous chapter as important to you as a None. Psychoanalytic understandings of the Self as a structure within the mind, since "it is cathected with instinctual energy and it has continuity in time,"[67] become even more complex and require an understanding of self-psychology that is beyond the scope of this book.

Spiritual and religious definitions of the Self can also vary greatly. In the Christian tradition, one might hear references to the "soul" more than the "Self" or references to the "heart" as the inner motivating part of a person's life. And even though there is not a "structural hypothesis" regarding the Self within Judeo-Christian Scriptures, there is a lot that resonates with the idea of an outer self and an inner self, and the need to change the inner heart and mind before there can be any real change in outward behavior. King David, who wanted to change his murderous external behavior that seemed to come uncontrollably from within him, prays, saying, "You desire truth in the inward being; therefore teach me wisdom in my secret heart . . . Create in me a clean heart, O God, and put a new and right spirit within me" (Ps 51:6, 10). The Apostle Paul, praying for agape-love to be the motivating force in the life of the early Christians, says, "I pray . . . that you may be strengthened in your inner being with power through his Spirit, and that Christ may dwell in your hearts through faith, as you are being rooted and grounded in love" (Eph 3:16–17). Jesus, speaking some of his harshest words to self-righteous religious leaders

---

65. Kegan, *Evolving Self,* 85.

66. Kegan, *Evolving Self,* 12.

67. Kohut, *Analysis of the Self,* xv.

who had failed to do the necessary inner spiritual work, says, "Woe to you, scribes and Pharisees, hypocrites! For you clean the outside of the cup and of the plate, but inside they are full of greed and self-indulgence" (Matt 23:25). And there is also resonance within the Christian Scriptures for seeing the Self as something that is in process and where growth can be described as losing the Self in order to redefine the Self at another stage. In the words of Jesus (where the word for "life" can also be translated as "soul" or "Self"), "Those who try to make their life secure will lose it, but those who lose their life will keep it" (Luke 17:33).

Can we at least acknowledge in our dialogue that there is an inward-ness and an outward-ness to the Self and that the Self is dynamic and changing? And can we find some language for talking about the inward Self that gives us real choice over the core motivating aspects of our lives, rather than canning it or letting it leak all over our lives and the lives of others? I will also say that *when* the church does not remember this simple, defined structure of the Self and does not model a path toward an inner and outer congruence, an apology is in order.

Unresolved Images of the Ideal Self

If we have an ambivalence about the Self and a difficulty in defining the Self, it follows that there is not much clarity or agreement on what an ideal Self would look like. What is the Self that is realized, actualized, ex-pressed, fulfilled, esteemed, developed, accepted, soothed, emancipated, focused, helped, identified, improved, or whatever other word comes after the hyphen and is attached to "self"? If, in fact, the Self is to grow or develop, in what direction are we headed and how do we know when we have arrived? Does it have something to do with a mood, an experience, a characteristic, an energy, or a process?

Every society and every religion have tried to answer this question in one way or another with ethical codes of conduct, commandments, communal stories, and constitutions. Embedded in the American psyche would be "Life, liberty . . . and the pursuit of happiness," penned by Thomas Jefferson, who would write at a later date (1819), "Happiness is the aim of life, [but] virtue is the foundation of happiness."[68] Researchers in positive psychology have looked at philosophical and religious tradi-tions from around the world and have found certain core virtues in all

---

68. As quoted in Peterson, *Positive Psychology*, 137.

of them. "Specifically, within these traditions there was near-universal recognition and praise of the virtues of wisdom, courage, humanity, justice, temperance, and transcendence."[69] These core virtues, when broken down into their components, according to researchers at the Values In Action Institute, contain twenty-four character strengths: creativity, curiosity, love of learning, open-mindedness, perspective, authenticity, bravery, persistence, zest, kindness, love, social intelligence, fairness, leadership, teamwork, forgiveness/mercy, modesty/humility, prudence, self-regulation, appreciation of beauty and excellence, gratitude, hope, humor, and religiousness/spirituality. These virtues and strengths come into play in decisions about core values in ten areas that are consistent around the world. They are values variously emphasized by individuals having to do with achievement, benevolence, conformity, hedonism, power, security, self-direction, stimulation, tradition, and universalism.[70] Would these give us some words for the ideal Self that we are in process of developing? Certainly, these universal categories might appeal to the Nones Cristel Manning interviewed, who said that they wanted their children to have strong moral values but added that "there is an element of our society here that says in order to be a good person you must be a Christian, and I reject that . . . [wanting them] to have moral values that are not the exclusive domain of Christians."[71]

Although these are contained in the virtues and values above, religious traditions might use additional words for the ideal Self, like: peace, love, compassion, bliss, patience, joy, light, goodness, knowledge, or having a calm and clear mind. David Bentley Hart reminds us that ultimately our desire for these things, if taken to their logical conclusion, can be reduced to "transcendentals" that can be reduced no further and that are:

> essential aspects of existence . . . the intrinsic perfections of *being* in its fullness. There are purely *ontological* transcendentals, such as being and unity, and critical or "*criteriological*" transcendentals, such as truth, goodness, and beauty; ultimately, though, they are distinct from one another only conceptually, from our necessarily limited vantage, but in themselves are wholly convertible with one another, each being only one name for the single reality of *being itself.*[72]

69. Peterson, *Positive Psychology,* 140.

70. Peterson, *Positive Psychology,* 182.

71. Manning, *Losing Our Religion,* 121.

72. Hart, *Experience of God,* 242–43, italics added.

Perhaps different from psychology or any scientific materialism, religious and spiritual traditions would say that the ideal Self in its "intrinsic perfection of *being* in its fullness" would somehow connect with that which transcends the individual human self. In other words, that the Self is more than a structural component of the mental apparatus.

However, what is interesting is the amount of energy given by religion to delineating what is the *non-idealized Self* in almost endless categories of sin and many commandments that start with "Thou shalt not . . ." Running parallel with this has been (until recently) psychology's focus on categorizing pathology. Its "Bible," *The Diagnostic and Statistical Manual of Mental Disorders*, is not a catalog of ideal human qualities but of disorders. And, while making the distinction from diagnosable disorders, there are some universal words that most of us agree on to describe the non-idealized Self, such as: hate, violence, jealousy, greed, anger, defensiveness, and being manipulative or petty. For most people, these are not qualities that we want in ourselves or in those with whom we live. They are qualities that we strive to move away from and not toward.

These non-idealized qualities seem to have an energy about them as well (as distinct from the understanding of energy with which this chapter began). This energy has the power of instinct and is often connected to ways in which one learns to survive. Jaak Panksepp and Lucy Biven, in their work *The Archaeology of Mind*, speak of seven basic affective circuits in the ancient subcortical region of the brain having to do with *seeking* (expectancy), *rage* (anger), *lust* (sexual excitement), *care* (nurturance), *panic/grief* (sadness), and *play* (social joy). In the *seeking* circuit alone originates all our desires. "It is a complex knowledge- and belief-generating machine . . . It has no intrinsic morals. It is just a super-efficient get-up-and-go-get-it system. Human cognitive aspirations, both for good and evil, spring forth from its vast affective 'energy.'"[73] They would say the neural roots for religion are found in how we train this affective circuit. Similarly, Sigmund Freud saw this instinctual energy coming from two drives. "There are two kinds of psychic energy, that which is associated with the sexual drive, and that which is associated with the aggressive one. The former has a special name, 'libido.' The latter has no such name, though at one time it was suggested that it be called 'destrudo' by analogy from 'destroy.'"[74] Again, this powerful instinctual energy could

---

73. Panksepp and Biven, *Archaeology of Mind*, 103.

74. Brenner, *Elementary Textbook*, 20–21.

be directed into constructive or destructive paths, depending on one's consciousness of these forces or the patterns one developed in formative relationships with others.

Someone like Thomas Keating would say that the imperfect ways in which we learn to relate, learn to survive, learn to program our seeking system, or learn to channel our libidinal and aggressive drives causes us to create "false programs of happiness," or what he calls the "False Self." This is the Self developed to cope with the imperfections and trauma of early childhood. "It seeks happiness in satisfying the instinctual needs of survival/security, affection/esteem, and power/control, and bases its self-worth on cultural or group identification."[75] It is distinguished from what he calls the "True Self," defined as, "The image of God in which every human being is created; our participation in the divine life manifested in our uniqueness."[76]

It is this energy that individuals have dealt with in ways as unique as a fingerprint and ranging from repression to release. It is an energy that, in the pursuit of the idealized Self, most religions have sought to guide or contain, often erring on the side of repression or canning the Self using draconian measures such as the approach taken by the fundamentalist parents of Deirdre Sugiuchi mentioned above. In all fairness, it is not only religions that have sought to contain this energy. For example, Nazi Germany, having come to understand the power of the instincts through the guidance of Edward Bernays (Freud's nephew), sought to channel that energy into complete loyalty to the state and the Aryan race, with the necessary side-effect of having to have a group of people to hate (i.e., the Jews). In America, also under the guidance of Edward Bernays, business interests sought to channel that instinctual energy into consumer capitalism, learning to tap into the desires of the Self for the purposes of marketing products as desirable even if they were harmful (for example, getting women to smoke as a sign of freedom).[77]

Your very presence as a None, with an emphasis on the importance of the Self, is a valuable reminder that we have unresolved issues and ambivalent attitudes about the meaning of the Self and the energies of the Self. Perhaps in our dialogue we can find ways to engage these energies that have nothing to do with binding, canning, or repressing, starting

75. Keating, *Intimacy with God*, 163.

76. Keating, *Intimacy with God*, 166.

77. *Century of the Self.*

with an apology from the Christian point of view when we get these things wrong. Rather than repression, perhaps we can think in terms of transformation, being aware in our dialogue that the energy of the Self and the energy of spirituality can be powerfully constructive *and* powerfully destructive.

3

The Transactional Captivity of the Church

Marketplace Religion and Spirituality

ONE ADVANTAGE OF A "canned" religion is that it is more easily brought to the marketplace, especially if that marketplace is experienced more as a place for the exchange of consumer goods and less as a public square for the exchange of ideas and beliefs. The former lends itself to the art of a business deal that is transactional. The latter lends itself to the possibility of transformation based on the "discovery of new areas of reality and meaning we were not aware of before."[1] Marketplace religion can go either way.

On the one hand, marketplace religion can be an expression of the Enlightenment ideals of individualism, privatization of religion, and freedom of choice that were built into the founding documents of the United States, where personal choice and personal expression in matters of faith are highly valued and where there is a vibrant religious and spiritual presence in the public forum of ideas and beliefs. This aspect of the marketplace seems to be very important to you as a None, and to some extent your very presence as a None is a reminder to all of us of these core values lying at the heart of what it means to be a United States citizen. Cristel Manning would go further, indicating that individualism and free choice consumerism have essentially created you as a None. She says,

> American individualism tells me I have the power to choose; consumerism promises there will be many choices. Given the

1. Augsburger, *Pastoral Counseling*, 42.

83

larger historical context, we can understand the growth in Nones as the inevitable outcome of individualization and commodification in religion. Declaring yourself to be None is the penultimate expression of personal worldview choice, a declaration that you are unique and will not be defined by somebody else.[2]

On the other hand, marketplace religion, rooted in the same Enlightenment ideals, can lead to marketplace competition with an emphasis on marketplace "share" and the selling of religion to the consumer. Craig Van Gelder and Dwight Zscheile point out,

> As articulated in the Declaration of Independence, the Constitution, and other founding documents of the United States, the American understanding of freedom is deeply indebted to the Enlightenment idea of individual expression—freedom *from* restraint. With the individual as the basic unit of society, America has tended to define freedom in individualistic rather than communal terms. Religious communities are seen as voluntary societies along the lines of John Locke's definition, where individuals contract to meet their spiritual needs and are free to dissolve such contracts when those needs are not being met. This has encouraged a variety of consumerist approaches to church, especially in recent decades.[3]

In a more pointed way, Paul Smith paraphrases the American scholar Sam Pascoe, who said, "Christianity began in Palestine as an experience; It moved to Greece and became a philosophy; It moved to Italy and became an institution; It moved to Europe and became a culture; It moved to America and became a business!"[4] While it would be easy to limit this critique to the unique context of "prosperity gospel" proponents who advocate a raw transaction between donations given and blessings of God received, and who have built business empires from those donations, the marketplace characteristics of religion are far more pervasive than these. For example, by the mid-twentieth century, the default narrative for the church in America was that of the modern corporation, and leadership became managerial. Marketplace *dialogue* was not a consideration, but the desire for marketplace *dominance*, often fueled by a missionary imperative to advance a particular understanding of ultimate truth, made it easy to see others as customers and to make transactional political and

2. Manning, *Losing Our Religion*, 149.

3. Van Gelder and Zscheile, *God's Mission*, 46.

4. Smith, *Integral Christianity*, 234.

business alignments to ensure market share. Regarding the consumer approach, Craig Van Gelder and Dwight Zscheile say,

> Neighbors tend to become objects of marketing, recruitment, or benevolence. The waves of renewal efforts in the late twentieth century operated within this basic modern managerial narrative. For instance, the church-growth movement sought to use the culture's best techniques (advertising, marketing, entertainment, consumerism) to attract unchurched and dechurched people to come back through the doors and to keep them satisfied long enough to stay . . . The modern managerial imagination formed people to seek the right technique or killer app that would secure a new future of prosperity and influence.[5]

Kenda Creasy Dean saw the effects of this on religiously affiliated teenagers who were taught an "almost Christian" perspective in church where there was more love for the market than love for the kingdom of God. "After two and a half centuries of shacking up with the 'American dream,' churches have perfected a dicey codependence between consumer-driven therapeutic individualism and religious pragmatism."[6]

The desire for marketplace dominance has also led to transactional alignments between religion, politics, and business for the purposes of power and influence which is now honed with digital precision to consumer preferences discovered on Facebook, Twitter, and online purchasing patterns. While the digital precision may be new, this general pattern of alignment is nothing new in the history of Christianity, where Christian missions have often gone hand-in-hand with Western colonial power and the "hegemonic narrative of American influence."[7] Such alignments in America are not unique to the religious left or the religious right and are often motivated by legitimate concern for others, whether it be for a Great Society, a Moral Majority, or a Focus on the Family. However, these transactional alignments are almost always costly to the church as it brokers an increase in transactional power and market share at a cost of sacrificing true transformational power.

A recent example of this is the alignment of conservative Christians with the Council for National Policy (CNP), the Republican party, and the money of the Koch brothers and others. Citing the work of Republican

5. Van Gelder and Zscheile, *God's Mission*, 301–2.

6. Dean, *Almost Christian*, 5.

7. Van Gelder and Zscheile, *God's Mission*, 33.

strategist Kevin Phillips in his 2006 book *American Theocracy*, Anne Nelson says, "The Republican party has slowly become the vehicle of . . . a fusion of petroleum-defined national security; a crusading, simplistic Christianity; and a reckless credit-feeding financial complex."[8] And with regard to Ralph Reed's (Chairman of the Faith and Freedom Coalition) victory lap at the National Press Club after the 2016 election, Nelson says, "Reed and his staff laid out the millions of interactions their coalition had delivered for the Trump campaign, and listed the policies they expected to be enacted in return. It was transactional politics in its purest form."[9] What I have heard from those of you who are Nones is that this form of marketplace religion that seeks *dominance* and not *dialogue* provides plenty of fuel for your anti-religious sentiments. In my opinion, it is something for which Christians need to offer an apology.

However, it is important to note, for those of you as Nones who are interested in spirituality, that this market share and consumer-driven focus is not limited to Christianity. Peter Williams, writing about America's religions, says that there is the "theme of Americanization"[10] of any faith that develops in the broader context of the American culture, and that any religious tradition significantly changes when it is transplanted on American soil. This might be an adaptation of the religion to the therapeutic culture of America much like what has happened with Buddhist practices of mindfulness. As Matthew Hedstrom says, "Such reformulations . . . wrest Buddhism out of traditional contexts—something akin to nineteenth-century archaeologists plundering the treasure of Asia for western museums—and thereby transform it utterly."[11] But this Americanization of a religion is often transformed by the predominant capitalistic culture, such as Bikram Choudhury's adaptation of yoga to American culture based upon the advice of Shirley MacLaine, who advised him saying, "In America, if you don't charge money . . . people won't respect you."[12] As Andrea Jain goes on to say, "Rather than allow capitalism to restrain him, Bikram became a master capitalist. He changed his

---

8. Nelson, *Shadow Network*, 266.

9. Nelson, *Shadow Network*, 223.

10. Williams, *America's Religions*, viii.

11. Hedstrom, "Buddhist Fulfillment," 68.

12. Jain, "Yogi Superman," 150.

approach, becoming one of the first entrepreneurs to build a commodified, franchized, and merchandized yoga brand."[13]

And then there are organizations like Goop. Alan Levinovitz, in a *Washington Post* article entitled "Goop Teaches Us We Can Be Pure—If We Spend Enough Money," writes, "Lost in the haze of mugwort steam, however, is an entirely different problem with Goop, which is religious, not scientific. Ultimately what Goop promises is purity: physical, moral and spiritual." And then he says, "Tellingly, Goop's first fragrance was 'Church.' Church perfume runs $165 for a 1.7 ounce bottle (Chanel No. 5 is a comparative bargain at $105), and a Church-scented candle costs a whopping $72. Why? . . . Goop's scents have 'healing properties.'"[14]

Goop may seem like an egregious example, but it really is the norm now for a marketplace spirituality in which the branding of a product using watered-down religious references has become big business and, as some would say, a religion unto itself. Melissa Wilcox, commenting on Jeremy Carrette and Richard King's book *Selling Spirituality: The Silent Takeover of Religion*, says,

> The book focuses on a supply-side analysis of what its authors term the "corporate takeover of religion" through the individualizing language of spirituality, the monetization of the term *spirituality*, the use of orientalist exotification to sell a fragmented and decontextualized mélange of Asian traditions as "Asian spirituality," and the corporate turn to spirituality as a way to improve profit margins.[15]

Andrea Jain goes further to say, "I suggest we should imagine commercial spirituality, not as a *takeover* or *replacement* of religion or as an *alternative* to religion, but as a modern *manifestation* of religion. What popular and scholarly assumptions about spirituality often miss are the ways commercial spiritualities share a lot with traditional religions."[16]

Tara Burton goes even further to say that spiritualized business is now our civil religion, seen at its worst in the COVID-19 pandemic where there was a willingness by some in power to sacrifice the lives of many on the marketplace altar. Following on from a prosperity gospel

13. Jain, "Yogi Superman," 150.
14. Levinovitz, "Goop."
15. Wilcox, "Consuming Spirituality," 133.
16. Jain, "Yogi Superman," 148.

theology and from the call of some politicians to get people back to work regardless of the collateral damage to others, she says,

> Within such a paradigm, the implication—however repug-
> nant—that in the midst of a pandemic, our capitalist system
> might require sacrificing the elderly to ensure future bounty for
> the young is sort of the next logical step. When the language of
> buying and selling, product and profit, so dominates our dis-
> course about our identities, our society and our metaphysics,
> capitalism becomes indistinguishable from religious faith. Once
> we made human sacrifices to appease the gods; now, we're told,
> we must do the same to appease the markets.[17]

We are in the midst of a dot-com bubble for spirituality in the marketplace with a form of "woke" capitalism now being taught in business schools in specialized courses focused on "spiritual entrepreneurship." With all of religion and spirituality in a state of change in America (change of which you as a None are a big part), Tara Burton says that new religions are emerging, and "the most successful new religions of 2020 and beyond are the ones that have taken this institutional turn and found ways to make it both communal and—in an increasing brand-driven age—salable."[18]

As a None, if you have been repulsed by a marketplace form of Christianity that has targeted you for conversion in an attempt to increase their market share and dominance in the culture, you might want to consider the degree to which there is a larger targeting of you in the commercial-spiritual marketplace that seems to be working. Tara Burton comments:

> Corporations have taken it upon themselves to become, in some
> instances, what churches and synagogues once were: arbiters of
> public morality. And the public agrees. A 2018 study by Vice
> Media's branding partnership arm, Virtue, found that 54 per-
> cent of millennials and Generation Z-ers said they prioritized
> spending money on brands that "enhance their spirit and soul."
> Seventy-seven percent said they sought out brands that shared
> their "values."[19]

We are in this together in the Americanization of all things sacred. Perhaps we can dialogue about the powerful marketplace preference for

17. Burton, "Civil Religion."

18. Burton, *Strange Rites*, 34.

19. Burton, "Civil Religion."

dominance rather than *dialogue*, and about the underlying religious and spiritual patterns that make us susceptible to transactional rather than transformational life practices.

Transactional Theologies

In this experience of Americanization, I wonder if the consumer-focused marketplace has created marketplace religion in America or if dominant marketplace religions have created the consumer-focused marketplace. Certainly, this latter idea was the theory of Max Weber, who in 1905 wrote *The Protestant Ethic and the Spirit of Capitalism*. Weber proposed that the Protestant faith, especially as taught by the sixteenth-century reformer John Calvin with his focus on predestination and a limited number of people (the "elect") being saved for heaven, created an approach to life involving hard work, discipline, and frugality (interpreted as tangible signs that one was a part of the "elect") and gave birth to capitalism.[20] Of course, this theory has been controversial since its inception, with clear evidence that capitalism existed before the Protestant Reformation, but the idea that a particular type of Christian belief might significantly influence the culture is worth pondering in our dialogue—especially if that particular (Protestant) Christian belief happens to have been dominant in the marketplace for centuries and happens to be particularly transactional.

As a None, whether you realize it or not, it seems from interviewers who have listened deeply to your stories (in what I would call the first phase of dialogue) that your reactivity to Christianity is fueled by this particular (largely) Protestant form of belief. Here is what Linda Mercadante found:

> Many interviewees homogenized and simplified core theological themes labeled as characteristic of Western religion—Christianity in particular—and then rejected or radically altered them. For example, as we have seen, people have rejected a God stereotyped as a judgmental overseer and instead have substituted the idea of a sacred force which is impersonal and benevolent. The positions disavowed by the majority of interviewees include:
>
> • an exclusivism that rejects all religions but one's own;
>
> • a wrathful and/or interventionist God;

20. Weber, *Protestant Ethic*.

- a static and permanent afterlife of glorious heaven and tortu-
ous hell;
- an oppressively authoritarian religious tradition;
- a non-experiential repressive religious community; and
- a view of humans as "born bad."[21]

I find it interesting—and it is certainly worth pondering in our
dialogue—that the particular form of the Christian religion described
in the bullet points above, being the religion rejected by you as a None,
is essentially the same (conservative and Calvinistic) Protestant belief
system that has dominated the religious marketplace in America since
the seventeenth century and that influenced Max Weber's theory of the
Protestant work ethic. This belief system has at its core an understanding
of how human beings are "made right" or "at-one" with God, and it has a
name: *The (Penal) Substitutionary Atonement Theory.*

While there are clear roots in the Bible for a number of theories of
atonement, no full theory can be found in Scripture, and only later were
complete doctrines developed. *The (Penal) Substitutionary Atonement
Theory* (some would call it a doctrine) was not fully developed until the
eleventh century by Anselm (1032–1109), an Italian Benedictine monk
who became the Archbishop of Canterbury. One cannot do justice here to
the intricacies of his argument written in the language of medieval scho-
lasticism and with the clear influence of "feudal ideas as to the relation
of king and subject, together with juridical conceptions drawn from the
customs of Germanic law and the penitential system of Latin theology."[22]
His argument unfolds in his book, *Cur Deus Homo*, in the form of a dialogue between Anselm and his student, Bono, who is representing people
who are unbelievers or who have difficulty understanding the faith. Anselm's argument goes something like this: While human beings are made
for blessedness, they cannot attain it unless there is forgiveness of sins.
Every person sins, and sin means not to pay to God what is owed to God.
Not to do so is to dishonor God. In order to maintain God's dignity, there
must be punishment for sin. Since everything good is already required
by God, there is nothing human beings can do to make satisfaction for
their sins. Therefore, God alone can make reparation for sin, but since the
reparation must be made by human beings, God must become man in

---

21. Mercadante, *Belief without Borders*, 230.
22. Mozley, *Doctrine of Atonement*, 128.

Jesus Christ so that when this sinless man obediently dies, he surrenders his life as a debt that is not due. This surpassing value that is in excess of what is due is then passed on to human beings in the form of forgiveness of sins and future blessedness by those who live according to the commandments of the gospel.[23] (I told you it was intricate!) The condensed version is found in the universal Christian phrase, "Christ died for our sins"—he takes the punishment for our sins in his death (our substitute), restoring our relationship with God and assuring us of eternal life in heaven if we have faith in Jesus Christ.

Depending upon the explanation of this theory, there can be an emphasis on the love of God for human beings, or the wrath of God; on the justice of God and the threat of Hell, or the mercy of God in a desire for the salvation of all; on the obedience of Jesus Christ only in the last three days of his life, or the full life of obedience that gives us an example of how to live life to the full. As a means of making clear distinctions in beliefs from the Roman Catholics in the sixteenth century, Protestant Reformers (e.g., John Calvin in his *Institutes* and in his attempts to set up a theocracy in his "Geneva experiment") accepted a more drastic penal interpretation of Anselm's theory. In the seventeenth century, the Puritans brought this form of the Christian religion to America. In the eighteenth century, this was the favored religion that enabled survival on the frontier, moving to the West with the idea of manifest destiny and fueled by the passion of the Great Awakenings. In the nineteenth century, this form of Christianity served as a "touchstone of truth" with the perceived threats of modernism and immigration (of Jews and Roman Catholics). In the twentieth century, this form of religion brought stability in times of war and the chaos of liberal rebellion and pluralism. In the twenty-first century, this form of the Christian religion continues to fuel what seems to be an underlying desire amongst some in our culture for a theocracy not unlike that of Calvin in Geneva. When understood "concretely" (which is where most people are in their spiritual development), it is *very transactional* (a debt paid to God to avert God's punishment) and produces a passionate missionary imperative to *dominate* in the marketplace of religion in order to ensure that people, through faith in Jesus Christ, are forgiven and will go to heaven. Evidently, it is the form of religion that gives definition to what you as a None do *not* like about religion (as seen in the bullet points above) and fuels your anti-religious sentiment when

23. Mozley, *Doctrine of Atonement*.

you are treated as an object in the marketplace and targeted to "buy" a religion that is more repulsive to you than appealing.

You might be interested to know that within the wider Christian community there are equally strong feelings of attraction and repulsion toward this way of understanding the purpose of Christ's life, death, and resurrection. For instance, in the Foreword to a book entitled *Pierced for Our Transgressions: Rediscovering the Glory of Penal Substitution*, John Piper writes:

> This is how I feel today about teachers of Christ's people who deny and even belittle precious, life-saving, biblical truth. When a person says that God's "punishing his Son for an offense he has not even committed" would be as evil as child abuse, I am angered and grieved. For if God did not punish his Son in my place, I am not saved from my greatest peril, the wrath of God.[24]

David Bentley Hart is equally passionate from a completely different point of view:

> And it is fitting that, among all models of atonement, Reformed theology so securely fastened upon a particularly sanguinary version of "substitution," one that finds in the cross of Christ not simply God's self-outpouring love, but also—and chiefly—the outpouring of his implacable wrath against sin. And then even this act of substitution turns out to be one of a peculiarly miserly kind, since its appeasements avail for only a very few. An eternal hell is still required for the great many, in order to reveal the glory of divine sovereignty in its fullness. Very well. So this side of Calvinism is nothing but a savage *reductio ad absurdum* of the worst aspects of an immensely influential but still deeply defective theological tradition.[25]

There are other theories of atonement, equally rooted in the Bible. For instance, Abelard (1078–1142), writing about the same time as Anselm, understood the death of Christ not as a substitute for our punishment to appease the wrath of God, but as an exhibition of love that might kindle a similar self-sacrificing love in the hearts of men and women. For Abelard, Christ came to earth to teach an incarnate wisdom and to provide an example on how to live a fully human life. If Anselm saw Christ's

24. Jeffery et al., *Pierced*, 14.
25. Hart, *That All Shall Be Saved*, 77.

death as "acting on God for men and women," Abelard saw Christ's life as "acting on men and women for God."[26]

My point here is not to create a course in theology for you or to cast blame on one religious belief or another, but to provide information which I hope will pique your interest in our dialogue. My hope is that you might have a sense of wonderment with me about two things. Firstly, I find it interesting that someone like Martin Luther in the sixteenth century started a movement of reform in Christianity in reaction to the *transactional practices* of the Roman Catholic church for the selling of indulgences to raise money for the extravagant lifestyle of Pope Leo X. This was a selling of the forgiveness of sins to get relatives out of Purgatory or to acquire blessings for their own future salvation. What pushed Martin Luther over the edge was the selling of indulgences by Johann Tezel, who allegedly had a marketing jingle that said, "As soon as a coin in the coffer rings, a soul from Purgatory springs!" In one of his key treatises, Martin Luther referred to these transactional practices, and others associated with the seven sacraments of the Roman Catholic church, as the "Babylonian Captivity of the Church."

I find it interesting that many of the Protestant reformers who followed Luther, in distinguishing themselves from the Roman Catholic church, adopted as their primary understanding of the Christ-event a penal substitutionary theory of atonement that has at is core a *transactional relationship* between God and human beings. And, further, I wonder how the predominance of this transactional way of understanding the relationship with God through the centuries in America has "leaked" into the culture, interacting with neoliberal capitalism to produce a consumer-driven *transactional culture* (hyper-Calvinism producing hyper-capitalism?) that values products over people and creates a meritocracy based upon the ability to buy. And, still further, I wonder how the dominance of this transactional way of understanding the relationship with God has produced what I call the *transactional captivity of the church* (Protestant and Roman Catholic) where an over-focus on a forensic, transactional relationship with God has impeded an emphasis on character-transformation in Christians, and the very reading and interpreting of the Bible is held captive to this transactional point of view. In a similar way, N. T. Wright says that a liberation of New Testament exegesis and theology is needed from the dark gravitational pull of the whole post-Enlightenment

---

26. Mozley, *Doctrine of Atonement*, 132.

European matrix of thought and belief which are "forms of slavery, captivity in which words, thoughts and documents from the first century have been compelled to make bricks from less and less historical straw," and in which "we need twenty-first-century answers to first-century questions, not nineteenth-century answers to sixteenth-century questions."[27]

Secondly, could I pique your interest in a dialogue that helps us move beyond a transactional culture, undergirded by transactional religion and transactional spiritualities in which we are both entangled, and that asks what comes next in the five-hundred-year cycle of change? The wonderment here is that you, as a None, seem to have made the first step in exploring what comes next. It is curious to me that you have intuitively put your finger on the transactional Christian theology that undergirds a transactional culture and have deliberately stepped away from that form of religion. Without having the language for this, you have intuitively stepped away from what is known as "embedded theology" (religious beliefs, values, and practices embedded during childhood) and stepped toward what is known as "deliberative theology" (an understanding of beliefs that comes after intense personal reflection),[28] which is in itself a movement away from a transactional narrative to a transformational one, and which is necessary for personal development and character-transformation. Are you intuitively inviting the Christian community and the wider culture to do the same?

And, adding to this wonderment, it is curious to me that as a None you have by your presence invited us to the next step in developing a new cultural narrative, beyond the transactional narrative, which is a step into an unknown "space between" in which, for a period of time, we will have to exist in the "nothingness" that comes when one story is ending and the other is not yet beginning. In that "space between," maybe we are called to hold together the truth of opposites—transactional truth and transformational truth, Anselm truth and Abelard truth, spirituality truth and religion truth, etc.—where we exercise a "dignity of difference"[29] instead of having a "despair of defensiveness," and where we learn to move beyond "taking a stand" to "securely standing" on something that (in my opinion) is transhuman, transrational, transcendent, and transformational.

27. Wright, *Paul*, 1307, 1477.

28. Doehring, *Pastoral Care*, 18–19.

29. Sacks, *Dignity of Difference*.

However, I realize that I may be jumping ahead in our dialogue by assuming the antidote for the transactional captivity of the church has something to do with transformation, and by implying that the role of the Christian religion in the marketplace has more to do with *disequilibrium* than *dominance*. So *why* transformation, and *what* needs to be transformed?

From Transaction to Transformation

From the Christian point of view (and for most religions), religion was never meant to be transactional. Transactional religion was a major part of the problem from Jesus' point of view, directing some of his harshest words to religious leaders of the day for being perfectionists at ritual practice while avoiding more difficult issues of change: "Woe to you . . . hypocrites! For you tithe mint, dill, and cumin, and have neglected the weightier matters of the law: justice and mercy and faith" (Matt 23:23). Writing a revised covenantal theology based upon his dramatic experience of a resurrected Jesus, the Apostle Paul issued a call to the world for the embodiment of a simple transformational practice: "Do not be conformed to this world, but be transformed by the renewing of your minds" (Rom 12:2). The Greek word translated as "transformed" in this text is one from which we get our word "metamorphosis," indicating that central to the Christian religion is a complete metamorphosis of our way of thinking and being in the world.

The "Why?" of Transformation

The simple answer to the "why?" of transformation from a Christian point of view, then, has to do with the intentions of those persons with whom the faith originated, especially Jesus Christ and the Apostle Paul. As a None, to some extent, your rejection of a transactional form of religion is in alignment with their intentions. And, their intentions were in alignment with some of the core realities of how the world (and cosmos) works, whether one is ritually religious or not.

For instance, change, growth, and development are basic realities of how the world (and cosmos) works. Most everything changes. That which flows through our minds is constantly changing. How we process sensory data is constantly changing with cognitive growth and development necessary for our survival. Our bodies are constantly changing, starting with a single cell and moving through the seasons of life. Along the way the cells of the body grow, develop, and are constantly renewed. And the body itself works to survive in changing environments with constant shifts to maintain temperature, blood chemistry, and blood oxygen through the homeostatic and allostatic processes.[30] Relationships must change, grow, and develop to survive. Love experienced "at first sight" may still be love, but it must become a different kind of love for a long-term relationship to survive. The parent-child relationship is permanent in terms of biology, but in terms of connection and relationship, it must change to be healthy. Our personhood—our very selves—may stay the same as identified on a birth certificate, but who we are and how we relate to the world rarely stays the same throughout our lifetime.

The weather changes. Fashion changes. Technology changes. Laws change. Politics change. The geographic boundaries of, or existence of, nations can change. Public perceptions change. Diseases change and, as we have seen with COVID-19, can bring extreme global change. Even that which looks permanent is changing, like mountains whose rocks become sand over time or glaciers which appear static but are cutting deep channels into the earth's surface. Even the stars and galaxies are in a continual process of being born and dying in a universe that is ever expanding. As many religious writers and poets have acknowledged, impermanence is an integral part of our lives.

Change, growth, and development are not synonymous words, but they are deeply interrelated and necessary for life. Looking through the eyes of quantum physics, chaos theory, and chemistry, Margaret Wheatley takes note of how living systems not only produce themselves but will change in order to preserve that self. In that process, dissipation, disorder, and disintegration are not signals of death, but signals of new life. Although this is true throughout creation, she applies this insight to organizations, saying, "growth appears from disequilibrium, not balance. The things we fear most in organizations—disruptions, confusion, chaos—need not be interpreted as signs that we are about to be destroyed. Instead, these conditions are necessary to awaken creativity."[31] She goes on to say that in classical thermodynamics, equilibrium is the end state of closed systems, "the point at which the system has exhausted all of its capacity for change, done its work, and dissipated its productive capacity

---

30. Kabat-Zinn, *Full Catastrophe.*
31. Wheatley, *Leadership,* 21.

into useless entropy . . . a place where . . . all life has died out."[32] Disequilibrium, even more than equilibrium, seems to be necessary for living
systems to continue to grow and develop.

When we ask about the "why?" of transformation in the Christian
religion, the intention has been from the beginning to align the faith with
the realities of life. On the one hand, why would anything of truth be
any different from the rest of the creation that is embedded with change,
growth, development, and ongoing transformation? On the other hand,
since life itself is dependent upon change, growth, development, and disequilibrium, how could a religion be life-giving if it did not speak into
these transformative realities about life? A transactional religion can
easily separate itself from these realities. As a None, you have noticed
this and have raised questions about the inherent truth of a transactional
religion and its ability to connect you with the energy and purpose of life.

To be fair, even a transactional religion seeks to answer questions
about how to live life to the full and how to minimize or avoid the pain and
suffering associated with change. But, when it is held captive by the combined narratives of a penal exchange to avoid God's wrath, a consumer-
driven success determined by numbers, and an over-focus on individual
salvation, it runs the risk of reducing change to more superficial shifts in
morality (often overly focused on sex), freezing the ability for deeper personal growth (spiritual bypass), and making one nearly blind to the need
for systemic change in families, organizations, and cultural institutions
(overly "bound" to the current culture). It can provide safety amid change
by providing guidance on how to avoid certain destructive ways of living,
with ritual actions thought to evoke God's blessing and with hopes of an
other-worldly afterlife, but in a way that so enforces equilibrium (seen in
the church's almost universal initial resistance to change) that it leads to a
closed-system entropy that ceases to be life-giving.

By contrast, the founders of Christianity (who, it is believed, were
revealing the heart of God for the world) advocated for a transformational religion that was not only in alignment with the change, growth,
and development necessary for life in the *physical* systems of the world,
but also emphasized that to be fully human, one must bring to the human
predicament a *spiritual* understanding of life, and in the very *spiritual*
understanding of life, one *also* had to change, grow, and develop. In the
spiritual life there is also development that progresses from being a child

32. Wheatley, *Leadership*, 76.

to being an adult, or as it says in one verse from the Christian Scriptures, "For though by this time you ought to be teachers, you need someone to teach you again the basic elements of the oracles of God. You need milk, not solid food; for everyone who lives on milk, being still an infant, is unskilled in the word of righteousness. But solid food is for the mature" (Heb 5: 12–14).

For example, transformational religion would advocate that to live more fully one might start by following certain guidelines for daily living that would minimize unnecessary change and pain; guidelines such as: do not murder, do not cheat, do not steal, do not covet or envy your neighbor's possessions or spouse, do not lie, etc. Of course, to follow these guidelines, other learned behaviors and other instinctual responses for survival would need to be transformed. Transformational religion would bring millennial wisdom to that process and would illuminate a path that could minimize the way in which we actually create pain in our lives.

However, beyond that, transformational religion acknowledges that change and pain inevitably come whether we create it or not and invites us to grow spiritually in the face of it. We are going to grow up and grow old whether we want to or not. Important relationships are going to have difficult moments whether we create them or not. Sickness and disease will strike without apparent cause. Natural calamities just happen. Injustice will rob us of power simply for being who we are. Transformational religion can bring comfort to those moments, but not simply be means of escapism. Rather, transformational religion brings to us a wisdom that teaches us how to engage pain, changing the way we understand and the way we experience change or pain. Transformational religion even says that we can become empowered to transform pain itself in the midst of change and, in exceptional cases, learn to rejoice in our sufferings because suffering can produce patience, character, hope, and a vital aliveness (see Rom 5:1–5).

Still further, transformative religion calls for continuing spiritual growth that moves us beyond avoiding unnecessary change/pain and beyond changing the way we engage change/pain to a place where we find fullness of life by being agents of change—being the embodiment of change even if it temporarily *increases* our pain! On the one hand, this might mean facing the pain of who we are and choosing to initiate change in our lives. On the other hand, this might be an intentional "speaking truth to power" whereby we put our lives on the line in order to nonviolently expose systems of injustice and the unseen forces that destroy the earth. It would mean that in the marketplace, transformational religion would not seek *dominance* but, at the right time, would seek *disequilibrium*, knowing that the world at times needs disorder in order to be alive and growing. Dialoguing with you as a None in the marketplace is one example of bringing disequilibrium to an overly transactional culture that is enmeshed with an overly transactional religion, for which an apology is needed. And, if we can dialogue about religion and spirituality, perhaps we can also dialogue about weightier matters of justice and mercy.

Why a religion of transformation and not of transaction? Because a religion of transformation says that to live fully involves more than dulling the effects of change or pain through moral living and a ritual performance that guarantees a painless afterlife. To live fully, one becomes a collaborator with change, aligned with the forces of creation that generate life and open us up to a power that can even transform pain and suffering. In the lofty Latin language of St. Irenaeus of Lyons (AD 120–202), one might find support of this when he says, "*Gloria enim Dei vivens homo, vita autem hominis visio Dei,*" translated more traditionally as "For the glory of God is a living man; and the life of man consists in beholding God,"[33] but more frequently quoted as, "The glory of God is a human being fully alive, and the life of a man is the vision of God."

Edwin Friedman gives a more practical illustration when he notes that, for the most part, a boat is safest when it is in the harbor. But that is *not* what a boat is made for![34] Transactional religion would be like having a boat in the harbor bound securely to the dock, with sailors following orders, keeping to their duties and roles, keeping the boat in good order, and interacting regularly with those on shore. But the boat never goes anywhere, and the sailors know how to sail only in theory. In many ways, out of fear or habit, they are chained to the land and captive to it, and captive to a way of thinking that avoids the risk of actually sailing. Transformational religion would create a *disequilibrium* that takes the boat out of the harbor where the sailors actually learn how to sail in the midst of unpredictable seas. But to do that, they have to change their thinking and the way they engage the disequilibrium.

33. Roberts and Donaldson, *Ante-Nicene Fathers*, 490.

34. Friedman, *Failure of Nerve*, 48.

The "What?" of Transformation

Continuing the boat metaphor, it would be obvious to say that what keeps the boat tied to the dock are the ropes or chains that are secured to the boat on one end and the dock on the other end. Untie the boat and it is no longer "held captive" by the land. Less obvious would be the *invisible forces* that keep the boat tied to the dock. Someone must give the order for the boat to sail. A sailor must be motivated to "weigh anchor." There must be purpose, desire, and courage to sail. There needs to be an evaluation of the weather and changes that are on the horizon but not yet seen. And, in some cases, there needs to be permission to sail from powers that are known to exist but nowhere to be seen. Transactional religion would "show us the ropes," teaching us how to follow orders and how to tie or untie the boat. Transformational religion would open our eyes to the invisible forces that keep the boat tied to the dock and would offer us a path that engages and transforms those forces. The "What?" of transformation has to do with identifying and changing (or changing our relationship to) these invisible forces.

Again, this would be in line with understanding how the world and cosmos work, at least from the perspective of quantum physics. Not only is it true that in the quantum world all particles are in relationship, making the whole cosmos relational to the core, but as Margaret Wheatley says,

> Something strange has happened to space in the quantum world. No longer is it a lonely void. Space everywhere is now thought to be filled with fields, *invisible, non-material influences* that are the basic substance of the universe. We cannot see these fields, but we do observe their effects. They have become a useful way to explain action-at-a-distance, a descriptor for how change occurs without the direct exertion of one element needing to shove another into place.[35]

Wheatley brings this insight back to earth, wondering about the invisible forces that operate in organizations in the space between people, in the silences, in the unwritten rules, unspoken values, attitudes, or "dances" that go on around personalities. By listening deeply to the stories of people within the organization, one begins to get data points that when plotted together make for patterns that are "fractal" in nature (repeated over and over again in the same pattern) and eventually reveal the "heart" or culture of the organization. Not until these invisible patterns are revealed can the

---

35. Wheatley, *Leadership*, 50, italics added.

organization be understood and transformed. Other attempts at change, such as getting a new website or getting a new employee, are transactional changes and have no chance at transforming the organization because the heart of the organizational system is not changed.

Families operate as systems with similar invisible forces—powerful unspoken dynamics around family values, personalities, generational influences, etc. that operate in the family relationships and the "spaces" that exist between persons. Many of you as Nones (nearly one-third of Linda Mercadante's interviewees[36]) have experienced twelve-step groups such as AA (Alcoholics Anonymous) or ACOA (Adult Children of Alcoholics) and have come to understand the invisible patterns in alcoholic family systems. The addicted person, the chief enabler, the children in predictable roles (e.g., family hero, scapegoat, mascot, loner, clown) all relate to each other and to the abused substance itself in patterned ways that last a lifetime until they are seen. Murray Bowen[37] and Edwin Friedman[38] would say that every family system operates with invisible forces having to do with how relationships are defined by togetherness or separateness, by the formation of triangles in relationships, and by how one relates to the family emotional processes around anxiety. Until one can see these invisible patterns, it is very difficult to transform the behavior of family members.

Similarly, couples have invisible patterns in their relationships that fill the "space between" them, sometimes referred to as the way they "dance" with each other in life. The central question in deciding about the way they "dance" is, "How close are we going to be?" In this "dance," issues of power, residual issues from childhood, and deep images in the mind of how we expect the other person to act are all invisibly present and cannot be transformed until they are seen.

And, of course, individuals have unconscious patterns, automatic thoughts, unspoken and unseen core beliefs, and their own private logic, all of which operate so habitually that they are like invisible forces not only filling the "spaces" in our head, but also extending with our minds outwardly into our relationships with others and into the world by way of patterned thinking that interprets life events and makes assumptions about the motives of others toward us. We do this automatically as a

36. Mercadante, *Belief without Borders*, 173.
37. Bowen, *Family Therapy*.
38. Friedman, *Failure of Nerve*.

means of survival, adapting as best we can to the unique world around us with all its joy and sorrow, beauty and imperfection, stability and unpredictability, which constitute the human predicament. We develop defensive strategies to make us less vulnerable as well as patterned reactions that invite others to either come close or go away. We develop images in our minds about what love is and about who is safe or who is not. These patterned ways of interacting with the world become a force of their own, operating automatically and determining what we can see and what we cannot see in the world, or as Margaret Wheatley says, "No one, not scientists nor leaders nor children, simply observes the world and takes in what it offers. We all construct the world through lenses of our own making and use these to filter and select. We actively participate in creating our worlds."[39] This is what the Apostle Paul was referring to in his simple transformational practice mentioned above when he said, "Do not be conformed to this world, but transformed by the renewing of your minds" (Rom 12:2). We all "conform" to the world around us to survive. We do so efficiently, but often imperfectly. In fact, we do it *so* efficiently that we no longer realize we are doing it. It operates as an invisible force to which we are held captive until there is a renewal (metamorphosis) of the mind that takes place in our unseen world and is far greater than a simple transaction.

However, it is important for us to remember that this "conforming to the world" and the reality of invisible forces is not limited to an individualistic understanding. As we have already seen, there are forces operating in organizations. There are forces operating in families. But there are also forces operating in cultures and subcultures that determine how we see the world and make meaning of life events in our journey to be fully human. Otto Scharmer says that these forces originate from what he calls our "blind spot," saying, "The blind spot is the place within or around us where our attention and intention originates. It's the place from where we operate when we do something. The reason it's *blind* is that it is an invisible dimension of our social field, or our everyday experience in social interactions."[40]

Again, our individual life experience can shape our "blind spot," but so can accepted cultural assumptions about reality. As a None, like much of the rest of American culture, you see the world through the lens

39. Wheatley, *Leadership*, 65.
40. Scharmer, *Theory U*, 6.

of psychology. It is a lens that opens us up to important understanding about ourselves as individuals, but it can also blind us to other ways of looking at individuals and the world as a whole. As a None, those of you who have an interest in spirituality often see the world through the lens of perennialism, which is a belief that all religions at their core basically teach the same thing and that there is one spiritual ultimate underlying everything. On the one hand, this opens you up to seeing commonalities and making comparisons, but it could also blind you to the uniqueness of religions and to the harder work that moves us beyond toleration to deeply engaging difference with dignity. Further, as a None, you are entangled in a consumer-oriented society with the rest of us as discussed above, and we are blind to the all-pervasive transactional culture in which we live, taking as normal the "greatest effort in mental manipulation that humanity has ever experienced"[41]—through advertising.

In this we live not only in our individual stories but also in the stories of the wider culture that shape the way we see the world. The stories just are. We dwell in them. We are blind to them. These are stories having to do with race, religion, gender, sexuality, power, family, nationalism, etc. Speaking to this from a Christian perspective, Craig Van Gelder and Dwight Zscheile say,

> Beneath organizational structures lie cultural narratives that reflect shared assumptions about how the world works. Such narratives are embodied in practices and behaviors in communities—the very patterns by which we participate and belong. These narratives are often implicit; they form the lenses through which people interpret reality. They are the "defaults" by which people go through their daily lives. Attempts to restructure without addressing these underlying narratives will inevitably fail. This is because defaults are too powerful: they operate at a much deeper level than do structure and organization, which are expressions, or embodiments, of their logic. One powerful default shaping life in American churches is the establishment of . . . the narratives reflected not only in the Euro-tribal denominations but also in conservative-evangelical churches focused on "making America Christian again." These narratives assume cultural privilege and centrality of the church in society, and their presumption is that Christianity is normative in American society (or should be).[42]

41. Carrette and King, *Selling Spirituality*, 160.
42. Van Gelder and Zscheile, *God's Mission*, 299–300.

Of course, this is a cultural narrative which you have questioned as a None, and, by your questioning, have opened up the possibility of seeing the invisible forces that are operating in that narrative; forces that cannot be transformed until they are seen. And perhaps they cannot be seen until we engage in marketplace dialogue where we move away from canned answers imposed through culturally bound transactional dominance and learn to live in the disequilibrium of transformation where there is the possibility of revealing still hidden truths. If, in that marketplace dialogue, we can talk about religion, maybe we can also talk about our culturally embedded narratives around race, gender, sexuality, power, and climate change, moving us away from transactional solutions when we need transformational change—like the metamorphosis of entire systems that lead to global warming instead of simply building higher sea walls.

Ironically, this idea of transformation was embedded in the very first public words of Jesus. As Richard Rohr says,

> In fact, the first public word out of his mouth was the Greek imperative verb *metanoeite*, which literally translates as "change your mind" or "go beyond your mind" (Matthew 3:2; 4:17, and Mark 1:15). Unfortunately, in the fourth century, St. Jerome translated the word into Latin as *paenitentia* ("repent" or "do penance"), initiating a host of moralistic connotations that have colored Christians' understanding of the Gospels ever since. The word *metanoeite*, however, is talking about *a primal change of mind, worldview, or your way of processing*—and only by corollary about a specific change in behavior.[43]

Until our minds are transformed at this "primal" level, we are held captive by the personal and cultural narratives embedded deeply within us, operating as invisible forces to which we are blind.

If this is the "What?" of transformation, then, in Part II of this book we will look at the "How?" of transformation, shared from a Christian point of view for consideration in our dialogue. As Linda Mercadante discussed when she interviewed some of you who are Nones, the "How?" of transformation will take more than techniques to improve the Self. She says, "It is unwarranted to believe that simple or even complex techniques for self-calming, self-healing, and self-improvement will bring about thorough

---

43. Rohr, *Universal Christ*, 92.

and deep-rooted personal transformation."[44] It may take faith, defined at one place in the Christian Scriptures as "the assurance of things hoped for, the conviction of things *not seen*" (Heb 11:1, italics added).

Part II

Apology as Appeal

[There] is the question of how you herd cattle in Australia. It gets exactly at this question: Do you build a fence, or do you build a well?

—WESLEY GRANBERG-MICHAELSON

4

Spiritual Technology as Grammar

Moving from an Apology of Admission to an Apology of Appeal

WHERE ARE WE IN the process of our dialogue? I have attempted so far to listen deeply to what you as a None have been saying through observable actions, such as your distancing from religious institutions and rituals, and through a multitude of meaningful interviews well documented in effective qualitative research over the last decade. This has led to some "passing over" and "coming back" between the different worlds of Nones and Somes with a genuine attempt to dispel misinformation and faulty assumptions (the *first step* in the process of dialogue), and it has allowed for the *overhearing* of an internal dialogue that has gone something like: "If I hear you correctly, I am hearing this . . . When you say that, it stirs this . . . inside of me. Have you ever thought about this . . . ? If that is how you feel, I need to apologize for this . . ."

Perhaps we have also experienced the *second step* in the process of dialogue in which we see value in the other's perspective and wish to appropriate it for our own, and, maybe, we have even glimpsed for a moment new areas of reality and meaning we were not aware of before (the *third step* in the process of dialogue). I know that I have seen value in your perspective and glimpsed new realities. I hope that I have communicated this to you in my validation of your disagreements with the church, pointing out positions with which I resonate and for which I offer an apology.

Of course, the process of dialogue is never linear, and we will circle back through the steps many times. Given this reality, I wonder if, in the continual "passing over" and "coming back" of the *second step* in the process of dialogue, for a moment you would be willing to listen to, attempt to understand, and perhaps find some value in an expression of my beliefs that are part of my core identity as a Christian Some. As we *overhear* the dialogue, it might begin with something like this: "Are you in a place where you can listen to something that is important to me? Are you in a place that is safe enough for me to share deep personal beliefs in a way that does not cause me to lose my very Self and does not devalue your very Self? And, from the beginning, can you understand that this is only *my* interpretation of something that I see as essential to Christianity (a core spiritual technology) with the expectation that you will question, disagree, or need some distance at times as the process of dialogue continues, and that what I share may be different from what you have understood as the essence of Christianity?"

If you are ready and willing, we would move in our dialogue *from* apology as admission, where I have attempted to hear, understand, validate, and apologize for those aspects of Christianity that have devalued you as a None and as a human being, and move *toward* an apology of appeal, where I would make an appeal for you to listen for a moment to something that I hope will resonate with, or appeal to, you. Of course, the word "apology" now shifts in its meaning *from* a confession where one expresses understanding and even regret, *to* an apology that speaks from the heart to convey what one deeply believes. Within the history of Christianity, this latter meaning has been referred to as "apologetics" and has often been offered in a "forensic" way as a "legal" (or "legalistic") defense of the faith. But it has also been offered in a "participatory" way in which one is invited to participate in a conversation about the faith, making an appeal that is appealing.

In making such an appeal, I have opened the second part of this book with a metaphor used by Wesley Granberg-Michaelson about herding cattle in Australia,[1] which on the surface is *not* very appealing and could appear to be insensitive to a core aspect of who you are as a None. The mental associations may fly in the face of your desire *not* to be a part of any herd, especially any religious herd. As Cristel Manning says, "The association effect is clearly at work among Nones for whom no religion

---

1. Quoted in McArthur, "Future of Christianity," 90.

means they are free thinkers rather than sheep that follow the herd."[2] Contrary to this, the quote is intended to illust ference between a forensic form of apologetics that tells y need to believe in order to be either "in" or "out" of the Chri... and a more participatory form of apologetics that offers an invitational appeal. Kenda Creasy Dean quotes an African Christian as saying, "You Americans think of Christianity as a farm with a fence. Your question is, 'Are you inside the fence or outside it?' We Africans think differently. We think of Christianity as a farm with no fence. Our question is, 'Are you heading towards the farm, or away from it?'"[3]

The Granberg-Michaelson metaphor about building a well and not a wall or a fence suggests that an appropriate apologetics to which you are being invited as part of our dialogue is about choice (which you value as a None). But not a forced choice; not a legalistic in-or-out choice. It may be a choice about moving toward or moving away from something, but it is more a choice coming from the realization that we all need to drink, and that we all need to find some place where we can drink what is healthy and satisfying. Obviously, this is true in the *physical* sense of having access to clean drinking water and the accompanying dysphoria we experience when that choice is not available. We all must drink. We all need a well.

But this is equally true in the *spiritual* sense. To survive, we all must drink at the well of essential nurture, of personal worth, of personal meaning, of love. Without it we die. At the thought of losing it, we become defensive, reactive, or violent. We all make choices around how and where we will find this well, and whether it is a true well that does not run dry or simply a leaking cistern. An apology of appeal would simply say, "Consider this spiritual well." It is a well which is alluded to in the wisdom literature from the Hebrew Scriptures where it says, "All people . . . feast on the abundance of your house, and you give them drink from the river of your delights, for with you is the fountain of life" (Ps 36:7–9). Or, from the Christian Scriptures, where Jesus says, "Out of the believer's heart shall flow rivers of living water" (John 7:38).

---

2. Manning, *Losing Our Religion*, 157.

3. Dean, *Almost Christian*, 65.

Technology as Grammar

Just as we are making a transition in the process of dialogue *from* an apology of admission *to* an apology of appeal, we are also making a transition *from* the question about the "What?" of transformation *to* the question about the "How?" of transformation. If a discussion of the "How?" of transformation is to be referenced as a "spiritual technology of freedom," we need to pause for a moment to be clear about what is meant by "technology" lest we be misled by the term into thinking of something that is transactional, mechanical, superficial, ritualistic, or reductionistic.

I would like you to think of "technology" in terms of its original meaning as "grammar." The word "technology" was first used as a noun in the English language in 1615 to refer to a discourse or treatise on the arts, borrowed from the Greek word *technología* which meant a systematic treatment of an art, craft, or technique and originally referred to grammar. As an adjective, the word was first used in 1627 by Captain John Smith in his book entitled *The Seaman's Grammar*.[4] Although I have not read Captain Smith's book, I imagine that it said something about the "how" of sailing a ship. In the language of our metaphor from chapter 3, perhaps he was providing a way of understanding not only the mechanics of sailing, the nomenclature of sailing, or the protocol of command, but also *how* to engage the *invisible forces* of nature involved in taking any boat out of the harbor.

Similarly, a *spiritual grammar* (or technology) would provide a language for, ways of thinking about, appropriate practices for, and illustrative stories of that which is essential for living, inclusive of, but going beyond, that which is physical or material. Returning to the metaphor for this chapter, a spiritual grammar might have implications for making physical wells and water available to all people in an equitable manner, but it would primarily be concerned with how people can drink freely from something like a *spiritual well* that supplies essential life-giving nurture, meaning, care, guidance, purpose, fulfillment, or love without which we become depressed, reactive, defensive, angry, or violent. Or, we die.

4. Barnhart, *Dictionary of Etymology*, 1120.

A Unique Language

Even to write the last paragraph assumes that we have something in common with our language, such as a very basic understanding of the word "spiritual." It also assumes that we can use that language to connect with or describe experiences or feelings that are not readily seen in a physical way. A spiritual grammar would help us develop a vocabulary for describing and engaging unseen realities that are essential for living, not unlike what had to happen in medicine to describe the unseen realities of germs in order to implement practices like handwashing to prevent the spread of disease. But even that example is, at best, a metaphor, which of course assumes that we understand what a metaphor is and that we have some comfort with language which is necessarily imprecise and evolving, not unlike the words of stories and poetry where words are often used on the edge of their meaning and with multiple resonance.

This is the language of any spiritual grammar. So, when the Hebrew poet writes, "As a deer longs for flowing streams, so my soul longs for you, O God. My soul thirsts for God, for the living God" (Ps 42:1–2), the language is associating with the biology of a material world, but the words are breaking open into another reality that is much less precise. Or, when Emily Dickinson writes, "Have you got a brook in your little heart, Where bashful flowers blow, And blushing birds go down to drink, And shadows tremble so—And nobody knows, so still it flows, That any brook is there, And yet your little draught of life Is daily drunken there—,"[5] the words are on the edge of their meaning, calling us to the unique place that gives definition to who we are and to what nourishes our being.

A Language for Stories

This kind of language is also connected with that mysterious place in the brain where the flow of energy and information coming into the brain becomes our own subjective (personal) experience. As Daniel Siegel says, "How this brain activity, this neural firing, becomes your subjective mental experience, no one knows. As we've mentioned, this is the big unknown for us humans, an unknown not often discussed."[6] Or, as David Bentley Hart says, "There is an absolute qualitative abyss between

5. Dickinson, *Complete Poems*, 63.

6. Siegel, *Mind*, 45.

objective facts of neurophysiology and the subjective experience of being a conscious self."[7]

The way we remember and organize the neural firing of the brain as it constantly processes the flow of incoming sensory data is to create stories or attach the incoming data to existing stories; stories that define who we are as persons. Our minds are narrating minds.[8] We create stories to simplify how we engage a complex world, stories that arise at the mysterious point of the electrical firing of the brain where they become the very substratum of our being, operating invisibly and powerfully to define who we are, filter what we see and believe, and strongly influence how we will behave. (Is this the "little brook" that nobody sees from which we drink daily?) A spiritual grammar uses language appropriate for these stories; a language which arises out of the mysterious unknown where physical energy becomes personal experience and where we construct and reconstruct stories that help us make sense of seen and unseen realities in our world.

For example, simple sensory data coming into the brain, such as, "I'm running late for work and on the way my tire goes flat," immediately becomes a story about getting fired from my job for being late again, or what is this going to cost me, or do I dare pull over in this neighborhood, or I've heard of people getting hit on the side of the road when stopped, or what if the police come and judge me for the color of my skin and something terrible happens? These are stories of possibility, stories of what is not yet seen created from simple sensory data and, in this case, connected to existing stories already stored in the brain. A spiritual grammar would invite us into an awareness of the language of our stories; stories arising out of the firing of the neurons in our brains and creating worlds of possibility having to do with yet unseen realities. Are we even aware of the stories we are creating? Are we aware of the underlying invisible stories that are dictating the limits of the story we are now creating, and hence, limiting our freedom and life-possibilities?

A spiritual grammar would not only invite us into the awareness that in any given moment we are creating stories in response to sensory data coming into the brain, but it would also invite us into a deeper reflection about the essential and necessary components available for any *life-giving story*. That deeper reflection might help us evaluate not only

7. Hart, *Experience of God*, 157.

8. Siegel, *Mind*, 73.

in-the-moment stories (e.g., my tire is going flat, and I am going to lose my job) but also deeper, pre-existing stories (e.g., the world is a dangerous place, and I am unsure of my abilities to survive in the face of a crisis) which may or may not be very life-giving. A spiritual grammar is most interested in dialoguing about the essential components of, the arrangement of, the flow of, and the creation of those foundational (often invisible) templates into which we align our moment-to-moment stories created from our experience in the "now." Are we leaving out key components in our stories? Are our stories big enough? Are there other ways to align the parts of the story? Is our language limited? Do we know the rules of the game in the construction of our stories?

Rules of the Game

The philosopher Ludwig Wittgenstein referred to any language as a "game" and that to play the game we need to know the "rules of the game."[9] Grammar can be thought of as "the rules of the game" (even here we are using words on the edge of their meaning). Grammar would not only inform us that to speak or write a sentence, we need to have some understanding of nouns, verbs, articles, adverbs, prepositions, etc., but also that we need to follow certain rules in the arrangement of these words in a sentence and in the punctuation that accompanies the words. Are we communicating a question? Are we giving a command? Are we making a statement? There are different rules to follow for each. Obviously, the rules of the game change with different languages, but they can also change using the same language, such as the difference in the English language between England and the United States, or the difference in the same language between the Bronx, New York, or Mobile, Alabama. Of course, for most people these rules of the game are invisible but foundational for the construction of their most basic life stories.

Wittgenstein used the game of chess as an illustration. Just showing someone a chess piece does not mean that they know how to play the game of chess.[10] In fact, on the same playing board one could play chess or checkers, depending on the rules of the game to which you have agreed. On a grassy level surface that is about one hundred yards long, one could be given a ball, but depending on the shape of the ball and the

9. Quoted in Foley, *Theological Reflection*, 25.
10. Foley, *Theological Reflection*, 27.

rules of the game, one could play football, rugby, or soccer. Similarly, all languages have rules of the game—the patterns, procedures, components that are the unspoken grammar holding the sentences together and conveying different meanings by simple punctuation, but also by unspoken cultural and subcultural nuances that sometimes only the "locals" know.

A *spiritual* grammar, using a particular kind of language with words on the edge of their meaning, has something to say about the rules of the game one might want to consider when creating *foundational stories* of meaning on the *playing field of life*; basic stories which become broad (invisible) templates into which our moment-to-moment stories are rooted. A spiritual grammar would give some *description* to the playing field of life (otherwise known as the human predicament), bounded by birth and death, rich with resources variably distributed, offering experiences of pleasure and pain, or joy and sorrow, or beauty and terror, experienced through physical bodies uniquely and (from the human point of view) unequally formed. Like it or not, this is the field on which we play the game of life. Are there ways to see, understand, engage, and order these given components of life that are more helpful or life-giving than others?

And, it makes a lot of difference how you play the game of life by what you understand as the *purpose of the game*. Is it simply to survive, to get to the end of the field, to accumulate the best equipment for the game, to make powerful and noticeable moves on the field, or to defeat an opponent? Is it about team building and relating, about character development and how one conducts oneself in the game, about sharing resources, or about teaching and helping others? Is it about choosing and creating, or about consciousness and waking up, such as when we realize that a well is not just a well, or breathing is more than just breathing, or there is something more to a playing field than just a playing field? What are the rules of this game, including the purpose of the game itself?

A spiritual grammar, using words on the edge of their meaning, would advocate for a wisdom that looks at the entire scope of the game being played (seen and unseen), with some indication of the purpose of the game and how best to align the unique components given to us to play the game. It would give essential input on how to embody in the core of our being a foundational story of meaning about life that is *not* a transactional template or fixed meta-narrative, but an evolving masterpiece formed in *conscious dialogue* with our deep existing stories, our cultural and subcultural stories, our moment-to-moment stories, and a wide array of existing spiritual maps, theories, philosophies, and religions. A

Christian spiritual grammar, or technology, would advocate for a particular way of identifying the playing field, for describing the purpose of the game, for the most effective way of ordering the components of life to play the game, and for a way of being that allows us to see invisible stories and have the power to make real choices in how we play the game.

For instance, as we saw in chapter 2, we are entangled as Nones and Somes in the American culture over issues of the Self, with you as a None particularly interested in self-development, self-fulfillment, self-esteem, and even self-spirituality. A Christian spiritual grammar would bring ancient wisdom to this interest in the Self with some input on the characteristics of an idealized Self and with a corresponding evaluation of a non-idealized Self. It would bring wisdom to the evaluation of stories we tell ourselves about our Selves, helping to identify the invisible stories operating in the depths of our hearts and minds. It would bring a spiritual grammar to the game of life that says change in the Self is necessary and normal for living fully with a certain pattern of change to be expected. It would also offer a spiritual technology for how change of the Self might happen. Or if, as Elizabeth Drescher has pointed out, you as a None find spirituality in Friends, Family, Food, and Fido,[11] a Christian spiritual grammar would offer wisdom about the nature of these relationships, the depths to which they can be experienced, what makes them healthy, the invisible stories being played out within them, and how to change them when things go wrong or when one suffers loss. There may be some wisdom to be shared about how one plays the game of life that is purposefully relational and necessarily transformational.

Of course, this is what all religions do, offering wisdom regarding the rules of the game on the playing field of life while using words on the edge of their meaning and providing a grammar for bigger stories about relationships and the Self. But their spiritual technologies differ, and even within Christianity the grammar is variously understood. In fact, there may be some Christians who are overhearing this dialogue between you as a None and me as a Christian Some, and who might want to increase their distance from the dialogue upon reading my understanding of a Christian spiritual technology and the nature of transformation!

11. Drescher, *Choosing Our Religion*, 44.

A Variety of Spiritual Technologies

A Variety of Interfaith Spiritual Technologies

I have some hesitation in using the term "spiritual technology" lest our dialogue inadvertently turn back to a discussion of simplistic spiritual techniques and the transactional trap so prevalent in the cultural stories of America. Hence, when I use the term "technology," I am inviting you to think in terms of "grammar" as opposed to "technique." But you might ask why I would use the term "spiritual technology" at all. I do so because it is a term that I found to be frequently used in the discussion of the essentials of any religion and may resonate with you as a None. For example, Krista Tippet, in describing the point when religion in America began to change dramatically, says, "And in the tumult of social upheaval in the 1960s, young Westerners began to make their way to India and Burma to learn to meditate . . . They came home not so much as evangelists but as importers of spiritual technologies that offer themselves with urgency to the twenty-first century."[12] But I also use the term because it helps to highlight some of the deficits in understanding the essentials of Christianity when that religion is presented apologetically.

I taught a class for over twenty years in which professional-counselors-in-training learned how to be present with, listen to, and understand those from other faith traditions without judgment and reactivity. During a semester, I would have guest lecturers from different faith traditions present their faith to the class in order to provide a basic understanding of a variety of faiths. For over a decade, Dr. D. C. Rao would present on Hinduism. In a brilliant and humble way, he reduced the complexities of Hinduism, with its 330 million gods, multiple yoga paths to Brahmin, and three answers to any question, to a two-hour lecture and one PowerPoint slide. He referred to his presentation as giving the "spiritual technology of Hinduism" and later wrote a book on the basics of Hinduism.[13] He often challenged me to do the same for Christianity, and I often wondered what a spiritual technology of Christianity would look like.

It was almost easier to think of the spiritual technologies of other faiths. I read Yongey Mingyur Rinpoche's book, *The Joy of Living*, and I could easily see with his integration of science and religion a spiritual technology of Buddhism summarized in his opening paragraph,

12. Tippet, *Becoming Wise*, 59–60.
13. Rao, "Understanding Hinduism."

When you are trained as a Buddhist, you don't think of Buddhism as a religion. You think of it as a type of science, a method of exploring your own experience through techniques that enable you to examine your actions and reactions in a nonjudgmental way, with the view toward recognizing, "Oh, this is how my mind works. This is what I need to do to experience happiness. This is what I should avoid to avoid unhappiness."[14]

And then there was Chade-Meng Tan's book, *Search Inside Yourself*, summarizing the curriculum of a twenty-hour course that he taught for the technology-consumed employees at Google and incorporating the essentials of Buddhist meditation practices packaged as mindfulness-based emotional intelligence. These books are just two examples from a plethora of books that convey the essence of, or spiritual technology of, Buddhism and its practices, arising out of the Four Spiritual Laws and Eightfold Practice, and usually focus on a clear spiritual path to happiness.

Although he never used the term "spiritual technology," my friend Mr. Salahuddeen Kareem came to my class to present on Islam. He would describe the seven core beliefs of Islam: the oneness of God (Allah); divine justice of the Creator; prophethood; a belief in all the Divine Books, culminating in the Qur'an; a belief in the resurrection on a judgment day followed by an afterlife; a belief in Unseen Entities including angels; and a belief in predestination. Then he would illustrate the Five Pillars of Islam: The *Shahada*, or profession of faith; *Salat*, or the ritual of prayer five times a day; *Zakah*, or the giving of alms; fasting in the month of Ramadan; and pilgrimage to Mecca, or *Haj*. Mr. Kareem would say that no matter what you say, you cannot be a Muslim if you do not practice the Five Pillars. And I thought to myself, here is the spiritual technology of Islam.

Again, she never used the term "spiritual technology," but a wonderful colleague, Rabbi Amy Scheinerman, opened up the world of Judaism to the class in what seemed to some an over-focus on history. But, of course, this is Judaism, which does not focus on doctrinal beliefs but on a way of living in history in a covenantal relationship with the one G-d. Time itself is sanctified through the keeping of Shabbat and through the participation in major festivals, such as the three pilgrimage festivals (Passover, Shavuot, Sukkot), the High Holy Days (Rosh Hashanah, Yom Kippur), the minor festivals (Purim, Chanukah), and the days of mourning (Tisha B'Av). Daily prayer, such as praying the Psalms or prayers of gratitude that count one hundred blessings a day, is a way of engaging in the covenantal

14. Rinpoche, *Joy of Living*, 11.

relationship with G-d, as well as a daily practice of committing to deeds of loving kindness. Central also to keeping covenant with G-d is the study of Torah, whether one is focused on the 613 commands of Torah or on the foundational stories of Torah that teach one how to live—all with the proviso that disagreements about and dialogue over the text is *good*. And I thought, this essential description of living in history in a Covenantal relationship with G-d is a spiritual technology of Judaism.

Of course, in each case mentioned, it is easy to think of the spiritual technology of each faith as the specific practices of the faith, or what can be referred to as "orthopraxy" (right practice). But with varying degrees of emphasis, there was also an underlying "orthodoxy" (right beliefs) that was demonstrated. And, above all, there was a clear demonstration of "orthopathy" (right feeling), or what others have referred to as "orthokardia" (right heart), and is picked up on only in the presence of someone who has embodied their faith with hand, head, and heart,[15] such as the presenters in my class. Their faith had become the grammar of their lives, the invisible force holding together the components of life and providing a foundational story by which every moment-to-moment story is evaluated and incorporated.

Others have done this in an "interspiritual" way. Rory McEntee and Adam Bucko have written their own spiritual technology, calling it *The New Monasticism: An Interspiritual Manifesto for Contemplative Living*. They draw upon the work of Brother Wayne Teasdale, who coined the term "interspiritual" as a way of denoting a movement beyond interfaith dialogue to a more intimate way of relating among the world's wisdom traditions. "Interspirituality, however, built upon those initial forays and deepened the sharing among traditions, moving them to begin sharing actual *'spiritual technologies'* and mystical realizations with each other on an experiential level."[16] Going beyond other advocates of an interspiritual approach to interreligious relating, they advocate a more radical path, saying,

> This interspiritual path may not include being fully embedded in any of the existing wisdom traditions. It stems from a universal recognition of the potential of the human being for spiritual maturity as the basis of one's path, and cognizes clearly the interspiritual vision of the wisdom traditions as a common heritage for humanity. It also hints at a more radical understanding

15. Foley, *Theological Reflection*, 65.

16. McEntee and Bucko, *New Monasticism*, 25, italics added.

of our spiritual traditions. Not only are they all paths to spiritual maturity, but in a mysterious sense one feels they may complete one another. Each wisdom tradition may hold a puzzle piece as to the ultimate flowering of humanity . . . A new monastic is one who feels the calling to her own evolution, her own depth of Spirit, her own transformational path, and responds.[17]

Clearly, the spirit of Brother Wayne Teasdale, who anticipated the "Spiritual But Not Religious" movement, is seen here and may have resonance for those of you as Nones who align with this category.

A Variety of Christian Spiritual Technologies

I still wondered what a Christian spiritual technology might entail. Were there earlier attempts at developing a spiritual grammar that communicated the most essential elements of the faith? Certainly, historical confessions of faith have been created. These are creedal statements, such as the Nicene Creed, the Apostles' Creed, or the Westminster Confession of Faith, that are recited regularly in Christian worship service or taught in confirmation classes. For instance, the Apostles' Creed says,

> I believe in God, the Father almighty, Creator of heaven and earth, and in Jesus Christ, his only Son, our Lord, who was conceived by the Holy Spirit, and born of the Virgin Mary, suffered under Pontius Pilate, was crucified, died, and was buried; he descended into hell; on the third day he rose again from the dead; he ascended into heaven, and is seated at the right hand of God the Father almighty; from there he will come to judge the living and the dead. I believe in the Holy Spirit, the holy catholic church, the communion of saints, the forgiveness of sins, the resurrection of the body, and life everlasting. Amen.

I can see how believing in these statements could form something of a grammar in one's life and contribute to a foundational story of meaning. But, of course, it is primarily focused on right beliefs and doctrine (orthodoxy) more than a spiritual practice. The same would be true for the core principles of faith espoused by John Calvin as a summary of Protestant reformed theology (mentioned in the previous chapter as Calvinism). We could say that the *TULIP* principle of Calvinism is something of a spiritual technology. *TULIP* stands for: *T*otal depravity of

17. McEntee and Bucko, *New Monasticism*, 28, 31.

man; *U*nconditional election; *L*imited atonement; *I*rresistible grace; and *P*erseverance of the saints. For sure, these beliefs could form a grammar for one's life and serve to develop a very different foundation story, but, again, even though Calvin wrote a lot about spiritual practice and a regenerate heart, the summary focus is primarily on right doctrine without much help on the "How?" of transformation.

Others who followed this type of theology developed spiritual technologies around the "How?" of conversion to Christianity. Bill Bright, founder of Campus Crusade for Christ, wrote what he described as the Four Spiritual Laws to teach people how to be "saved" quickly and efficiently. Written in the form of a tract that has been reproduced over a billion times and distributed around the world, the four laws are: 1) God loves you and offers a wonderful plan for your life; 2) Man is sinful and separated from God. Therefore, he cannot know and experience God's love and plan for his life; 3) Jesus Christ is God's only provision for man's sin. Through him you can know and experience God's love and plan for your life. 4) We must individually receive Jesus Christ as Savior and Lord; then we can know and experience God's love and plan for our lives.[18]

Although it is uncertain whether it originated with Charles Finney, Billy Sunday, Billy Graham, or Jack Hyles, the Roman Road Plan of Salvation was a reduction to seven verses of the Apostle Paul's letter to the Romans (Rom 3:10; 3:23; 5:12; 6:23; 5:8; 10:9–10). It created a spiritual technology focused on the "How?" question for being "saved" and followed an evangelical understanding of theology which, when combined with the right questions, could guide someone in the process of conversion. The selected verses indicate that every person sins, the wages of sin is death, Christ has paid the price for our sin, and confession of Jesus as Lord opens one to salvation.

Search the internet for "The Roman Road to Salvation" and you will get millions of entries. It is obviously a popular way of approaching the essential grammar of evangelical Christianity. It assumes that if one follows the scriptural progression and makes a confession with the lips about Jesus Christ that one will not only be saved but also transformed. However, as we have seen in previous chapters, it is possible through one's religious confession to be bound to a particular theology and a particular culture without changing the underlying (invisible) stories that are the templates into which we fit our moment-to-moment sensory experience. Hence, it

---

18. Bright, "Four Spiritual Laws."

is possible to make a confession (which might be an important first step in transformation) while still being unbound to agape-love and blind to things like racism, sexism, materialism, etc. It seems to me that a spiritual technology that answers the question regarding the "How?" of transformation must include a wider understanding of the rules of the game.

Although one cannot say that it is succinct (over eight hundred pages), the *Catechism of the Catholic Church* (1995) could certainly be considered as a spiritual technology of Christianity from a Roman Catholic point of view. It is organized around four pillars: 1) The Profession of Faith (with a major focus on the Apostles' Creed); 2) The Celebration of the Christian Mystery (with a major focus on the sacraments of the Roman Catholic Church); 3) Life in Christ (with a major focus on the moral life and the Ten Commandments); and 4) Christian prayer (with a major focus on the Lord's Prayer).

There is definitely plenty of input here on the rules of the game from a Christian point of view regarding the purpose and meaning of life and how the components of the human predicament are to be understood and aligned for living fully. There may be an over-focus on orthodoxy (right believing) at times, but there is plenty of material on orthopraxy (right practice) that is not limited to ritual performance and is inclusive of moral behavior that brings about justice for all creation. Orthopathy (right feeling) and orthokardia (right heart) are implied throughout, especially in the section on prayer. In fact, it is in the extensive development of prayer within the Roman Catholic tradition where one might find clues to the "How?" of transformation, provided one does not get stuck in ritual practices and transactional performance characteristic of a Roman Catholic faith that has become overly bound to the obligations (*religiones*) of the church. In the richness of the Dominican, Franciscan, Benedictine, Augustinian, Carmelite, Salesian, Ignatian, and Mercy traditions,[19] as well as the Prayer of the Heart tradition coming from the Eastern Orthodox Church, one engages a variety of Christian spiritual technologies capable of evaluating and transforming our foundational stories that serve as the basic grammar of our lives and influence our moment-to-moment way of being in the world.

These traditions of prayer all have their roots in the desert fathers and mothers who, in the early centuries of Christianity, retreated to the desert to focus solely on their relationship to God. As Richard Rohr says,

19. Wicks, *Prayer in the Catholic Tradition.*

The Desert Fathers and Mothers focused on these primary practices in their search for God: 1) leaving, to some extent, the systems of the world; 2) a degree of solitude to break from the maddening crowd; 3) times of silence to break from the maddening mind; and 4) "technologies" for controlling the compulsivity of mind and the emotions. All of this was for the sake of growing a person capable of love and community.[20]

Summary

In my opinion, a spiritual technology from a Christian point of view would, using words on the edge of their meaning and a unique vocabulary, advocate for a spiritual grammar that helps us understand the rules of the game of life in such a way that allows us to maximize the freedom and possibility in our life-stories and, therefore, to drink deeply from the "spiritual well" that supplies essential life-giving nurture, meaning, care, guidance, purpose, self-fulfillment, or love. It would advocate for a wisdom that looks at the entire scope of the game being played (seen and unseen), with some indication of the purpose of the game and how best to align the unique components given to us to play the game. It would give essential input on how to embody in the core of our being a foundational story about the meaning of life that is *not* a transactional template or fixed meta-narrative, but an evolving masterpiece formed in *conscious dialogue* with our deep existing stories, our cultural and subcultural stories, our moment-to-moment stories, and a wide array of existing spiritual maps, theories, philosophies, and religions.

Implied in this spiritual technology is the reality that our stories, in order to be life-giving and in line with the rest of creation, are regularly in a state of *disequilibrium* or change and are *relational* to the core. While not dictating what an individual's, organization's, or culture's story must look like (for these stories are as unique as a fingerprint), a Christian spiritual technology would have something to say about what is life-giving or not, as well as *how* the stories are transformed. Included in this would be an openness to see what might be operating *invisibly* in our lives, as well as opening to an *experience of the energy* that 1) holds the components of the stories together, 2) is the creative force behind any new stories, and, at the same time, 3) is the very essence of our Being or Self.

20. Rohr, "Contemplative Consciousness."

As we discussed in chapter 1, our lives as Nones and Somes are entangled in stories with themes emerging from an American culture that involves religion, individualism, secularism, social science, spiritual experience, etc., played out in the wider context of the unavoidable "givens" of the human predicament. Frequently the themes of our stories are played out with different plots. Even more often, we have cultural aspects to our stories that operate like a grammar we can no longer see—such as a marketplace mentality or a mechanistic approach to performance—and that invade the stories of the religious and nonreligious alike in ways that are not very life-giving for ourselves or for the planet. David Bentley Hart says, "Martin Heidegger . . . was largely correct in thinking that the modern West excels at evading the mystery of being precisely because its governing myth is one of practical mastery."[21] This is so in a culture where there is "one truly substantial value at the center of our social universe: the price tag."[22]

Our continuing dialogue is one way in which we begin to see the grammar of our stories and open ourselves to the disequilibrium that brings about creative change, asking, "What's the story going to be?" A spiritual technology would offer a grammar of understanding that creatively links "What's the story going to be?" to "How's the story going to change?" It recognizes that in changing our stories there may be certain ways of being religious that one can, and probably should, move to the periphery of one's life or be eliminated altogether. But it also advocates for a wisdom which can see that there are irreducible "transcendentals,"[23] having to do with being itself, which one cannot remove from one's life without experiencing loss so great that one becomes depressed, reactive, defensive, angry, or violent. We all have to drink. We do not need more fences. We need more wells.

Are you still willing to be in the role of the listener in our dialogue?

21. Hart, *Experience of God*, 310.
22. Hart, *Experience of God*, 313.
23. Hart, *Experience of God*, 242.

5

A Spiritual Technology of Freedom

Toward a Pedagogy of Interiority

THERE ARE SO MANY British murder mysteries streaming on American televisions and digital devices, each with multiple murders in a single episode, that I wonder how anyone is still alive in Britain. A similar comment was made by Queen Elizabeth when she made John Nettles an Officer of the Order of the British Empire (OBE) in 2010 for his lead role in *Midsomer Murders*, as she jokingly wondered if anyone was still alive in Midsomer. In addition to *Midsomer Murders*, there are shows like *Morse, Inspector Lewis, Endeavor, Vera, Father Brown*, and *Grantchester* that are more accurately classified as detective dramas, with shows like *Miss Marple* and *Poirot* being more classical murder mysteries in the style of Agatha Christie. While the latter involve more independent sleuths solving complex murder cases, the former usually involve a detective chief inspector (DCI) and a younger detective sergeant (DS) who solve the case together with clues emerging by way of dialogue between them in a relationship not unlike teacher (pedagogue) and student. In an interesting twist, sometimes a clergy person is positioned as the dialogue partner with the DCI, and the teacher-student roles are mixed.

There are clear rules of the game for the development of a murder mystery or detective drama. For example, there will always be multiple murders that are not serial killings but are related by way of covering up a family secret or some impropriety arising out of human greed, loss of status or fortune, illicit relationship, jealousy, etc. The DCI will always solve the case in a final flash of insight after processing the clues with a DS, who

126

does the grunt work, and after engaging in a conflicted debate with the department superintendent, who is concerned about the public's reaction to the case. When a clergy person is cast as an undercover detective, the dialogue about clues is the same, but the roles are reversed or mixed. It is almost always the case that the first person who appears to be guilty is not the real murderer, and there are enough red herrings and subplots to tease the brain and ensure that the audience overhearing the drama will not solve the murder before the star of the show does. There is a certain grammar to the story that becomes familiar and invites the overhearing audience to participate in the drama for the purposes of entertainment and brain stimulation to figure out "whodunnit."

But there is more to the grammar of these stories than a familiar form of entertainment and brain teasing. Firstly, the detective dramas go beyond the classical murder mysteries in the development of "dramedy," which combines drama with comedy, often with a subtle and sometimes dark form of humor. Secondly, as with most art, there is a story being told that is both reflective of and critical of the surrounding culture. As the detective dramas unfold, there is almost always a critical commentary being offered on class distinctions in British society, and the brilliance of the DSI is usually portrayed as being far superior to the intelligence of any Oxford or Cambridge don. Racial issues in British society are often addressed, although early episodes of the shows were criticized for being insensitive to racial disparities in casting and character portrayal. Still further, religion is usually portrayed as silly superstition or antiquated ritual on the margins of society and certainly nowhere to be found in the life of the DCI. (This is ironic given the fact that, at a basic level, the detective drama follows the story line from the biblical book of Genesis in which the immediate human response to misbehavior by Adam and Eve is the attempt to hide and cover things over with fig leaves, creating further human hardship that progresses to the murder of Abel by his brother Cain.) When clergy play a leading role, their clerical roles are merely a cover for their true detective interests and sometimes for their less-than-spiritual inclinations. Often, the clergy add words of simple morality to the story line, but at times their words can evoke deeper thoughts about the joy and suffering found in the human condition. These grammatical influences on the detective drama may be less visible, but they are constantly flashing meaning-making images to the participating audience about how the culture is or should be; about how life is or should be; about the rules of the game of life.

Thirdly, even less visible in the rules of the game is the underlying grammar of how the murder will be solved. The solution always involves a rational and psychological technology mixed with street-smart experience and intuition. The solution to the murder case can always be rationally understood once the clues are rationally aligned and the psychological motives (usually tied to defensive protection of the non-idealized Self) are brought to conscious light. Perhaps the wisdom of the DCI in putting it all together with a mix of rationality and intuition comes closest to something of a spirituality, but nowhere in the rules of the game or the underlying grammar of the detective drama is there a place for how murders could be stopped in the first place or how one might be liberated from the wheel of death-producing thought and behavior. Of course, that would require changing the rules of the game; changing the grammar and technology of the detective drama. And, certainly, this would include changing one important rule of the game—namely, the requirement to produce something that will sell in the marketplace by way of enticing an audience to overhear and participate in the story being sold. For that, you need more murders and for the wheel of death to continue.

Other forms of media art have similar rules of the game tailored for a particular type of story, but always with less visible cultural implications shaping the story line and with underlying technologies that are culturally conditioned. All of these stories are *good at* revealing the flawed and complex nature of the human condition and at pushing the envelope on the degree to which that raw human reality can be openly portrayed in the public eye. They are *good at* offering reasons for the mysterious violations of basic societal values by the application of a rational and psychological technology, and they are *good at* using art as commentary on current cultural beliefs and issues by weaving these into the grammar of the stories. However, much like a religion that is overly bound to culture, they are better at reflecting culture than changing culture. Almost by default, they employ rules of the game that rule out other grammars and technologies that are available for playing the game of life and that can free us from the repetitive patterns of human imperfection found in stories as ancient as the biblical book of Genesis.

To some extent, the detective drama is a paradigm for our own culturally-bound stories that have been created by our brains to simplify the constant inflow of sensory data and to make meaning of our experiences as best we can. More often than not, we *live in our own repetitive dramas* with consistent themes dictated by our egos in learned patterns of survival. Our dramas have fixed rules of the game, producing stories that cycle over and over again and are revealed in our moment-to-moment experiences and relationships. These stories, among other things, are entangled in cultural issues such as individualism, secularism, religion, spirituality, and ideas about the Self, as well as issues around sexuality, race, gender, power, and climate change that we are good at naming but not changing. We turn to "experts" for rational explanations of life's problems and operate with an inner understanding of human thought and behavior that is mostly limited to pop psychology, inclusive at times of spiritual practices that calm our anxieties but rarely rise above Americanized versions of Eastern religions or a moralistic therapeutic deism[1] devoid of transformative power.

Whether our stories are influenced by cultural art, such as detective dramas, or our stories create the milieu from which these dramas emerge, I am not sure. In either case, there seems to be a "cap" on the level to which we can rise within any given culture in order to name the repetitive stories operating invisibly in our lives and become liberated to see other grammars, other technologies, and other possibilities for the game of life. The "cap" remains in place because it is less anxiety-producing to see the world the way we have constructed it, even if that construction is false and limiting. If one has only lived in a culture where the story is told that the earth is flat, it is far safer to stay close to home than to venture forth and discover that we have lived with a false story. And there are those who benefit from the "cap" that keeps us imprisoned in our repetitive, life-limiting stories of human imperfection, whether it be church authorities who need to control the story of imperfection in order to offer salvation, or politicians who limit the options for societal change in order to get reelected, or conspiracy theorists who gain control over our minds by making us afraid, or educators who push agendas while controlling the grades for success, or a business that undermines the innovation of outsiders in order to keep market dominance, or a film production team that needs more murders to keep the show going.

But, in all fairness, the cultural "cap" remains on what we can see and know about our constructed stories because we lack what some have referred to as a "pedagogy of interiority." Such a pedagogy would provide some form of instruction on how to navigate the mysterious interiority where the brain turns sensory data into subjective experience and

---

1. Dean, *Almost Christian.*

generates stories about reality. Traditional churches and cultural institutions together have failed to provide clear and comprehensive instruction on how to understand and participate in an inner life that is inclusive of, but is not limited by, religious obligations, psychology, or scientific observation of the material world. David Bentley Hart calls for instruction in the "metaphysics of the transcendental,"[2] which focuses less on convincing arguments and more on experience. John O'Donohue calls for a return to valuing and understanding the interior work involved in experiential rites of passage, or what he calls "threshold experiences." He says,

> Today many people describe themselves as "being in transition." In a culture governed by speed, this is to be expected, for the exterior rate of change is relentless. This "transition" can refer to relationships, work, and location; or more significantly, to the inner life and way of viewing the world. Yet the word *transition* seems to be pale, functional, almost inadequate and impersonal, and does not have the same intensity or psychic weight as perhaps the word *threshold* evokes. The word *threshold* was related to the word *thresh*, which was the separation of the grain from the husk or straw when oats were flailed. It also includes the notions of *entrance, crossing, border,* and *beginning.* To cross a threshold is to leave behind the husk and arrive at the grain. A threshold is a significant frontier where experience banks up; there is intense concrescence. It is a place of great transformation.[3]

As part of the development of a pedagogy of interiority, might there be a *spiritual technology* that could move us beyond the repetitive cycle of human tragedy and imperfection that more education, more information, and more cultural stories have helped us to name but not change? If so, might it help us to navigate the threshold experiences of life where there is a "shattering of our carapaces," or the breaking open of the earth to find a well from which springs the water of life?

Can we continue to dialogue about this? As a None you are important in this dialogue because you not only have the ability, like the murder mysteries, to name the blatant manifestations of human imperfection in the world, but you also have a keen sensibility to name that which is *not* working in our culture to change the cycle of human tragedy (such as transactional religion). In my opinion, and perhaps beyond what you have overtly shared in our dialogue, your very presence is an invitation

2. Hart, *Experience of God,* 83.

3. O'Donohue, *To Bless the Space,* 193.

into a creative space of "nothingness" where there might emerge an energy and pedagogy for real change. I simply want to introduce into that space some options from a Christian point of view. Are you still willing to be in the listener role in our dialogue?

Core Operating Systems of the Mind

A Christian spiritual technology would suggest that the reason we cannot rise above the cultural "cap" on our conscious awareness and step out of the cycle of our repetitive dramas is because we do not understand the degree of change that is being asked of us in the game of life. As well, we have no grammar or language to help us decipher the nature of our own interior depths and the methods of inner transformation. As mentioned in an earlier chapter, the Apostle Paul called for a complete metamorphosis of the mind (Rom 12:2). He built on the earlier work of the Hebrew prophets who called for any instructions concerning rules for the game of life to be written on the heart (Jer 31:33). In what we now understand as a heart-mind entrainment or a "heart-centered cognition"[4] involving the cognitive, emotional, and physiological systems of our being, a Christian spiritual technology would define real change as a complete transformation of the core operating systems of our hearts *and* minds. The change being called for has to do with the very way we *process* information and sensory experience. We can change partners, we can change our politics, we can change our religion or opt out of religion, we can change our location, we can change our friends, we can change our nationality, we can change our job, we can change from negative to positive thinking, we can change our education or increase our knowledge, we can change the plots and subplots in our stories, etc., but none of this is true transformation because the *core operating system* by which we process all of life has not changed.

Although all analogies are limited, we might think of the core operating system of a computer. A computer is simply a machine that uses basic technological hardware, but how that machine operates is determined by the core operating system. For example, the mechanical hardware works differently if it is an Apple product or a Microsoft product. These operating systems have their default settings that are repetitive and, once learned, can even create people who operate with an "Apple brain" or a "Microsoft brain" when turning on the computer. The point here is not

4. Bourgeault, *Centering Prayer*, 153.

to argue that one system is better than the other. The point is to illustrate that true transformation in our lives would not be like simply moving from one Apple product to another or from one Microsoft product to another. It would be more like moving to a completely different operating system—in other words, moving from an Apple system to a Microsoft system or *vice versa*.

Similarly, we might think of the operating systems of a search engine on our computers. We might have a personal preference for using Google or Bing to conduct an internet search, but usually we are not thinking that there are certain formulas being used that determine what "pops up" first (or at all) in our search. These formulas are created by employees and owners of the techno-organizations who are influenced by money and who knows what else. These formulas operate like invisible forces that determine what we see and what we do not see in our search. To change what we see in our search, we would need to change the formulas that are operating as foundational filters of the information that is in the world. Again, the analogy might be imperfect, but a Christion *spiritual technology* would say that true transformation involves changing the default formulas in our brains that are filtering all the information available in the world and determining invisibly and slavishly what "pops up" on the screen of our minds.

As another example, think of algorithms that take basic data from our lives and mathematically generate interpretive recommendations on how we should think, or live, or be seen by others. One year the blood work done in my annual physical said that my circulatory system was operating just fine. The next year the blood work produced equally good results, but this time the report came back recommending that I start medication. The only thing that had changed in the way the data was being interpreted was my age. The algorithm, inclusive of what happens to most people on average when they age, produced a different result from the same basic physiological data.

And what about those algorithms used to run the computers that now determine a lot of investing in the stock market and have some determination regarding our financial security? Or, what of the algorithms used to create our credit scores or whether we can get a loan? This is not simply an issue of unbiased mathematical formulas as can be seen by loan requests with identical financial information being interpreted favorably or unfavorably for approval with only one differential data point being entered into the algorithm—race! Or, what of the information that appears on our Facebook feeds? What are the algorithms being used to determine what we see or do not see based upon the "invisible" collection of and interpretation of our personal data for the purpose of influencing our thinking and behavior? By way of analogy, we might say that true transformation does not occur until we change the algorithms being used to interpret the "data" flowing into our lives at any moment. A Christian *spiritual technology* would have something to say about the algorithms we are using (our grammar, our rules of the game) to determine the basic stories of our lives. As well, it would have something to say about the necessity of change and the process by which those algorithms are changed.

Data Collection

Of course, if the rules of the game or the grammar of our core operating systems operate automatically or invisibly in our lives, how are we ever going to change those systems? How can we assess the difference in core operating systems if we cannot see them, name them, or know them? It seems that an important aspect of any pedagogy of interiority would be to find some way to bring to our awareness what is happening in the *interior of the heart or mind*. The danger of *not* doing so is well documented by psychology and all religions in theories ranging from a "leaking" of unconscious material to the toxicity of spiritual bypass or "canned" religion. Then there is the prophet who proclaims, "The heart is devious above all else, it is perverse—who can understand it? I the Lord test the mind and search the heart, to give to all according to their ways, according to the fruit of their doings" (Jer 17:9–10).

Where might we "collect data" on the interior operations of the heart and mind? The logical conclusion from physics, psychology, and religion seems to indicate that such "data" *emerges in relationships*. The operational heart of the universe emerges in the relationship of quantum particles.[5] The unconscious emerges in the transference between therapist and client.[6] The nature of the Self at any developmental stage is seen in the relation between subject and object.[7] The highest achievement of human development, according to Jesus, could only be observed and developed in intentional communities focused on a particular quality

---

5. Wheatley, *Leadership*.
6. Brenner, *Elementary Textbook*.
7. Kegan, *Evolving Self*.

of relationships: "By this everyone will know that you are my disciples, if you have love for one another" (John 13:35). "Data" on how one was doing as a follower of Jesus could only be observed in the relationships that emerged in communities later described by the Apostle Paul as the "body of Christ," where differences were likened to different parts of the human body functioning relationally at its best with one spirit or mind (1 Cor 12:12–27).

So, it seems natural that if we want to have some understanding of what is operating (sometimes invisibly) in the core of our hearts and minds, we would do well to become observers of our relationships—*all of our relationships*—paying attention not only to what we say but also to what we do and how we behave. How do we relate to our neighbors, friends, or spouses? How close will we allow ourselves to be? What are the patterns? Can I set boundaries? Do I become enmeshed? What is my style of relating that repeats itself over and over again? How do I relate to my very Self? Is there self-care and appropriate self-love, or self-sabotage, self-doubt, or self-hate? How do I relate to nature, whether with care and a sense of oneness or with abuse and unthinking dominance? How do I relate to problems, whether with curiosity or reactivity? What is my style? How do I relate to enemies or those who dislike me? How do I relate to power or those in authority? How do I relate to God—if I were to believe in God?

All of these relationships (and more) provide "data" on what is happening in the human heart. Or, as it says in the wisdom literature, "Just as water reflects the face, so one human heart reflects another" (Prov 27:19). But we can only begin to see the core operating systems that are functioning dynamically in our interior Self *if*, in the process of observation, we 1) cease to critique and blame someone else for what is happening, and 2) nonjudgmentally begin to ask what my observations are telling me about the core operating systems, the foundational stories, the functional grammar of *my* heart, mind, and very Being. If I am committed to a religious community but repeatedly get angry about doctrine, practices, or others in the pew, what is this telling me about the core operating systems of *my* heart? If I value family but suffer from cut-offs that seem irreparable, what is this telling me about *my* interior stories or basic grammar? If I deeply love someone but periodically display condescension or irrational anger, what is this telling *me* about the deepest rules of the game which I expect people to follow? Often our relationships are speaking loud and clear about the nature of our interior Selves, our deepest heart and mind, which is usually different from the exterior Self that I try to present to others and want to believe that I am. Can I look honestly at the "data" that emerges from these observations, and can I do so without sliding into non-productive guilt or self-condemnation, which simply produces another cyclical story with its concomitant bondage?

As a None, your interest in the Self is an advantage here because in your curiosity about self-development, self-fulfillment, self-esteem, self-help, self-improvement, etc., you have already begun to develop strategic observational skills regarding the functioning of the Self. The challenge might be to prioritize the observation of the Self-in-relationship over the individual Self or the Self-in-isolation. As well, you would have to consider that current ideas about self-development, self-fulfillment, self-esteem, self-help, self-improvement, etc. are also culturally conditioned as much as any canned religion that is bound to culture, and that these ideas can be very different from the *transformation of Self*, which requires a different core operating system than the one learned for survival or cultural accommodation.

Assessment

If we become observers of the Self-in-relationship and have some enlightened interest in the transformation of Self or some genuine human interest in avoiding pain and enhancing pleasure for ourselves and others, then we must have some way of *evaluating* what we are observing about our relationships and what they are telling us about our deepest heart and mind. Using the unique spiritual language of parables to make the distinction between an external form of religion focused on strict dietary rules and true inner transformation, Jesus says to his disciples,

> It is not what goes into the mouth that defiles a person, but it is what comes out of the mouth that defiles . . . Do you not see that whatever goes into the mouth enters the stomach, and goes out into the sewer? But what comes out of the mouth proceeds from the heart, and this is what defiles. For out of the heart come evil intentions, murder, adultery, fornication, theft, false witness, slander. These are what defile a person (Matt 15: 11, 17–20).

Not only is Jesus indicating that the way we communicate with others reveals what is in our deepest hearts, but he is also making an *evaluation*, based upon the "data" emerging from our mouths, concerning the transformation of our hearts, the purity of our hearts, the liberation of our hearts—or not! If the "data" emerging from our Self-in-relationship includes evil intentions, murder, adultery, fornication, theft, false witness, slander, etc., then our assessment would be—no matter how religious or culturally accomplished we are—that our deepest heart, mind, or Self has *not* been transformed and is functioning with a core operating system that is *not* liberated.

The *means of assessment* are fairly universal among religions and cultures and are related to what was referred to in chapter 2 as ideas about the idealized Self and the non-idealized Self. Regarding the non-idealized Self, one can find a lengthy list of amoral psychological categories in the *Diagnostic and Statistical Manual of Mental Disorders* used to assess the interior Self in Western cultures. Religions have come up with lengthy lists of moral categories of the non-idealized Self, usually lists of vices such as the seven deadly sins of pride, greed, wrath, envy, lust, gluttony, and sloth. As well, every culture has encoded in its laws what is socially acceptable or not, including the cultural prerogative to change what is "socially acceptable" without changing the core operating system within a person. Whatever one's starting point, whether with psychology, religion, or culture, there are means of assessment that are used to evaluate the interior functioning of a person, with nearly universal agreement that manifestations in one's relationships of things like hate, violence, abuse, jealousy, manipulation, etc. are indicative of something amiss in the interior or core operating system of a person.

The same thing applies to the means of assessment of the idealized Self. Positive psychology can speak of the nearly universal recognition of the core virtues of wisdom, courage, humanity, justice, temperance, and transcendence, and the accompanying character strengths of creativity, curiosity, love of learning, open-mindedness, perspective, authenticity, bravery, persistence, zest, kindness, love, social intelligence, fairness, leadership, teamwork, forgiveness/mercy, modesty/humility, prudence, self-regulation, appreciation of beauty and excellence, gratitude, hope, humor, and religiousness/spirituality.[8] The Christian religion can speak of the seven heavenly virtues: prudence, justice, temperance, courage, faith, hope, and charity. Most cultures would value honor, courage, valor, honesty, trust, faithfulness, a sense of duty, etc. Again, while there may be some differences depending on one's starting point for assessment, there are clear methods of assessment that all humans use, based upon

---

8. Peterson, *Positive Psychology*.

the observation of a person's relationships, to give some indication of who a person is in the deepest part of their being and when that person is functioning in a healthy or acceptable way.

Where differences emerge from a religious/spiritual point of view is not so much in the means of assessment but in *what the assessment means*. Without denying the validity of other interpretations of what the "data" mean when observing the Self-in-relationship, a Christian spiritual technology would have something unique to say about what the external "data" are telling us about the interior Self. (Lest I am misunderstood, let me repeat that a Christian spiritual technology does *not* invalidate other interpretations of what the "data" mean, such as an interpretation that supports the work of mental health or facilitates brain science or supports the cooperation of law-abiding citizens. At its best, a Christian spiritual technology will provide a supportive superstructure for work in these areas.) A Christian spiritual technology (as understood by this author, limited by his context, and overly simplified for the purpose of explanation) would say that the means of assessment are telling us something about the core operating system of the heart and mind. The core operating system will always "bear fruit"—i.e., it will manifest in predictable ways. When there is evidence of the non-idealized Self, then the core operating system either needs transformation or is in the process of transformation. When there is evidence of the highest virtues of the idealized Self, then the core operating system has made a transformational shift or has reached a tipping point in its ability to function with a different grammar for the foundational stories of life.

For instance, in one of the early letters of the Apostle Paul to the church in Galatia we see his presentation of the *means of assessment* of the non-idealized Self and the idealized Self. The first he calls the "works of the flesh," which include "fornication, impurity, licentiousness, idolatry, sorcery, enmities, strife, jealousy, anger, quarrels, dissensions, factions, envy, drunkenness, carousing, and things like these" (Gal 5:19–21). The second he calls "the fruit of the Spirit," which includes "love, joy, peace, patience, kindness, generosity, faithfulness, gentleness, and self-control" (Gal 5:22–23). The first gives evidence of a mind that is enslaved to the instinctual passions of the Self (referred to as the "yoke of slavery" in Gal 5:1). The second gives evidence of a mind that is liberated and lives by only one basic rule of the game of life, "You shall love your neighbor as yourself" (Gal 5:14). He refers to this "second mind" elsewhere as being the "mind of Christ" (1 Cor 2:16; Phil 2:5). Based upon his *means of assessment* (which is fairly consistent with universal themes), the Apostle Paul seems to be saying that *what the assessment means* is that the external "data" are giving evidence as to the "yoking" of the mind to a core operating system that is either the *mind of ego* (rooted in the ego-defensive system of survival and cultural accommodation) or the *mind of Christ* (rooted in agape-love). This change in the core operating system to which the mind is "yoked" means that the mind now has a new way of processing any sensory data flowing into the brain. How this change happens from a Christian point of view involves the death of the ego-mind and the resurrection of the Christ-mind in us. In the language of the Apostle Paul (where the Greek word for "I" is *egó*), "I have been crucified with Christ; and it is no longer I who live, but it is Christ who lives in me" (Gal 2:19–20). Others would call this process a "cruciform divinization,"[9] and it is one way of talking about the purpose of the game of life.

A Cruciform Divinization

If, in fact, there are *means of assessment* (almost universal) that emerge from observed thoughts, words, actions, etc. in all of our relationships having something to do with qualities of an idealized Self or a non-idealized Self, and if that *assessment means* something about the most interior operating system of our mind, then it would be helpful to say more about what "mind" is and about the different operating systems being proposed in the process of "yoking" and the process of transformation of the mind (remembering that mind is more than brain and that there is a heart-mind entrainment).

For instance, using the language of Daniel Siegel, we might think in terms of *energy* as the essence of reality, and what the mind does with this energy determines who we are. "If we imagine that energy is the fundamental essence of the universe, that even matter is condensed energy, then patterns of energy are the essence of reality."[10] The mind, then, would have something to do with how we manage the flow of energy that is here and now in our bodies and relationships—both within us and between us. In response to the question "What is Mind?" Siegel says it is "an embodied and relational, self-organizing emergent process that regulates the flow of energy and information both within and between . . . What is

9. Wright, *Paul*, 1023.

10. Siegel, *Mind*, 273.

it? At least one aspect of mind . . . can be seen as a self-organizing process that emerges from, and regulates, energy and information flow within and between us."[11] How the mind organizes and regulates this energy flow *determines who we are.* Siegel says,

> Who are we? We can say simply we are our minds. But what is this mind exactly? At a minimum we can say that from a bottom-up experience, we are our sensory flow of energy that arises from the outer world and from our inner, bodily world including its brain. This is how we function as a conduit of sensory experience, immersing ourselves in the miracle of being here, in this moment. We are also our top-down experience—ways we filter energy flow into information, symbolic meaning that stands for something beyond the pattern of energy we experience. This is how we are also a constructor of information, not merely a conduit of energy.[12]

In this definition, who we are is determined by our minds by a process in which the mind is *perceiving the essence of reality in the energy of life* as it comes to us in our bodies and our relationships (within us and between us). But also, who we are is determined by our minds by a process in which our minds *filter and interpret that energy* to make meaning of reality through symbolic expression, such as the stories created by our narrating minds. *The core operating system of our minds* has to do with the basic grammar and the rules of the game that influence the way in which we filter and process the essential energy of life as it comes to us moment-to-moment. In reality, this perceiving, filtering, and story-construction process is as unique as a fingerprint, but according to a Christian spiritual technology, it makes a difference how our minds go about this filtering and constructing of the basic energy of reality; it makes a difference in determining who we are; it makes a difference in terms of the "fruit" that emerges from the energy that is ours; and it makes a difference in terms of our Selves being imprisoned or being liberated to be fully human.

The Ego-Mind

Being alive (our reality) means that there is a basic, *universal energy* incorporated into all aspects of who we are, and our minds have something

11. Siegel, *Mind*, 37.
12. Siegel, *Mind*, 143.

to do with how that energy is organized, regulated, and expended. One way in which that universal energy flows to us and through us might be described as a basic *instinctual energy* that propels us toward life. This is not the only way to talk about the universal energy of life, and it may represent a very early (even ancestral) and biological organizing mechanism hard-wired into the brain, but there does seem to be an instinctual energy that automatically drives us to survive. For example, when mammals are born, there is an energy that instinctually manifests in the phenomenon of sucking in response to a source of food. The energy that drives us to eat, and later to reproduce, might be referred to as a basic instinctual energy of life that is programmed toward survival and is accompanied from the beginning with organizing and self-regulating mechanisms such as avoiding pain and enhancing pleasure, also described as "our most basic instinctual behavior patterns—approach and avoidance."[13] We would be ignorant to pretend that this hard-wiring is not a foundational grammar shaping the stories we create about life and shaping our rules for playing the game of life. It is also unfortunate when those constructed stories imply that this energy, as it is organized, regulated, and expended through our minds and in our bodies, is inherently evil. For example, Christianity has a long history of sending mixed signals about this energy when it involves the physical body—especially with regards to reproduction— going so far as to suggest that the generational transmission of evil/sin is through the sexual act, in contradiction to the biblical story in Genesis of God looking at all of creation and saying that "it was very good" (Gen 1:31). For this, we need to apologize.

Closely linked to the hard-wired biological responses that instinctually organize the universal energy of life toward survival are the *ancestral passions* whose systems reside in the ancient subcortical regions of the brain. These are affective systems that have to do with raw emotion and that have also helped us survive. These raw emotions are like instinctual energy because they are automatic, and they profoundly influence the higher regions of the brain such as the cerebral cortex, where our executive decision-making abilities reside. This is why it is possible to find very intelligent people making poor decisions in areas such as relationships (high IQ but low emotional intelligence). Or, we hear of clergy who make decisions that are contrary to their value systems and have no idea from where this behavior came. Or, we see refined civilizations committing

13. Panksepp and Biven, *Archaeology of Mind*, 23.

horrendous crimes such as the killing of six million Jews in Nazi Germany or the systemic racism in the United States. The raw emotions can influence or override logical reasoning and the thinking part of the brain. As Jaak Panksepp and Lucy Biven say,

> The primary-process emotional feelings are raw affects that automatically make important decisions for us, at times unwise decisions, at least based on views of our upper cognitive minds . . . The intrinsic evaluations that affective feelings convey to the higher brain enable humans and animals to determine how well or how badly they are doing with respect to survival. But at times, they simply get us in trouble.[14]

These ancestral passions are really energy systems that significantly affect the organizing, regulating, and expending of the universal energy that flows into our minds and makes us who we are. This is true to the extent that Panksepp and Biven say, "We will make the case for the conclusion that raw affective feelings lie at the primordial foundation of the mental apparatus—that they are the primal biological substrates of a core-SELF—perhaps the neural foundation for the concept of 'the soul.'"[15]

There are seven basic affective systems that constitute the ancestral passions: the *seeking* (expectancy) system; the *rage* (anger) system; the *lust* (sexual excitement) system; the *care* (nurturance) system; the *panic/grief* (sadness) system; and the *play* (social joy) system.[16] These core energy systems are not intrinsically bad. They are part of how we survive. They significantly affect who we are and how our minds process the flow of universal energy and all life experiences. But they must be trained, or they can get us into trouble. *It is no surprise, then, that every religion in the world has something to say about the regulation of these passions.*

For instance, take the *seeking* (expectancy) system wherein lie all aspects of "desire." Panksepp and Biven say that this system is the "brain sources of eager anticipation, desire, euphoria, and the quest for everything."[17] This seeking urge is an anticipatory eagerness, which is a "goad without a goal" and motivates almost every energized thing we do. We can seek food, water, shelter, a mate, an experience, and much more. The seeking system can respond to greed as well as need and is

---

14. Panksepp and Biven, *Archaeology of Mind*, 15.

15. Panksepp and Biven, *Archaeology of Mind*, 46.

16. Panksepp and Biven, *Archaeology of Mind*, 34–37.

17. Panksepp and Biven, *Archaeology of Mind*, 95.

very sensitive to any and all rewards that are within one's grasp. Even when bodily needs are satisfied, we can still be drawn to enticing stimuli. It can solidify our addictive desires and can easily urge us to indulge in a wide range of activities without stopping to carefully consider what we are doing. It needs to be trained well in order to reduce human tragedies. "It has no intrinsic morals. It is just a super-efficient get-up-and-go-get-it system. Human cognitive aspirations, both for good and evil, spring forth from its vast affective 'energy.'"[18]

Is it any wonder that this primary-process energy system in the subcortical region of the brain that gives energy to everything we do is acknowledged in narrative form through ancient religious stories about a Garden of Eden (Hebrew *eden* meaning "delight") and a tree standing in the middle of the garden called the tree of the "knowledge of good and evil" (Gen 2:9)? And, further, is it any wonder, with such a powerful energy system designed for survival but with the potential for either creation or destruction (psychology would call it *libido* or *destrudo*), that religion would be interested in the "training" of this influential energy system for human fullness? And, still further, is it not this training of the seeking system to which the Apostle Paul is referring when he makes the distinction between the "desires of the flesh" and the "desires of the spirit" (where the Greek word for "desire" is '*epithumía*, meaning a "strong impulse, eager longing, or craving" and came to be regarded as intrinsic to the "passions")? How we train these systems that profoundly influence our decision-making can easily lead either to bondage or to liberty. These systems *are* being trained one way or the other from the very beginning of our existence, and they *are* influencing our choices whether we consciously realize it or not and no matter how educated or rational we claim to be.

The way we train these affective systems in the subcortical regions of the brain contributes to the organization and regulation of the flow of universal energy at an instinctual level, profoundly affecting our minds and who we are. The unique way in which this instinctual mind gets trained has to do with the genetics, particular context, social isolation, personal experiences, relationships, challenges, sorrows, joys, etc. of an individual person—an individual "I" or "ego"—and can in its uniqueness be referred to as the *ego-mind*.

Just as we acknowledged with the ancestral passions, it would be unwise to say that the ego or the ego-mind is altogether bad. In fact, the

18. Panksepp and Biven, *Archaeology of Mind*, 103.

development of the ego is quite necessary in becoming human; it is an important part of the journey of life, and it is important in understanding the purpose of the game of life. Difficulties arise when the development of the ego gets stuck and when it operates from a limited perspective that highly constricts the possibilities for organizing, regulating, and expending the energy of life and for more completely training the ancestral passions. Acknowledging the influence of transpersonal psychology on her perspective, Kathleen Singh speaks of human development in three broad stages of life:

> The progression in the psychological reality of a typical, healthy human being is always from a stage that is prepersonal, preegoic, prerational, undifferentiated, and unindividuated to a stage of consciousness and identity that is personal, egoic, rational, differentiated, and individuated and beyond to one that is transpersonal, transegoic, transrational, integrated, and whole.[19]

The movement from preegoic to egoic is a journey that all of us seem to manage, but often without full awareness of the degree to which we have become a separate "I" or "ego." Firstly, we learn early on that we are separate from other beings and other objects, but we have less awareness of how we, secondly, separate being from non-being (life and death) in our consciousness of time, how we, thirdly, separate our ego-minds from our bodies, and how we, fourthly, separate our acceptable self-image from the parts of ourselves that we disown. Singh calls these the First, Second, Third, and Fourth Dualisms on the way to becoming a personal, egoic, rational, differentiated, and individuated Self that is dominated by an ego-mind obsessed with its own "identity project," supported by an incessant inner, mental dialogue that continuously makes up stories about who we are. According to Singh, that is where most of us get stuck, usually failing to enter the next stage of the journey (the transpersonal and transegoic)—until we begin to die.

In addition to being stuck on the journey of life as it obsesses with its own identity project, the ego-mind has a limited understanding of the possibilities for living that exist outside of its own context-specific experience and its self-constructed stories. The ego-mind is often unaware of how it is stuck in its own repetitive dramas, having inherited and trained the ancestral passions for the purpose of survival by way of influence from the context in which it developed. These patterns of survival tend to

19. Singh, *Grace in Dying*, 24.

be reactive, repetitive, and protective of the ego. The young child who is teased a lot learns to withdraw or fight back, and the style becomes part of the ego-personality that lasts into adulthood and can be seen in all relationships. The child of an alcoholic may become the "perfect child" who meets the needs of everyone but lets no one get too close and never talks about repressed feelings of guilt over the inability to fix the parent. An abused child carries the trauma in her body that can manifest in destructive acting out or hyper-sensitivity to fear of abandonment. A child of privilege may design systems of law and learning that protect his/her power and wealth while being addicted to success and blind to how this is impacting others.

Further, there is the cultural overlay absorbed by the ego-mind—the symbols, stories, rituals, relationships, and worldviews that we pick up from our experience of the world around us and that become part of our "tool kit" for how to survive in the world and define the ego. As Kenda Creasy Dean writes, "Culture, to use a computer analogy, is humanity's operating system, and like a computer operating system, culture gets installed with certain 'default' settings that, unless overridden, determine how humans view their world and structure their everyday behavior."[20]

In fact, very personal experiences *and* cultural embeddedness combine to create the core operating system which we are referring to as the ego-mind. It is this ego-mind, operating with a stuck-ness on its journey, with limited perception, and with ancestral passions whose algorithms have been set very early to filter the energy of life into defensive, reactive, and protective strategies of survival that needs to be transformed. It is our ego-mind that is determining who we are in ways that limit our possibilities and our freedom, a "yoking" of the mind that is a form of slavery. And, if the ego needs to die, it will mean the transformation of the ego-mind and the concomitant transformation of the ancestral passions; the transformation of the way we automatically organize, regulate, and expend the universal energy of life; and the transformation of the stories we have created to keep these systems in place, which are revealed in all of our relationships. That would mean having a different energy-regulating mind.

20. Dean, *Almost Christian*, 47.

The Mind of Christ

To some extent it is easier to say what the *mind of Christ* is *not* than to say what it is, just like it is often easier to say what God is not than to say what God is. From the above paragraphs, we can conclude that what the mind of Christ is *not* is a mind controlled by the ego with its stuck-ness, its limited perspective, its repetitive dramas, its incessant inner dialogue focused on an identity project, its well-crafted system of defenses tied to untransformed ancestral passions, and its tendency to blame others for whatever is wrong in the world. That which is not transformed is transmitted to others in our relationships, or as Richard Rohr is famous for saying, "If we do not transform our pain we will always transmit it."[21]

We can also say that the mind of Christ is *not* equal with the mind of the church. At best, the church can guide us to the mind of Christ and can be the "body" that manifests the working of the Christ-mind on earth, but to know correct doctrine or to be a doctor of theology does not necessarily equate to having the mind of Christ.

In a similar fashion, having the mind of Christ is *not* the same thing as knowing all the teachings of Jesus. For instance, one might be able to memorize all of Jesus' Sermon on the Mount but still be living with an ego-mind. The memorization could serve only as a spiritual bypass and leave the religious person resembling a "white-washed tomb full of dead men's bones." As well, it is worth noting that the Apostle Paul, who "invented" the term "mind of Christ," seems to know very little of the teachings of Jesus besides "you shall love your neighbor as yourself." His experience, which informs the majority of what is written in the Christian Scriptures, is not of the earthly Jesus but of the resurrected Christ. This is not to minimize the teachings of Jesus, which are a profound guide to finding the mind of Christ. It is just to say that "Christ" is not Jesus' last name; it refers to something inclusive of, but far bigger than, the earthly Jesus, something that goes back to the beginning of creation and is the source of life and light for all things (see, for instance, John 1:1–5; Col 1:15–17) and, hence, has been referred to by some as a name for everything.[22]

Of course, it is impossible to adequately describe "everything," and at best one can only give pointers to what might be understood as the mind of Christ. Since I am making an apology for a Christian spiritual

21. Rohr, "Wounded Healers."
22. Rohr, *Universal Christ*, 9.

technology, these "pointers" come largely from the Christian Scriptures. For those of you who are Nones, some of this language may come with "baggage" because of the way Christian concepts have been introduced to you. Are you still willing to remain in the listener role in our dialogue and look for new meaning? For those of you who identify as Christian and who are "overhearing" this dialogue, it may be hard for you, too, to hear this language unencumbered by your own subcultural interpretations of the faith.

Building on what was said earlier, it could be said that the mind of Christ is a *non-conforming mind*. When the Apostle Paul speaks of the complete metamorphosis of the mind, he alludes to how our minds have been conformed to our very specific "worlds." He says, "Do not be conformed to this world, but be transformed by the renewing of your minds, so that you may discern what is the will of God—what is good and acceptable and perfect" (Rom 12:2). Although it is etymologically questionable, I like to highlight the letters for the word "schema" in Paul's Greek word for being "conformed" (*suschématizo*) to the world because in the worlds we inhabit, whether it is the world of our families, our friends, our communities, our subcultures, or cultures, we develop schemas or images in our minds about how relationships work, how the world ought to be, and how we will survive in those worlds. Our minds conform to and are shaped by these worlds automatically. Because of this, when we come to make choices in life, we are *not* starting with a clean slate. We are filtering our choices through a mind that has been "conformed to our worlds" at a very basic level. The mind of Christ is a mind that has an awareness of and has stepped back from the "conformed mind" and has stepped toward an aware mind that is seeking to align with the irreducible transcendentals often named as "the good, the true, and the beautiful."

Following from this, we might next say that the mind of Christ is an *emptied mind*. In another passage where the Apostle Paul makes reference to the transformed mind, he writes, "Let the same mind be in you that was in Christ Jesus, who, though he was in the form of God, did not regard equality with God as something to be exploited, but emptied himself" (Phil 2:5–7). Although what needs to be emptied from our minds is different from what was emptied when Jesus emptied himself, the pattern is the same for developing the mind of Christ and is often referred to as the process of *kenosis* (coming from the Greek word for "make empty"). What needs to be emptied from our minds (among other things) are the automatic schemas, images, and stories that have come from our being conformed to the world. Unlearning is as important as learning. Unknowing is as important as knowing. Naming, watching, catching, and emptying the thoughts, patterns, defenses, reactions, etc. of the ego-mind is a necessary part of the development of the mind of Christ. This "emptying" is not a one-time event but a continual process, acknowledging the wisdom of referring to the mind of Christ as an *emptied* and an *emptying* mind. Necessary for the process of emptying the mind would be the congruent characteristics of an *awake* and *watchful* mind that turns on a light to shine on the invisible, automatic patterns of the mind and remains watchful of their incessant attempts to return. Or, in the words of Scripture, "but everything exposed by the light becomes visible, for anything that becomes visible is light. Therefore it is said, 'Sleeper, awake! Rise from the dead, and Christ will shine on you'" (Eph 5:13–14).

Waking up to and having an awareness of what needs to be emptied from our ego-minds implies that we have *open minds* which are especially open to revelation about our life patterns and our severely constricted Selves, but also open to revelation about worlds which we have not yet seen. In referring to the mind of Christ, the Apostle Paul writes,

> But as it is written, "What no eye has seen, nor ear heard, nor the human heart conceived, what God has prepared for those who love him"—these things God has revealed to us through the Spirit . . . Those who are spiritual discern all things, and they are themselves subject to no one else's scrutiny. "For who has known the mind of the Lord so as to instruct him?" But we have the mind of Christ (1 Cor 2:9–10; 15–16).

So, it could be said that the mind of Christ is an *open mind*. In particular, it is a mind *open to revelation*: open to revelation about ourselves and who we really are, and open to revelation about "what no eye has seen, nor ear heard, nor the human heart conceived." According to the Apostle Paul, it is this openness to revelation in a two-fold sense that makes the difference between the natural or psychological person and the spiritual person. It also makes a difference in the energies available to us in playing the game of life.

Finally, it can be said that the mind of Christ is a *oneness mind*. If our minds are energy-regulating minds, this would imply a movement away from the filtering of the universal energy of life by our limited ego-minds and an increasing alignment (oneness) with the unfiltered universal energy itself. We move toward an *at-one-ment* with the universal energy and discover that the universal energy in its creative fullness has definition to it. *It is not only an infinite source of possibility, but even more, an infinite source of love and light.* In the language of state and stage development, this might be described as the eighth level of human consciousness, a causal consciousness in which one becomes aligned with the original "causes" behind the structure of the universe and is followed by non-dual consciousness. Jim Marion says,

> Christ Consciousness is the Christian term for causal consciousness. At this level the Christian is identified with his or her true Christ Self, which is seen as in a spiritual union with God the Creator. At this level one can truthfully say, "I live, now not I, but Christ lives in me," as St. Paul said. The person with Christ Consciousness sees all other human beings as the Christ and treats them accordingly. This is the level of true Christian love . . . One is able to commune silently with God . . . from which all creation and creativity arises.[23]

Using the language of the Christian mystics, Martin Laird refers to this as developing a "luminous mind" in which one becomes part of an "ocean of light" and moves into an "unknowing" that is beyond the limited knowledge of the ego-mind. He says, "This unknowing and oneness are a piece. The tenth-century Byzantine monk St. Symeon the New Theologian says, 'He is then totally within the depths of the Spirit, just as if he had been dropped into a bottomless abyss of illuminated waters.'"[24] It is as if we not only learn how to drink from a spiritual well, but even bathe in it. We dwell in it. We abide in it. We become one with it. It is as if the Self becomes saturated with the universal energy defined as an infinite light and love. This light and love correspondingly *saturate* the ancestral passions, *saturate* all the stories created by our narrating minds, and *saturate* all our relationships. Jesus said it this way: "Abide in me as I abide in you. Just as the branch cannot bear fruit by itself unless it abides in the vine, neither can you unless you abide in me . . . abide in my love" (John 14:4, 9). He also says, "The glory that you have given me I have given them so that they may be one, as we are one, I in them and you in me, that they may become completely one, so that the world may know that you have sent me and have loved them even as you have loved me" (John 17:22–23).

23. Marion, *Mind of Christ*, 183.

24. Laird, *Ocean of Light*, 147.

It is interesting that the Christian word for "repentance" comes from the Greek word *metánoia*. It is made up of two words: *noia* meaning "mind" and *meta* meaning "after" or "behind." It is unfortunate that the word "repentance" has become equated with a culturally conditioned feel-bad-about-yourself ritual necessary for entry into the church. We need to apologize for this when the meaning is conveyed in this way. The word really means having a change of mind. On the one hand, it is having a *mind* that comes *after* we have had an encounter with Christ. It is the mind that comes after we become aware of the ego-mind and choose to move toward the Christ-mind. But it also refers to the *mind* that is *behind*; the "behind-mind." This is the mind that exists behind the limited and culturally conditioned filters of the ego-mind. It is the mind that is in touch with the creative causes or energy of the universe; that which is behind all of creation itself. Christianity would call this mind the "mind of Christ," which has existed from the beginning of creation. When we get *behind the filters of our ego-minds to the Christ-mind*, we find a new Self (sometimes referred to as the "naked Self" or "true Self") which transcends the idealized or non-idealized Self and becomes what Scripture calls a "new creation" with a mind that is "reconciled" to the mind that is behind all of creation (2 Cor 5:17–18) and operates out of a completely different core operating system. How this change of mind happens follows a particular pattern. Are you still able to be in the listener role in our dialogue?

Cruciformity

The symbol of the cross is central to Christianity for many reasons, and we will speak of it here in a limited way with relevance to its schematic power to reveal the inner pattern of how the transformation of the ego-mind to the Christ-mind happens. This follows the Apostle Paul's call for the crucifixion of the ego and an inner divinization of the Self that equates to Christ living inside us in oneness. "I [*ego*] have been crucified with Christ; and it is no longer I [*ego*] who live, but Christ who lives in me" (Gal 5:19–20). This "divinization" is one way of describing the purpose of the game of life, following the dictum attributed to St. Athanasius (AD 328–73) that "God became man, so that man might become God." It is a process of deification (or *theosis*),

> not limited to a point in time but is a lifetime synergistic process,
> involving not only God's presence and activity, but also one's
> own personal struggle (*ascesis*) to be open to and cooperate with
> the energies of Grace. Through this grace-infused effort, as St.
> Anthony observed, you "become yourself." Despite overtones in
> modern English idiom, the word *deification* does not mean that
> the person becomes what God is in the divine *essence*, nor that
> he or she is dissolved into God as a drip in an ocean . . . The dei-
> fied person becomes a partaker of the divine nature (2 Pet 1:4)
> *and* his or her personhood is kept intact.[25]

As N. T. Wright reminds us, this *theosis* is "a *cruciform* 'divinization', involving the constant life of putting to death the flesh and coming alive to
the spirit"[26] and is the hard moral work that is not an automatic developmental progression, but follows from a "helpless trust"[27] in the love of
God revealed in Christ.

There is a pattern with a purpose in a world where change is necessary for one to be alive. The purpose has to do with human growth and a
particular goal of divinization which involves a lifting of a "veil" that is over
our minds so that we might "wake up" to the automatic functioning of the
ego-mind and see the possibility of transforming the core operating system
of our minds so that it is more and more saturated with light and love. In
a striking passage, the Apostle Paul says it this way: "But when one turns
to the Lord the veil is removed. Now the Lord is the Spirit, and where the
Spirit of the Lord is, there is freedom. And all of us, with unveiled faces,
seeing the glory of the Lord as though reflected in a mirror, are being transformed into the same image from one degree of glory to another, for this
comes from the Lord, the Spirit" (2 Cor 3:16–18).

What exactly the "degrees of glory" are as we move from one to
another is up for debate. As a contribution to the pedagogy of interiority,
many have advocated for maps of the stages of development in cognitive,
psychological, and spiritual human growth. Do the "degrees of glory" refer to the natural stages of cognitive development, stages of the evolving
Self, stages of faith development, stages in our level of consciousness, or
something else? Ken Wilber has compiled hundreds of these maps referring to the teachings about the different stages as "psychotechnologies of

---

25. Gassin and Muse, "Beloved of God," 53.

26. Wright, *Paul*, 1023.

27. Wright, *Paul*, 954.

consciousness transformation"[28] and indicating that our stage of development gives us a unique "grammar" for understanding the world. He says, "These stages of interpretive frameworks are just like grammar—they are 'hidden maps' that determine how we see, think, and generally experience the real territory around us."[29] This is why, even with a religion like Christianity, people at different stages of development (or "degree of glory") can see the faith so differently. For instance, the very experience of and understanding of Jesus will be quite different depending upon whether one is developmentally at the magic, mythic, rational, pluralistic, integral, or super-integral stage.[30] According to Wilber, the failure to understand these stages of development with their unique grammars is contributing to the exodus from institutional religion by many people around the world. As a None, you might understand this!

In whatever way one understands the degree of change from "one degree of glory to another," a Christian spiritual technology would advocate a pattern to be applied at any point of change in our lives or at any point in the process of divinization. It is the pattern of cross, death, and resurrection exemplified by Christ. It is a cruciform pattern.

Cross

As indicated above, the *cross* represents many things to Christians, not the least of which is the atoning work attributed to Jesus. But with regard to the "How?" of transformation in which we are being changed from one degree of glory to another, it represents the place of *disruption* or *disequilibrium*. In saying this, we are not limiting the importance of Jesus' life to its last few days or hours. Jesus' entire earthly life was a life of disruption. According to Brian McLaren, Jesus repeatedly introduced "disruptive technologies,"[31] calling for educated people to go back and start over as if they were to be born again and calling for worship to be located anywhere there is spirit and truth in a tabernacle that is now located within us. He lived on the margins of society, representing disequilibrium to the ones who held power. He met people at places of disruption in their lives; places of sickness, rejection, and pain, but also places of great joy such

---

28. Wilber, *Religion of Tomorrow*, 3.

29. Wilber, *Religion of Tomorrow*, 8.

30. Wilber, *Integral Spirituality*, 91–92.

31. McLaren, *Great Spiritual Migration*, 192.

as a wedding feast or a great banquet. These are the places where change is happening or change is possible. These are the places that hold the potential for "threshold experiences." These are places in life where we have the greatest potential to "wake up," or, as it was said in Jesus' parable of the Prodigal Son after the son had lost everything, finally "he came to himself" (Luke 15:17). Change happens, and transformation has great potential at the place of disruption and disequilibrium, especially if we see the disruption (even suffering) not as the cosmos being against us, but as part of a process of being changed from "one degree of glory" to another. There is a great freedom when these disruptions are seen in the context of transformation and are *saturated* with love.

Death

But it can feel like *death,* and, in fact, the experience of death, is essential to transformation at any point of change. Ilia Delio says, "Without death there is no fullness of life; hence, death is integral to life. The whole Christian message based on death is simply this: without death there is no new life."[32] Taking her cues from an evolutionary universe where death is integral to the process of creation, Delio goes on to say,

> The only way to evolve toward greater wholeness is to let go and die to those things that hinder the emergence of love from within. Such death involves suffering, accepting pain as part of the birthing process to richer life. Pain rends, but it is in separating that love gathers the scattered pieces and creates anew. The very thing we fear—death—is the beginning of what we desire—wholeness.[33]

In the unique spiritual language of parables, Jesus said it this way: "Very truly, I tell you, unless a grain of wheat falls into the earth and dies, it remains just a single grain, but if it dies, it bears much fruit" (John 12:24). He follows this up with rather harsh language in which he says we must move from loving the psychological life as we have known it to hating it, so that we might find a greater life. Whether we are moving from one stage of development to another or are moving from the ego-mind to the Christ-mind, the process of letting go of the world as we have constructed it and stepping away from the defenses we have used to protect

32. Delio, *Emergent Christ,* 77.
33. Delio, *Emergent Christ,* 122–23.

the Self is experienced as a death. At some point, there is a realization that the opinions and beliefs we have held might not be completely true.

In the language of a dystopian novel, Margaret Atwood describes the moment when one of the Handmaids, whose construction of reality had been formed by the powerful theocratic regime of the Republic of Gilead, gets a key and is able for the first time to read the Bible on her own. She says,

> It came as a painful shock: kind, helpful Aunt Estee had lied to us. The truth was not noble, it was horrible . . . Up until that time I had not seriously doubted the rightness and especially the truthfulness of Gilead's theology. If I'd failed at perfection, I'd concluded that the fault was mine. But as I discovered what had been changed by Gilead, what had been added, and what had been omitted, I feared I might lose my faith. If you've never had faith, you will not understand what that means. You feel as if your best friend is dying; that everything that defined you is being burned away; that you'll be left all alone. You feel exiled, as if you are lost in a dark wood. It was like the feeling I'd had when Tabitha died: the world was emptying itself of meaning. Everything was hollow. Everything was withering.[34]

Even in "normal" change, there is a moment when we must empty our minds of the meaning we have created and step into an unknown that is experienced as "nothingness." It is like the trapeze artist who must let go of one swing before grabbing the other, doing so with one's back turned to the other swing and, while suspended in midair high above the ground, pivots in trust that the other swing will be there to grab onto when she turns around. In these moments, there are many of voices crying out within us saying, "Don't let go!" These are the voices inside us that must be appeased or silenced (more so than appeasing an angry God), which is done as we evaluate any moment using the pattern of cross, death, and resurrection; saturate the moment with light and love; and remember that death is not the end of the story.

Resurrection

Resurrection is still coming. Resurrection is not just about the next life. It is part of the process of transformation in this life as we are being changed

---

34. Atwood, *Testaments*, 303.

from "one degree of glory to another." When light and love are applied with faith at any moment of change (often experienced as a death), a new creation happens. The faith referred to here is (among other things): 1) a belief in the purpose and pattern of life described above; 2) a faith in how the story goes—i.e., its unique grammar; 3) a trust in the underlying energy of love; and 4) a belief that we can participate in the creation of something new if we wait and watch in love while suspending the automatic and reactive responses of the ego-mind. In my opinion, there is a creative "miracle" that occurs when, in the face of any joy or sorrow, success or suffering, we saturate the moment with light and love. This act of faith produces a very different "fruit" than if we apply egoic fear, pride, jealousy, greed, or judgment at the point of change and the impending unknown. It creates a very different process in the mind and frees the mind to organize (or be organized by) the universal energy of life in new and creative ways beyond what "eye has seen or ear heard." This transformation, in large and small ways, is like a resurrection.

The conscious application of light and love by faith when facing moments of crisis or change produces something like a "carbon arc."[35] Remembering that in a spiritual technology we are using words on the edge of their meaning and metaphors that will always be imprecise, I think of these moments like the scenes in old sci-fi movies in which a scientist is in the laboratory working on a new creation, and there are electrodes with sparks arcing between them. Holding the present experience of change, crisis, pain, or the unknown side-by-side with the experience of light and love, apprehended and applied by faith, creates a "spark" between them. This "arcing spark," in my opinion, replicates the original "spark" of creation in some small way and becomes the nexus point where heaven and earth meet in us, not only transforming the ancestral passions, but also opening up possibilities for our stories that, before now, our eyes have not seen and our ears have not heard. In these "arcing" moments, people will often say, "Oh, I had not seen that or thought of that before." More deeply, people will simply rest in a "peace that passes understanding," and it does not matter if they have immediate answers or not. In that moment, there is new life that can be referred to as a *resurrected* life.

Such "arcing" moments do not usually come out of the blue and can be misunderstood, on the one hand, as supernatural events beyond our control or, on the other hand, as the result of exceptional human effort. If

---

35. Bourgeault, *Centering Prayer*, 83.

this is a nexus point between heaven and earth, I cannot deny that there is a transcendental component to this which is beyond words and beyond human control, and which can only be apprehended by faith and helpless trust. Neither can I deny that there is an important human participation which requires a regular "laying of the groundwork" for these "arcing" moments to occur. For me, there are two helpful ways to understand how we participate in this process that leads to resurrection moments and our own divinization.

Firstly, I like to use the mnemonic "ARCS" to help me remember how I might best participate in the "arcing process." In that process, "A" stands for *awareness*. This awareness includes my willingness to be an observer of my life, especially my relationships, and collect data on what is occurring. This awareness must be a nonjudgmental awareness and is connected to the important theme of "paying attention," coming from both neuroscience and mystical prayer. Daniel Seigel reminds us that "where attention goes, neural firing flows and neural connection grows."[36] Jacob Needleman says that this is an important part of the "missing link" that has been lost in Christianity and that "the teachings of Christianity as we know them were not intended to be put into practice without . . . 'the accumulation of the force of inner attention.'"[37] Or, Symeon the New Theologian (d. 1022) could say, "God demands only one thing from us—that our heart be purified by means of attention."[38] "R" stands for *responsibility*. I take responsibility for whatever is happening in my life, especially for my response to anything that occurs. I do this without blaming others, but also without the distracting energy of guilt so that the ego and its defenses might be brought to light. "C" stands for *compassion*. Consciously having compassion toward myself and others in any circumstance is one of the ways that I bring the energy of light and love to any moment, activating the calm-and-connect energies of the parasympathetic nervous system. Doing this regularly retrains the ancestral passions in the subcortical regions of the brain and is an essential movement from the ego-mind to the mind of Christ. "S" stands for *silence*. I hold the awareness, responsibility, and the compassion together and wait in silence. Holding all of these together produces some "heat" which may be uncomfortable. But I stay in it. I wait. I watch. I rest in it

36. Siegel, *Mind*, 179.
37. Needleman, *Lost Christianity*, 119.
38. Kadloubovsky and Palmer, *Writings from the Philokalia*, 160.

without running away and without defaulting to the old patterns of the ego-mind.

Secondly, I find that my ability to participate in the "arcing process" is best supported by a form of praying that underlies my ability to remain in the silence and opens a space for the nexus point of heaven and earth. Although, in my opinion, any prayer can be helpful, not just any prayer will do for this level of transformation. In the world of neuroscience, it has been shown that prayer can change the brain, but not just any prayer does so. It is deeper prayer or meditation that changes the brain.[39] But, beyond the physiological change of the brain, there is praying that changes our inner attention and the inner place from which all aspects of our being come. This prayer changes the mind and in the Christian tradition is often referred to as *apophatic* prayer.

The word "apophatic" comes from the Greek *'apóphasis*, which has roots in the verb *apóphemi* with the meaning of "saying no" or "saying negatively." But others believe that it has its roots in the verb *apopaíno* with overtones of "revelation."[40] As I wrote elsewhere,

> The apophatic approach (*via negativa*) to prayer differs from the kataphatic (*via positiva*) approach to prayer. The apophatic approach to prayer strips away all of the attitudes, mental images, and ideas that are considered to stand in the way of a relationship with God because God transcends all human language. It is the "unsaying" (*apophasis*) of language for God, and it leads eventually from the negation of knowing to the "negation of negation," where the mind shifts beyond unknowing to an inexpressible, hidden union with God (Howells, 2005). Conversely, the kataphatic approach to prayer emphasizes God's immanence. "Kataphatic" means "with images," and kataphatic praying focuses on things like the beauty of nature, the Gospels, the symbols of faith in the creed, an affective relationship with Christ, and participation in the liturgical life of a faith community . . . Many would argue that the fullness of prayer includes a dialectical dynamic between affirmation and negation, *via positiva* and *via negativa*.[41]

---

39. Davidson and Begley, *Emotional Life;* Newberg and Waldman, *How God Changes Your Brain.*

40. Coakley and Stang, *Rethinking Dionysius,* 9n30.

41. Rodgerson, "To Diagnose or Not to Diagnose," 106.

Interestingly, it is this *apophatic* approach to praying and to life that seems to resonate with you as a None, especially those of you who identify as "Spiritual But Not Religious."[42] This way of praying in the Christian tradition has a long history and is variously described as contemplative prayer, or centering prayer, or the prayer of the heart (the complete methodologies of which are beyond the scope of this book). Ironically, it is a way of praying that takes us to a place of "nothingness"—meaning a place beyond images and words—and to what some describe as an "objectless awareness."[43] The difficulty immediately arises of trying to describe something that is beyond words, with most writers usually defaulting to words like "light," "love," or "energy." Symeon the New Theologian (d. 1022) can speak of "an incomprehensible, inaccessible, and formless light."[44] Teresa of Avila (d. 1582) can speak of "love melting into love."[45] Cynthia Bourgeault can speak of an "alchemical agape," and a movement beyond the "carbon arc" to a fountain of "spondic energy."[46] In this, there is a movement of our attention from the descriptors that we normally use to identify our Selves to a "free attention" in which we align with pure Being. Quoting Beatrice Bruteau, she says,

> When you are perfectly empty of all predicates—including the description of yourself as a "receiver"—then you are intensely full of pure "I am." And just as this point is reached, it explodes into the creative outpouring energy . . . I call this energy spondic because it pours out like a sacred libation, and this perfect liberty I call "creative freedom."[47]

This place of perfect freedom found in *apophatic* prayer has the potential for revelation by definition and the "possibility of revealing still hidden truths . . . which, being real, will bear surprising fruit indefinitely."[48] But even more than a place of new insight, it becomes the place where our being is connected to Being. It becomes the place where we *dwell* or *abide* and *from which* our thoughts and actions have their origin so that: 1) we are at-one with the universal energy of life, and our

42. Ceriello, "Toward a Metamodern Reading," 200, 203.

43. Bourgeault, *Centering Prayer*, 127.

44. de Catanzaro, *Symeon*, 365.

45. As quoted in Laird, *Sunlit Absence*, 1.

46. Bourgeault, *Centering Prayer*, 76, 83.

47. Bourgeault, *Centering Prayer*, 87.

48. Polanyi, *Science, Faith, and Society*, 17.

seeking system desires primarily to drink from this luminous well; and 2) our perceiving, organizing, regulating, and directing of life's energies no longer default to our ego-mind, but to the Christ-mind, giving a very different "flavor" to the stories we create about reality and to the "fruit" that we produce in our words and actions. With the practice of prayer, we return to this wordless, luminous, loving fountain of energy every day, and it becomes the source of a *resurrected* life.

The Grammar for a New Story

A valid argument can be made that the complete transformation of the ego-mind to the Christ-mind is not possible, or at least is very rare. For instance, our very use of language embeds us in a culture, and that culture can contribute to the ego-mind. On the one hand, those Christians who advocate for a conversion experience in which they receive the mind of Christ through the Holy Spirit are correct in the implication that his kind of transformation cannot be limited to human performance. But they have a lot of explaining to do when the collection of "data" from their relationships shows that the ego-mind is still in control long after this supernatural transaction has occurred. And, when there is not a clear pedagogy of interiority or spiritual technology outlined for the longer journey of transformation, an apology is in order.

On the other hand, those who cast off all traditions and elevate the Self and individual free choice to a sacred place in their lives (clearly influenced by the philosophies of Bacon and Descartes taken to the postmodern extreme)[49] are often blind to the ways in which their mind is operating to give them very little free choice, being subjected to far more punishing gods of the ego than the God of heaven they have foresworn. As David Bentley Hart says, "I do in fact believe in hell, though only in the sense of a profound and imprisoning misery that we impose upon ourselves by rejecting the love that alone can set us free . . . Practically all of us go through life as prisoners of our own egos."[50] Or, again, he says, "We are free not because we can choose, but only when we have chosen well. And to choose well we must ever more clearly see the 'sun of the Good' (to employ the lovely Platonic metaphor)."[51]

---

49. Mitchell, *Limits of Liberalism*.

50. Hart, *That All Shall Be Saved*, 63.

51. Hart, *That All Shall Be Saved*, 173.

A Christian spiritual technology would say that we must choose the Good every day and that this is a continuous process for a lifetime. And while it is a stretch to think that we can ever be free completely of the ego-mind, it is well within the realm of possibility to tip the balances in favor of the mind of Christ by means of a moment-to-moment watchful awareness of the flow of energy through the mind and the application by faith of light and love to every situation we encounter as we move from "one degree of glory to another." It is not unlike what Daniel Siegel suggests from the point of view of neuroscience and psychology when he says,

> We can learn, with intention and practice, to move more freely from particular peaks and plateaus that may be restricting us, limiting our identity, imprisoning us in habits and beliefs that keep us in rigid states of depletion and stagnation, or chaotic states of overwhelm and flooding. How can we do this? By intentionally training the mind to access the open plane of possibility, we can learn new ways that energy can emerge from its space of open possibility and uncertainty toward manifestations as the actual, toward certainty and realization . . . Awakening the mind is freeing the movement of energy along these new patterns of probability, shifting from paths that have become stuck or chaotic in our lives by gaining the freedom to experience new unfoldings, a liberation that often requires we let go of a need to control and instead relax into the embrace of the unknown and empower the natural drive toward integration and harmony to be realized.[52]

A Christian spiritual technology suggests that the infinite "plane of possibility," to which we train the mind to be open, has an opening itself into an infinite plane of love and light, which gives definition to the universal energies of life (sometimes referred to as the Good, the True, and the Beautiful). We can choose to align ourselves every day with these energies as we begin to see this as the purpose of life and adopt the simple and elegant spiritual technology of collecting data, assessing the nature of our interior Selves, and following the pattern of cross, death, and resurrection in the transformation from glory to glory. This allows us to create new stories for our lives; stories that have removed the cultural "cap" set by the ego-mind; stories that maximize our freedom and incorporate the essential grammar of light and love; stories that become part of our own

52. Siegel, *Mind*, 286–87.

evolving masterpiece formed in conscious dialogue with ourselves, others, creation, and that which is transcendent.

Our stories can be nourished by a form of prayer that is beyond words and images. The Apostle Paul describes this prayer as one "with sighs too deep for words," and as the "necessary prayer" that we "do not know how to pray as we ought," requiring assistance from the Spirit that "helps us in our weakness" (Rom 8:26). The "sighing" that is too deep for words can also be translated as a wordless "groaning." It is a groaning beyond words that not only connects us with the Spirit, but also connects us with all of creation that "has been groaning in labor pains until now" (Rom 8:22). Creation groans, we groan, and the Spirit groans with the labor pains of new stories, new birth, and new creation.

This groaning would imply that the experience of transformation is not only like drinking from a luminous well, but at times can be experienced as falling into a well. The fictitious character of Jayber Crow likens the man of faith to a man who has fallen into a well. Our human tendency is to think of this as a tragedy and to wonder how the story will end. Does he save himself? Does somebody hear him? Does he truly pray for the first time in his life?

> Listen. There is a light that includes the darkness, a day that shines down even on the clouds. A man of faith believes that the Man in the Well is not lost. He does not believe this easily or without pain, but he believes it. His belief is a kind of knowledge beyond any way of knowing. He believes the child in the womb is not lost, nor is the man whose work has come to nothing, nor is the old woman forsaken in a nursing home in California. He believes that those who make their bed in hell are not lost, or those who dwell in the uttermost parts of the sea, or the lame man at the Bethesda Pool, or Lazarus in the grave, or those who pray, "*Eli, Eli, lama sabachthani.*" Have mercy.[53]

In the sighing/groaning that is beyond words and beyond knowing, there is a different grammar for different stories of freedom.

---

53. Berry, *Jayber Crow,* 357.

6

Creation Groaning

What About Suffering?

IF I AM WRITING an apology of appeal to those of you who are Nones, it probably is not very attractive to introduce a form of praying that is characterized by deep sighing or groaning and an image of falling into a well rather than just drinking from a well. These images raise the specter of suffering which, at best, has not been considered and, at worst, is simply off-putting. For example, Kaya Oakes cites the work of Candace Chellew-Hodge, who gave the millennial college students in her comparative religion class the assignment of creating their own ideal religion. Most of the students included some aspects of meditation, pilgrimage, or rituals of prayer in their ideal religion, but they had no career clergy, no dogma, no punishment or hell, and no regular meetings of the faithful. Oakes goes on to say,

> Chellew-Hodge admits that this idealized version of religion is missing a significant element: it fails to address the question of why human suffering exists. "By ignoring the question of the suffering of humanity and the role of religion in addressing that suffering," she writes, "I am afraid that this new generation is denying itself the opportunity to truly connect not just with the divine, if that's their thing, but with each other."[1]

Of course, it would be unfair to generalize this finding to all Nones or to imply that Nones have no concern for those who are hurting and

---

1. Oakes, *The Nones Are Alright*, 173–74.

have not struggled with their own suffering characterized by deep sighing or groaning. In fact, as I listen more deeply to you in our dialogue, I hear you saying something more profound about religion and suffering by the action you have taken to strategically unaffiliate with any religion—namely, you do not want a religion that is a mindless "opiate of the people" (to use Marx's term) which numbs one to the pain and hardship of an unpredictable and often unjust world. On the one hand, this mindless religion seems disingenuous to you as a None. On the other hand, to be quite blunt, there are plenty of other "opiates" available in our culture to serve as numbing agents if we want one, such as consumerism, addiction, busyness, or social media. Obviously, Christians are entangled here, unwittingly finding many ways to numb their pain and often defaulting to a religion that, if not an "opiate," is primarily a way of coping with life's unpredictability and injustice. This is not all bad and is one way to live a life that minimizes painful consequences or painful experiences that come our way. Essentially, as a None, you have said that you do not need religion for this.

Further, in what I am hearing from some of you who identify as a None, neither do you feel that you need religion in order to be a good person who upholds good values that minimize any suffering inflicted on the rest of the world. For instance, in Cristel Manning's interview of religiously unaffiliated parents, she found the approach of Lori to be typical: she said that she wanted her children to have strong moral values, "but, she added, 'there is an element of our society here that says in order to be a good person you must be a Christian, and I reject that.' She wants them 'to have moral values that are not the exclusive domain of Christians.'"[2] To some extent this corresponds with the Pew Research Center report which focused on world-wide responses to the question of whether people felt it was necessary to believe in God in order to be moral and have good values. They found that answers to this question varied by economic development, education, and age, but that 19- to 29-year-olds, who were less religious by several measures (i.e., Nones), were the *least likely* to say it was necessary to believe in God in order to be a moral person.[3]

In our dialogue, I can validate your position that you do not necessarily need religion to cope with the unpredictability and suffering that life brings. Neither do you necessarily need religion to be a "good" person

2. Manning, *Losing Our Religion*, 121.

3. Tamir, "Global God Divide."

who seeks to minimize any suffering that one might personally inflict on the rest of the world. However, I would ask you to consider the question that any human needs to ask, whether one is religious or not, having to do with *where* one's coping mechanisms or "good" moral values have come from in the first place. To ask this question helps us to live with a greater awareness of how we are making decisions in life and helps us to be less under the control of automatic thinking and the ancestral passions. If we are to make an assessment about the idealized or the non-idealized Self, where does that assessment come from? In what is it rooted? What does it mean to be a good person? How does a good person respond to any pain that might come his/her way? Does my "goodness" have limits, or does it extend even to my enemies?

Even if we think that we have freely chosen our own particular "good" values, many of them have come to us by way of the cultural traditions in which we are embedded and the nature of the very language we are using.[4] We do make choices, but we do not start with a blank slate. We are embedded in traditions influenced by nonreligious sources (e.g., Aristotle's *Nicomachean Ethics* or ancient English law) and religious sources (e.g., the commandments, noble truths, sutras, and pillars from every major religion). In my opinion, we would do well, at the very least, to give a deferential nod to the wisdom traditions whose adherents have wrestled with how to become fully human and by experience have hammered out a grammar for living that goes beyond instinctual pain-avoidance-survival strategies so that we can minimize suffering for ourselves, for others, and for the entire creation.

You do raise a good point that many Christians have not wrestled with or resolved: that the Christian faith is to be more than a coping mechanism in the face of suffering or a list of rules on how to be a good moral person. Not that these intentions are "bad," but they must come with two caveats: 1) the definition of who is a "good moral person" can become so culturally conditioned that it loses the energy and life perspective of the founders of the faith (see chapter 2 on a "type-two binding error" of religion); and 2) an over-focus on coping and being "good" can blind us to an essential point about suffering from a Christian point of view in which we are called *not* to avoid suffering but to *move toward and engage suffering* for the benefit of self, others, and creation. There is a reason why an intentionally-chosen event of enormous suffering lies at

4. Mitchell, *Limits of Liberalism.*

the heart of Christianity—the cross of Christ. The intent is not to make us feel guilty so that we are motivated to be better persons. The intent is to illuminate a path by which we are transformed as we follow in the way of Christ, who is the pioneer and perfector of salvation through suffering (Heb 2:10) and whose life was interpreted through the lens of the prophet Isaiah as a "suffering servant" providing healing through suffering; "and by his bruises we are healed" (Isa 53:5). This different approach to suffering was adopted by the Apostle Paul as a way of continuing or "completing what is lacking in Christ's afflictions" (Col 1:24) and could result in a mindset where one actually chooses to *rejoice in suffering* because of the transformation it can produce. He says, "Not only that, but we also boast [rejoice] in our sufferings, knowing that suffering produces endurance, and endurance produces character, and character produces hope, and hope does not disappoint us, because God's love has been poured into our hearts through the Holy Spirit that has been given to us" (Rom 5:3–5). This path of illumination teaches us to intentionally choose to enter into the groanings of creation.

At a simple level, this might be nothing more than an affirmation of the maxim, "No pain, no gain." There is truth in choosing the harder path at times so that one might grow, as long as the harder path is not the martyr path where we seek attention more than growth. The caterpillar struggling to emerge from its chrysalis as it is transformed into a butterfly provides a symbolic representation of this path. Anecdotal wisdom points out that without the struggle, the wings of the butterfly will not fully strengthen, and the butterfly will die. The path to new life includes moving toward and through the necessary pain.

At another level, this choice to enter into the groaning of creation has similarities to what others have called "conscious suffering." John Wellwood sees this as essential to the sacred path of any intimate relationship. The "gold" in any relationship is found not by avoiding difficulties, defending one's ego, or blaming the other but by intentionally engaging any relational difficulties with love and with a conscious awareness of a higher purpose. Quoting the Sufi master Hazrat Inayat Khan, he says that one of the greatest sins against loving is "shrinking from all sorrows, pains, troubles, and difficulties that come in the path of love."[5] This non-avoidance of difficulties can be done only if those in the relationship have a higher guiding vision regarding the meaning of their life together. Wellwood says,

---

5. Wellwood, *Love and Awakening*, 8.

> What can sustain a couple through the most difficult times is
> knowing that they are together for a larger purpose—helping
> each other refine the gold of their essential natures by working
> through obstacles in the way of their deepest unfolding. Such
> a vision can help them convert ordinary tribulations into what
> the Russian teacher Gurdjieff called "conscious suffering"—will-
> ingly making use of the pain of encountering inner obstacles, as
> motivation to work on overcoming them.[6]

Wisdom gleaned from the way of Christ would apply this choice for conscious suffering to all our relationships, including our relationships with
our enemies. Of course, this, too, requires a vision of a larger purpose for
our lives if we are to include conscious suffering as an essential grammar
for our core stories of freedom.

One way to envision the higher purpose of our lives as we journey
to full humanity is to become aware of our call to diminish all suffering
in life *by transforming it*. We cannot transform any difficulty, pain, or
suffering without entering into it or engaging it. At one level, this engagement is simply *a place to practice*; to practice our ability to override
the instinctual passions of the ego-mind, which is programmed for pain
avoidance and fight-flight. The transformation implicated here is not in
the elimination of the instinctual response. If we are chased by a lion,
we still need to have the adrenaline rush that enables us to run. No, the
transformation of suffering has more to do with the freedom of choice
when our ego-minds are interpreting the behavior of someone else, or
any random event, as life-threatening (or ego-threatening) even when it
is not. The angry response of a spouse, the annoying actions of a neighbor, the irresponsible behavior of a teenager, the accident that comes
out of nowhere, the election that seems disastrous, or the unexpected
arrival of an illness can all be interpreted as a direct assault upon our
existence (with the accompanying fear or other emotional reactivity). Or,
these events can be seen as an *invitation to practice* the application of
awareness, responsibility, compassion, and stillness until the moment is
saturated in love (as described in chapter 5). In the words of Scripture,
this is to abide in love until "there is no fear in love, but perfect love
casts out fear" (1 John 4:18). There is no real freedom of choice until we
have the freedom to override the programmed instinctual passions of the
ego-mind. If needed, we may choose to run. If not, we consciously accept
the higher purpose of engaging the difficulty with a different awareness,

6. Wellwood, *Love and Awakening*, 8.

seeking to transform the suffering. In reality, there is usually a back-and-forth-ness between the instinctual response and the higher awareness until the presence of love opens up new possibilities for growth and we are able to see what we could not see before. As Richard Rohr says, "Suffering is the only thing strong enough to break down your control systems, explanatory mechanisms, logical paradigms, desire to be in charge, and carefully maintained sense of control. Both God and the guided soul know to trust suffering, it seems."[7]

At another level, this higher vision that involves *moving toward suffering* to *transform it* is more than a simple practice when random experiences come our way. It is more proactive than that. For example, in the documented studies of those who engage in compassion meditation, Richard Davidson and Sharon Begley report that "rather than becoming depressed by suffering, people who are trained in compassion meditation develop a strong disposition to alleviate suffering and to wish others to be happy."[8] Tonglen meditation practice, for instance, intentionally visualizes taking in the pain of others on the in-breath and sending out confidence, hope, or healing on the out-breath.

Even more, from a Christian point of view, the proactive aspect involves our choice to engage suffering by *being with it*, whether the suffering is solely our own, that of others, or of the creation itself. Especially, this means *to be with it* even when we have no answers, and all seems lost: whether we are facing our own tragic loss or someone else's; whether we are facing an impossible relationship; whether we are facing an incurable illness; whether we are engaging an intractable social issue; whether we are facing injustice or a misrepresentation of our character; whether we are working to alleviate poverty; whether we are trying to mediate peace; whether we are trying to prevent the destruction of the planet; etc.

This type of experience runs parallel to that of Jesus on the cross as the Scriptures record, "And about three o'clock Jesus cried with a loud voice, 'Eli, Eli, lema sabachthani?' that is, 'My God, my God, why have you forsaken me?'" (Matt 27:46). This is the place where the suffering is real and profound, with no apparent answers or any sufficient rescue in sight. Those who can stand in this place where they 1) embody suffering in some form, 2) honestly lament its reality, and 3) *still engage the Transcendent*—"Father, into your hands I commend my spirit"

---

7. Rohr, *Divine Dance*, 125.

8. Davidson and Begley, *Emotional Life*, 223.

(Luke 23:46)—actually *participate in the disempowerment* of all forms of negativity, darkness, suffering, or evil. Removing the fuel of fear and the constriction of control at the place of suffering robs any negativity or darkness of its power and opens us to an infinite plane of possibility supported itself by an infinite plane of love. The place of deep sighing and groaning, then, becomes the nexus place where heaven and earth meet; where the husk is "threshed" or flailed and the grain is revealed in this threshold of transformation.[9] As the Scriptures say, all of creation is groaning as it awaits the revealing of those who live in this illumined *Way* (Rom 8:18–25). In other words, creation is waiting for the emergence of those who have developed the interior capacity to see, hear, and engage the suffering of self, others, and creation without fear, and who, in doing so, become those who "are not overcome by evil, but overcome evil with good" (Rom 12:21).

Beyond Individualism

This is one way of talking about "the Good" to which we are called, and it is an essential element in understanding the purpose of the game of life. It is far greater than simply being a good person, especially if that person prefers religious reliquaries over religious wrestling or prefers the type of individual self-fulfillment/happiness that comes by insulating one's Self from the suffering of the world by a chosen cultural "opiate" (the Epicurean way) or non-feeling bravado (the Stoic way). Unlike the ancient philosophies (still extant in our culture) that suppose we come to true knowledge and the good life by individually learning to avoid suffering, Christianity calls for us to "embrace it"[10] individually and with others. "The Good" to which we are called, then, is greater than an individual salvation event, an individual identity project, or a personal self-fulfillment goal, and it must grow from a personal good to a common good to a good for all creation as we are increasingly attuned to the deep sighing and groaning that emerges within us, in others, and in all of creation.

Although we are all called to a private moment-to-moment practice in which we choose how we will think about the inevitable suffering, pain, or difficulty that comes our way, the higher purpose here is *not* to do this simply for personal growth, superior spiritual achievement, or to be

9. O'Donohue, *To Bless the Space*, 193.
10. Wright, *Paul*, 1377.

happier than our neighbors. An over-focus on the individual free choice aspect of this practice is almost unavoidable in the North American culture where personal achievement and individual rights usually trump community awareness in an atmosphere of individualism supported by our religions, psychologies, philosophies, and politics.[11] Ironically, this over-focus on individualism actually restricts our choices at a deep level and skews our understanding of freedom and what it means to be fully human.

Alternatively, the proactive embrace of suffering from a Christian perspective, as it begins to free us from the constraints of the ego-mind, develops within us a deep interior awareness of suffering as we learn to *be with it* without fear. In turn, this *being with it* creates a soulful capacity within us to *be with others* and to profoundly connect with others at the point of pain (theirs and ours). In so doing, this proactive embrace of suffering becomes a doorway, a threshold experience, that leads us out of the isolation and the illusion of the individual Self (some would call this the False Self). We begin to see that we exist fully not as high-achieving individuals who compete with others, but as interdependent beings who become aware of a greater Self (True Self) through experiences where great suffering and love are held together. These experiences remove the blinders created by the ego-mind that has focused on our individual survival. All self-constructed divisions of nation, tribe, race, culture, gender, religion, etc. fall away in the moment where great suffering and love are held together without fear, revealing the interconnection with other beings that has existed all along. And, we find ourselves in alignment with Being itself, the essence of which was revealed as the name of G-d[12] to Moses in the context of great suffering and love, where G-d says to Moses, "I have observed the misery of my people who are in Egypt; I have heard their cry on account of their taskmasters. Indeed, I know their sufferings, and I have come down to deliver them" (Exod 3:7–8).

The moment when we can see the misery of others, hear their cries, and proactively engage their suffering becomes a gateway, or a threshold experience, in which we begin to see our very Selves more fully. We also gain in that moment a wider understanding of our purpose in the game of life that aligns with Being itself in a great interdependent, interconnected, interbeing[13] system constantly energized by the proactive giving

11. Mitchell, *Limits of Liberalism*.

12. The name of G-d revealed as the unspeakable Tetragrammaton—YHWH—translated with the verb "to be" as "I am that I am" or "I will be who I will be."

13. Hanh, *Heart of Understanding*, 3.

and receiving of compassionate love applied at the point of pain without fear. However, the potential for the energy of this created system to be diminished in our lives comes about in at least four ways that require our constant attention.

Firstly, there is the truism that *we cannot give what we have not received*. If our own cries have not been heard, how are we going to hear the cries of others? If our own cries have not been heard, our default setting will always be to return to the ego-defensive patterns of survival that maintain the illusion of an individual or autonomous Self. These patterns are rarely changed by a simple act of moral will or rational choice. The spiritual and psychological superstructure that allows us to hear the cries of others is usually built out of those experiences when someone has heard *our* cries. This begins in infancy and never stops. The unique construction of our ego-defenses and the specific training of the ancestral passions in the ancient subcortical regions of the brain are directly influenced by the way in which someone hears *our* cries—or not! It is not rocket science to imagine how an inconsistent or negative response to our own cries for help produces a limited or non-existent ability to hear the cries of others, or, alternatively, how profound experiences of being heard in a time of real pain creates in us a unique empathetic awareness with regards to the cries of others.

This simple psychological truth was not first discovered in the modern era, but has emerged repeatedly in religious wrestling over thousands of years along with the profound underlying question: "How is it possible for us to develop the capacity to hear the cries of others if, in fact, we have never consistently experienced a compassionate response to our *own* cries?" Those who wrestled deeply with this loss in their own lives regularly found that there was another infinite source of these compassionate experiences *not* dependent solely on human caretakers. So, the Psalmist could sing, "If my father and my mother forsake me, the Lord will take me up" (Ps 27:10). And, while admitting the language of the wisdom traditions clearly anthropomorphizes this infinite source, these traditions constantly speak of the ears of God that hear us (we can be heard), the face of God that sees us (we are not invisible and can be seen), and the hands of God that hold us (we can be held). For example, in the words of God to Moses mentioned above, the cries of the people have been heard (Exod 3:7–8); in the later words of blessing given through Moses, God's seeing is invoked: "The Lord bless you and keep you; the Lord make his face to shine upon you, and be gracious to you; the Lord lift up his countenance upon you, and give you peace" (Num 6:24–26); and often in the Psalms an essential experience of trust is equated with being held by God's hands: "But I trust you, O Lord; I say, 'You are my God.' My times are in your hand" (Ps 31:14–15).

Since it is very difficult to proactively give compassionate love to others at the point of pain without first receiving that compassionate love ourselves, and since the imperfect human condition predicts an inconsistency in our own ability to receive this compassionate love from other human beings and pushes us to hide behind our individual ego-defensive survival strategies, these pioneers in the wisdom traditions give witness to a reliable infinite source to help with this predicament. It is always available. There is a path we can follow to find it. It often emerges for us when we wrestle with suffering. Metaphorically, we are invited to drink from this well, even if it means that at times we will fall into it.

The second potential for the diminishment of compassionate energy in the interdependent, interconnected, interbeing system is the flip side of the first. If the first is a failure on the receiving side of compassionate love at the point of pain, the second is a *failure on the giving side*. My spiritual mentor in Scotland would always say that the reason the Dead Sea is "dead" is because it takes in from the Jordan River on one end and is unable to give out at the other, resulting in "bitter waters."[14] The wisdom writers saw this as spiritual hoarding, symbolized by the Israelites in the wilderness hoarding the manna they received from heaven each day, and when they did "it bred worms and became foul" (Exod 16:20). In the Christian tradition, the cry for bread, both spiritual and physical, is always in the context of "us"—"give *us* this day our daily bread" (Matt 6:11) and implies that we always need to look around and see how everyone is being fed. The danger of living in a society defined by individualism is that we may become over-focused on our own fulfillment, including everything from our own spiritual filling to our individual achievement or physical acquisitions. Since this over-focus violates the very nature of the interdependent, interconnected, interbeing system, there will always be a diminishment of any transformative energy until we look around and have a compassionate look at how others are doing and how they are crying out to be fed or filled.

Thirdly, even if we have made a proactive decision to engage suffering for the good of ourselves and others, our ability to participate in the

---

14. Rushforth, *Something Is Happening*, 137.

energy that transforms suffering is diminished if we attempt to eliminate suffering without *first listening deeply to the cries of others*. Good people with good intentions attempting to apply their good solutions for the good of others ironically can create *more* suffering rather than transforming the energy of suffering into that which aligns with the Good and with Being itself. What looks like a proactive engagement with suffering when it does not truly and fearlessly hear the pain of the other can be nothing more than a spiritualized pain-avoidance strategy with a pious face plastered on it. While I appear to be helping *you*, I am really helping *me* create a defensive barrier against your pain in the very act of bringing superior solutions to your problems. Assessing your problem and what you need from my position without truly hearing *you* ensures an automatic distance from your pain. I may be choosing to engage your pain at some level, but without truly being with it and without being with you at the necessary level where suffering is disempowered. Our attempts to help the poor, the homeless, the dysfunctional family down the street, or the "third world" can turn into acts of shaming, mission tourism, or colonization when our proactive efforts sidestep the costly engagement where we truly hear the cries of the other in their own voice.

This is similar to what Paulo Freire spoke about in his unique approach to working with the poor and the oppressed. He said that those who attempted to help the oppressed, whether from the left or from the right, usually came with their own "truth" and "certainty." This "circle of certainty" always imprisoned reality and worked against true liberation of the oppressed. On the contrary, what was needed was someone who "enters more fully into reality so that, knowing it better, he can better transform it. He is not afraid to confront, to listen, to see the world unveiled. He is not afraid to meet the people or to enter into dialogue with them."[15] This dialogue was to be undergirded by love. "If I do not love the world—if I do not love life—if I do not love men—I cannot enter into dialogue."[16] The dialogue was to fully humanize all participants to the degree that the oppressed, in the process of "*conscientizacao*,"[17] no longer saw themselves as the oppressed needing liberation given *to* them but as humans participating in a freedom found *with* them. In this dialogue,

15. Freire, *Pedagogy of the Oppressed*, 24.
16. Freire, *Pedagogy of the Oppressed*, 78.
17. Freire, *Pedagogy of the Oppressed*, 54.

oppression itself is disempowered, and both the oppressed and the oppressor find freedom.

When we start our proactive engagement from the position of our own certain truth rather than from a compassionate love that listens, it is easy to end up dehumanizing the other or, even worse, judging the other. Whether this is done consciously or unconsciously, it moves the starting point of our engagement away from the suffering of others to the sin of others. At that point, it is hard for the one on the receiving end of the engagement not to feel judged and not to hear the message (whether spoken or implied) that your suffering is connected to your sin. If you correct the sin problem, the suffering problem will go away.

What I hear from you as Nones is that this point in particular has given a lot of energy to your exodus from the church. You can see this in the very title of Michelle Scheidt's unpublished dissertation, "Out of the Closet and Out of the Church: The Spiritual Lives of Queer People Who Are Spiritual But Not Religious." Scheidt documents how hard it was for the subjects in her dissertation to have their pastoral needs met and how there was not even an adequate language existing for them to express their spiritual needs and experiences. But, of course, that would necessitate deep listening at the point of pain without any hint of dehumanizing judgment.

That inability to apply compassionate love at the point of pain is seen repeatedly in the essays written for Chrissy Stroop and Lauren O'Neal's book with the striking title, *Empty the Pews: Stories of Leaving the Church.* In his essay from that book Garrard Conley writes, "It became impossible to take seriously the notion that I could continue communicating with a God who seemed to prefer me dead to gay."[18] The title of Conley's own book speaks volumes as to the experience of not being seen or heard: *Boy Erased: A Memoir of Identity, Faith, and Family.* Mel Wells writes in his essay that it is almost impossible for him to believe that anyone's experience of Mormonism could be different, milder, or more positive than his own since his experience "was such a potent, violent version, delivered through the knuckles and barbed words of my stepdad, heavy on Patriarchy, Obedience, and Ways You Are Doing It Wrong."[19] Picking up on this essay in a *Washington Post* article, Megan Marz says,

> This passage is one of many reminders that the equation of Christianity with homophobic, racist, misogynist and false

18. Conley, "Land of Plenty," 33.
19. Wells, "Burden of Proof," 158.

beliefs did not originate with any of these writers. It's an equation that some parents, teachers, and church leaders make again and again: To be a good Christian you must not be gay. To be a good Christian you must submit to your husband. To be a good Christian you must believe that the Earth is six thousand years old. To be a good Christian you must vote Republican. Their children have simply taken them at their word.[20]

Thomas Merton writes about the repeated temptation in Christianity to move from understanding absolute truth as "love" to absolute truth as "knowledge," which one must impose upon others under the guise of love. He says, "God has revealed himself to men in Christ, but he has revealed himself first of all as love. Absolute truth is then grasped as love: therefore not in such a way that it excludes love in certain limited situations."[21] He goes on to say that the one who believes in this absolute gospel truth will be concerned about losing the truth with a failure of love and not a failure of knowledge, and such a concern will bring both humility and wisdom. On the other hand, an over-concern for having the truth of correct knowledge that everyone else must share produces a different result. "It then becomes his duty, he thinks, by virtue of his superior knowledge, to punish those who do not share his truth. How can he 'love' others, he thinks, except by imposing on them the truth which they would otherwise insult and neglect? This is the temptation."[22] This, of course, underlies all attempts to legislate morality and the temptation to become advocates of a moral law that focuses on a target population who needs to be changed or disempowered. The result is not the disempowering of suffering, but the increase of suffering: more division, more hatred, more family cut-offs, more partisan identity politics, etc.

This should be our clue when the approach is off track—when it increases suffering rather than disempowers suffering and moves us away from the interdependent, interconnected, interbeing system where we find our True Selves united with others. It is not that we should ignore sin and its consequences; it is that we need to follow the model given to us in Christ (if we claim to be Christian). That model is of a God who starts with love and with hearing the cries of the people, and then takes on the sin/suffering of the world to disempower it. It would seem to me that those who are committed to the absolute love revealed in Christ might

20. Marz, "Exodus from Christianity."
21. Merton, *Conjectures*, 37.
22. Merton, *Conjectures*, 38.

do the same (as best we can from a human point of view)—namely, hear
the cries of the people with the ears of compassionate love and *be with*
the suffering in such a way that we take it on, including taking on a responsibility for imperfections that are creating the current pain. Have I
personally contributed to the problems by my "circle of certainty" that
imprisons reality? Have I knowingly or unknowingly contributed to systemic forces that are now manifesting in the suffering of the other? Similar to what Paulo Freire suggested, both the oppressor and the oppressed
need liberation. In the dialogue of love where suffering is disempowered,
doesn't everyone's "sin" need to be on the table? And if we find ourselves
"off-track" by creating more suffering rather than less, perhaps that could
be a reminder for us of the real meaning of the Greek word for "sin" in
Scripture, which is "missing the mark."

Fourthly, there is a diminishment in the energy that can disempower suffering in the interdependent, interconnected, interbeing system
when we fail to *hear the cries of creation.* Creation does have a "voice." The
psalmist writes, "The heavens are telling the glory of God; and the firma-
ment proclaims his handiwork. Day to day pours forth speech, and night
to night declares knowledge. There is no speech, nor are there words;
their voice is not heard; yet their voice goes out through all the earth, and
their words to the end of the world" (Ps 19:1–4). When the ecology of
justice, truth, and equity reigns in the human sphere, then all of creation
rejoices: "Let the heavens be glad, and the earth rejoice, let the sea roar,
and all that fills it; let the field exult, and everything in it. Then shall all
the trees of the forest sing for joy before the Lord" (Ps 96:11–12). Alternatively, when humans are separated from the interdependent, interconnected, interbeing system of Being and channel the flow of life's energy
through their limited ego-minds, all of creation groans as if in bondage.
As the Apostle Paul writes, "For the creation waits with eager longing for
the revealing of the children of God . . . We know that the whole creation
has been groaning in labor pains until now; and not only the creation but
we ourselves" (Rom 8:19, 22–23).

Creation does have a "voice," and when we fail to hear it, we can
easily contribute to the exponential increase in suffering and not to the
disempowerment or transformation of suffering. But it does require us to
hear differently. In considering the future of Christianity, Diana Bass cites
the example of the Methodist church on Tangier Island in the middle of
the Chesapeake Bay. This Methodist church has been in existence since
Europeans settled on the island before the Revolutionary War. As she says,

It is a good church. It has been so for many generations. As church goes these days, it is a successful small community, having done what it needs to do to last well into the future. But there is a problem: the island is sinking. In the next three decades or so, Tangier will slip into the bay, taking everything to a watery grave, including the church.[23]

As she goes on to say, the future of the church can no longer be separated from questions about the future of the planet. If we do not hear the groanings of climate change, the church will sink along with everything else. But this would require us to hear differently; to hear the unique way in which creations speaks; to hear the cries of creation.

To hear those cries would require us to remove the noise-cancelling headphones of anthropocentrism and individualism that cause us to hear only the music that soothes our egos as we listen to the utilitarian rhythms of unlimited progress, competition, consumerism, and unregulated markets. Christians are entangled here with the wider culture to the point that even Scripture cannot be heard clearly. For instance, "salvation" gets heard as "me being saved to go to heaven" rather than as a "restorative justice for the whole creation." As N. T. Wright says,

> Of course "salvation" matters. What is being said, however, is (a) that salvation doesn't mean what the western tradition has often taken it to mean (escaping to a disembodied "heaven"), (b) that it is in any case not the main topic of most of the texts, and (c) that it is not the main narrative which they are trying to explicate. In the New Testament the rescue of human beings from sin and death, which remain vital throughout, serves a much larger purpose, namely that of God's restorative justice for the whole creation.[24]

Or, as another example, in the creation narrative God says, "Let us make humankind in our image, according to our likeness; and let them have dominion over the fish of the sea, and over the birds of the air, and over the cattle, and over all the wild animals of the earth, and over every creeping thing that creeps upon the earth" (Gen 1:26). With our noise-cancelling headphones on, we have heard the word "domination" of nature instead of "dominion." On the one hand, this comes from our acceptance of "dominion" without owning it in the context of our having

---

23. Bass, "Future of Faith," 50–51.

24. Wright, *Paul*, 164–65.

been created in the likeness of the God who always hears the cries of suffering. On the other hand, we have not owned it in the context of the reality that we are *not* God. In his encyclical letter entitled *Laudato si'*, Pope Francis states this clearly:

> We are not God. The earth was here before us and it has been given to us. This allows us to respond to the charge that Judaeo-Christian thinking, on the basis of the Genesis account which grants man "dominion" over the earth (cf. Gen 1:28), has encouraged the unbridled exploitation of nature by painting him as domineering and destructive by nature. This is not a correct interpretation of the Bible as understood by the church. Although it is true that we Christians have at times incorrectly interpreted the Scriptures, nowadays we must forcefully reject the notion that our being created in God's image and given dominion over the earth justifies absolute domination over other creatures. The biblical texts are to be read in their context, with an appropriate hermeneutic, recognizing that they tell us to "till and keep" the garden of the world (cf. Gen 2:15). "Tilling" refers to cultivating, ploughing or working, while "keeping" means caring, protecting, overseeing and preserving. This implies a relationship of mutual responsibility between human beings and nature. Each community can take from the bounty of the earth whatever it needs for subsistence, but it also has the duty to protect the earth and to ensure its fruitfulness for coming generations.[25]

In a later passage, he says that we are not to hear "dominion" as "domination" but as "stewardship,"

> Modernity has been marked by an excessive anthropocentrism . . . An inadequate presentation of Christian anthropology gave rise to a wrong understanding of the relationship between human beings and the world. Often, what was handed on was a Promethean vision of mastery over the world, which gave the impression that the protection of nature was something that only the faint-hearted cared about. Instead, our "dominion" over the universe should be understood more properly in the sense of responsible stewardship.[26]

To hear more clearly, we will not only need to remove our noise-cancelling headphones so that we might balance anthropocentrism with biocentrism, but also we will need to learn the language of creation as it

25. Francis, *Laudato si'*, 49.
26. Francis, *Laudato si'*, 87.

speaks loudly with a "voice" that is "no voice" as mentioned in Psalm 19. At one level, "we are speaking of an attitude of the heart, one which approaches life with serene attentiveness . . . an inner peace . . . with a capacity for wonder which takes us to a deeper understanding of love."[27] At another level, this "no-voice voice" is the language of the Spirit "who prays for us with sighs too deep for words" (Rom 8:26). In the mystery of the trinity (beyond the reach of this book to explain), this would be the language of the pre-existent Christ who "is the image of the invisible God, the first-born of all creation; for in him all things in heaven and on earth were created . . . He himself is before all things, and in him all things hold together" (Col 1:15–17). The language of creation and the language of the one who holds all things in creation together is the language of the "no-voice voice" and the language of "sighs too deep for words." It is the language of the interdependent, interconnected, interbeing system of Being where spirit and creation are held together. It is the language of "sighing" beyond words, which, as we saw in the last chapter, has overtones of "groaning" and which lies at the heart of "apophatic praying." And in that sighing and groaning, suffering and beauty resonate together like vocal folds where the real cries of Self, others, and creation vibrate in oneness with infinite love, ready for new stories, new birth, and new creation to be heard.

Caroline Fairless suggests that it is on the "apophatic pathway" where church and not-church might meet. It is the pathway of unlearning, unsaying, and self-emptying where out of the "nothingness" we find something new emerging in the space between things. It is a pathway that might be taken together around a common concern for the planet. She says,

> What if the people who love the earth and fear for its future begin to meet in a space that is neither church or not-church—a space where ideas, living experience, and the sacred "unspeakable" would be exchanged and celebrated to deepen human-to-human and human-to-nonhuman contact?[28]

Could it also be that the apophatic "language" and experience become the connecting grammar of our stories, connecting us to one another and creation at the same time? Could it be that the "no-voice voice" and the "sighs too deep for words" connect us to the energy by which all things are created and through which all things hold together? If so, that would be appealing. However, it would also place us in a unique

---

27. Francis, *Laudato si'*, 164–65.
28. Fairless, *Space Between*, viii.

relationship to other powers that claim to hold things together, powers
that have other ideas about suffering.

Getting Political

If "the Good" to which we are called as Christians has something to do
with our ability to hear the cries of all creation and to engage suffering
in order to transform it, then it is bound to affect how we participate
as citizens in the *marketplace* of energy and ideas where the cultural
rules of the game are established, resources are distributed, and the lines
of power and authority are drawn. Since, by definition, being a citizen
involves politics (coming from the Greek *polītikós* and meaning "relating to a citizen"[29]), our involvement in the marketplace inevitably gets
political, especially when one lives in a democracy where one holds the
right and responsibility to vote. For the church, this has historical prece-
dence in the Apostle Paul, who entered into marketplace discussions in
Athens but also used his rights as a Roman citizen to his advantage. He
reminded those who were about to torture him that it was unlawful to
do so because he was a citizen of Rome (Acts 22:25–29) and he appealed
an unjust case against him all the way to Caesar himself (Acts 25:12).
While awaiting his trial in Rome, Paul argued for Christians in that city
to be good citizens by obeying the governing authorities, exercising good
conduct, and paying their taxes (Rom 13:1–7), but with a unique purpose
to "owe no one anything, except to love one another" (Rom 13:8) and in
the context of having their primary identity as "citizens with the saints
and . . . members of the household of God" (Eph 2:19). As Ched Myers
and Elaine Enns remind us, the appropriate question for Christians is not
whether they will be involved in politics, but *how* they will be involved
in politics. Citing the appeal of Martin Luther King Jr. for churches to
be a "headlight" leading people to higher levels of justice rather than a
"taillight" supporting the *status quo* and following behind other agen-
cies, they say, "King and Paul could not be more explicit, yet modern
Christians still imagine that our churches should 'stay out of politics'—as
if that were possible! The question is only what *kind* of politics the church
should embody."[30]

---

29. Barnhart, *Dictionary of Etymology*, 813.

30. Myers and Enns, *Ambassadors of Reconciliation*, 106.

According to Robert Putnam and David Campbell, the way the church has gotten political in the last several decades has influenced many of you to unaffiliate with the church and to self-identify as a None. They say,

> After 1991, increasing numbers of Americans of all ages expressed deep concern that religious leaders should not try to influence either people's votes or government decisions . . . This change was visible across all parts of the religious spectrum . . . and most strongly among the growing number of Nones, those who rejected all religious identification. Young Americans came to view religion, according to one survey, as judgmental, homophobic, hypocritical, and too political.[31]

Later they say, "a growing number of younger Americans have come to equate religion with 'Republican,' and react by turning away from religion."[32]

In the decade since their book was published, this trend has only continued for those of you who are Nones. The number of Nones in the population has increased exponentially and, interestingly, the involvement of Christians in politics has increased frenetically. But Christians are highly divided on *how* they are involved in politics and what *kind* of politics would be congruent with being a Christian citizen. For instance, White Evangelical Christians and Black Christians generally are compellingly different when it comes to politics. And even when churches try to stay out of politics, Putnam and Campbell found that political leanings were communicated in various ways and that people tended to sort themselves into congregations based upon political affiliation. They say,

> Politically relevant information, mostly subtle but occasionally overt, reverberates through the social networks formed in and through one's place of worship. The salience of this information is amplified by the political like-mindedness of people who share a given faith. That political congruence, in turn, is owing to the switching, mixing, and matching in American religion. People sort themselves—whether conscious or not—into congregations with politically simpatico members, through a self-reinforcing process . . . All of this sorting makes many religious social networks into political echo chambers.[33]

31. Putnam and Campbell, *American Grace*, 121.
32. Putnam and Campbell, *American Grace*, 401.
33. Putnam and Campbell, *American Grace*, 442.

In the last decade, this has moved from politically sympathetic relationships to politically sycophantic relationships that strive to increase
marketplace domination. In turn, this has contributed to the rise of identity politics (on the left and the right) with their all-consuming and totalizing ideologies, acting as "pseudoreligions with confessions, catechesis,
soteriologies (theories of salvation), ecclesiologies (theories of membership), eschatologies (theories of the future), heretics, and martyrs."[34]

Of course, no marketplace dialogue is possible with totalizing ideologies that are pseudo-religions. Even for Christians (maybe especially
for Christians!), all perspective gets lost, such as that of Richard Niebuhr,
who pointed out long ago that Christianity has a long and varied history
of determining how it will interact with culture and become involved
in politics. He says, "Given these two complex realities—Christ and culture—an infinite dialogue must develop in the Christian conscience and
the Christian community."[35] He identified five different ways in which
Christianity, over the centuries, has interacted with culture, which he
names as: (1) Christ against culture (e.g., monasticism); (2) Christ of
culture (e.g., culture-Protestantism); (3) Christ above culture (e.g., the
synthesis of Thomas Aquinas); (4) Christ and culture in paradox (e.g., the
polarity and tension of duality in Luther); and (5) Christ the transformer
of culture (e.g., the conversionist solution of Augustine).

Admittedly, politics is only one aspect of culture with particular reference to the nature, use, and purpose of governing power. But Niebuhr's
point is well taken that there is not one right, totalizing approach that
Christianity has historically taken in relation to politics or culture. How
could it? The context is always changing. For example, the politics of a
Christian citizen in a totalitarian state would be very different from that
of a Christian citizen in a democracy. Even more confusing would be to
discern the appropriate politics of a Christian citizen in a supposedly
"Christian" totalitarian state. Hence, "an infinite dialogue must develop in
the Christian conscience and the Christian community."[36] In that infinite
dialogue, Christians are called to be wary of an over-identification with
hot-button political issues of the day in favor of a discerning wisdom that
looks for timeless principles involving *process, power, and position.*

---

34. Mitchell, *Limits of Liberalism*, 19.

35. Niebuhr, *Christ and Culture*, 39.

36. Niebuhr, *Christ and Culture*, 39.

Firstly, Christians would bring to their political involvement a particular *process* that is congruent with their spiritual technology of freedom—collect data, make an assessment, and apply a cruciform pattern of
change. The *collection of data* comes from all our relationships and, in this
case, includes not only looking at how individuals relate to each other, but
also how individuals and groups of people relate to the market, to places
of employment, to educational institutions, to social organizations, to the
state, and to nature. What is the hard evidence (the data) that emerges
from these relationships? For instance, in the United States politics has its
beginnings in some "self-evident" truths about equality and unalienable
rights as stated in the Declaration of Independence, but we have often re-
fused to look at the evidence concerning these self-evident truths. When
you look at the data for all relationships, what is relationally evident is that
certain individuals and groups of people are treated unequally or left out
completely in the creation of a more perfect union. In their political involvement, Christians are called not to ignore the hard relational evidence
that emerges from any form of government, especially one theoretically
rooted in self-evident truths and unalienable rights.

Not only are Christians called to look at the hard relational evidence,
but also to *make an assessment* on how to be politically involved based
upon core principles that are inclusive of, but go beyond, self-evident
truths about equality and unalienable rights such as life, liberty, and the
pursuit of happiness for all people. For example, Christians are also called
to look at the evidence and ask how any political decision affects the "least
of these": those without power or resources, those who are helpless and
weak, those who are marginalized or suffering, those who have no voice
(human beings and all creation alike). Christian political involvement
brings an assessment that starts by looking at the implications for those
on the bottom and not at the top. Are those on the bottom being treated
justly? As the prophet Isaiah said,

> Is this not the fast that I choose: to loose the bonds of injustice,
> to undo the thongs of the yoke, to let the oppressed go free, and
> to break every yoke? Is it not to share your bread with the hun-
> gry, and bring the homeless poor into your house; when you see
> the naked, to cover them, and not to hide yourself from your
> own kin? (Isa 58:6–7).

Or, in the words of Christ,

> For I was hungry and you gave me food, I was thirsty and you
> gave me something to drink, I was a stranger and you welcomed
> me, I was naked and you gave me clothing, I was sick and you
> took care of me, I was in prison and you visited me . . . Truly I
> tell you, just as you did it to one of the least of these who are
> members of my family, you did it to me (Matt 25:35–36, 40).

Jonathan Sacks says that this is essential to what he calls covenantal politics. "One of the great historical lessons is that societies become strong when they care for the weak. They become rich when they care for the poor. They become invulnerable when they care for the vulnerable. That is the beating heart of the politics of covenant."[37]

These are examples of the *means of assessment* that Christians are called to bring to their political involvement, which, when paired with the hard relational evidence emerging in society, brings the still harder evaluation of *what the assessment means*. What does it tell us about our core operating systems individually and corporately; personally and politically? For example, it is not enough to look at the data and make political assessment from the perspective of those on the bottom, but we are called to go further and ask what is creating "the top" and "the bottom" in the first place. We not only need to change the filters in our minds, but also change the mental filters and legal algorithms in our political and cultural systems that by design favor those at the top and ensure inequality for the "least of these."

To change these does require a commitment to a *cruciform pattern of change* because those who advocate for changing the corporate and political core operating systems usually get "crucified" in one way or another. Only when we have committed to an internal pattern of crucifixion that leads to a radical change of mind and have proactively chosen to engage the suffering of the world will we be able to see how the invisible core operating systems of society are functioning, including how we ourselves may be benefitting from some of those systems. Only then will we have enough character to sacrificially make these systems visible in the marketplace. We become something of a "town crier" bringing to the town square a call—made with a combination of faith and reason that speaks without hostility—to look at the relational data, make an assessment based upon moral principles, and ask what this means regarding *which* "invisible hand" we are empowering to make our union more

---

37. Sacks, *Morality*, 322.

perfect. As Jonathan Sacks points out, the "invisible hand" of the market suggested by Adam Smith in *The Wealth of Nations* is not neutral and is not morally balanced, as seen in the ratio of executive-to-worker pay that has gone from 20:1 in 1965 to 312:1 today. As Sacks says, "the market is better at creating wealth than distributing it, and equitable distribution requires something other than self-interest. It needs a sense of the common good, of the 'We' not just the 'I.' Markets need morals."[38] We have a *process* by which we can make visible any unjust "invisible hand."

Secondly, Christians are called to bring to their political involvement a wider understanding of and a different relationship to *power*. More specifically, Christians are called to name the different kinds of power existing in the marketplace and to become free agents of the kind of power that can transform all core operating systems, especially those that limit our freedom to be fully human.

For example, a clear illustration of the radically different forms of power existing in the marketplace of life can be seen in the moment near the end of Jesus' life when he is being interrogated by the fifth governor of Judea, Pontius Pilate. Already Jesus has demonstrated his preferred form of power when being accused of blasphemy by the religious authorities: he remains silent. In an appeal to political power, the religious leaders send him to Pilate. Pilate asks Jesus about the charges against him, "Are you the King of the Jews?" Jesus offers no defense and simply says, "You say so." Pilate becomes frustrated and reactive, asking if Jesus is implying that he is a Jew. He questions Jesus further: "Pilate asked him again, 'Have you no answer? See how many charges they bring against you.' But Jesus made no further reply, so that Pilate was amazed" (Mark 15:4–5). Finding no fault in Jesus, Pilate next makes a political move to "pass the buck" by sending him to Herod, citing an issue with jurisdictional authority. Herod shrewdly sends Jesus back to Pilate. Pilate questions Jesus further but still receives no answers. "Pilate therefore said to him, 'Do you refuse to speak to me? Do you not know that I have power to release you, and power to crucify you?' Jesus answered him, 'You would have no power over me unless it had been given you from above" (John 19:10–11). Fearing a riot of the people that would question his ability as a leader by the Roman authorities, Pilate turns to the opinion poll, classically saying that he is washing his hands of the matter and letting the people decide if

38. Sacks, *Morality*, 91.

Jesus should be killed. Prodded into a frenzied crowd mentality by their leaders, the people cry, "Crucify him!"

Jesus standing before Pilate. Who has the power? What form of power do they each embody? If he plays the political game shrewdly, Pilate has the power of the empire, the power of domination, the power of weapons, the power of destruction, the power of death, the powers of violence, force, and fear. Certainly, he is part of the *Pax Romana* (peace of Rome) that allowed for great technological advances and beautiful art, but it was a peace that needed enemies to defeat, scapegoats to blame, slaves to do the grunt work, gruesome entertainment to divert the masses, and great walls to keep out the barbarians. His is the power of a system that replicated ancient religious sacrificial systems which required some form of violent sacrifice to keep the gods happy or, in this case, to soothe the ego of the emperor. But, of course, this power had no ability to transform the ego of the emperor or to alter the character of bloodthirsty gods.

Jesus standing before Pilate. Who has the power? What is the evidence? Clearly, Pilate has the power of empire, but ironically, with all that power, it is Pilate who is afraid and reactive. It is Pilate who is trying desperately to get Jesus off his hands. It is Pilate who is afraid of blame. Jesus could have chosen the power of empire. His disciples tried to prevent his capture by wielding a sword, but Jesus said, "Put your sword back into its place; for all who take the sword will perish by the sword. Do you think that I cannot appeal to my Father, and he will at once send me more than twelve legions of angels?" (Matt 26:52–53).

But Jesus makes a conscious choice for a different kind of power that in the eyes of the world looks like no power at all; a power that the Apostle Paul would later hear through mystical experience as "power made perfect in weakness" (2 Cor 12:9). It is the power not associated with empire, but with the "kingdom of God" to which Jesus constantly referred in his parables. It is the power of a "peace that passes all understanding" so that we have "no anxiety about anything" and can use our minds to think about "whatever is true, honorable, just, pure, lovely, and gracious" (see Phil 4:4–8). It is the power to overcome "dividing walls of hostility" (see Eph 2:11–22) between us and God, between different ethnicities and religions, between genders, and between enemies. It is the power of non-violence that has the power to break the powers of the old sacrificial systems, not by appeasing an angry God with a scapegoat but by a God who joins in solidarity with the victim on the cross to absorb the violence of the adversary[39] and completely disempower the cycle of violence kept alive by the untransformed ancestral passions of humans. It is the power of silence where one has become so rooted in the power of Being beyond words that even death loses its power, whether that be our physical death, or the death of our ego, or the death of our false stories, or the death of the way we have done relationships, or the death of a career. Jesus is standing before Pilate, but he is standing in the silence that brings a rootedness in agape-love to the point that he can withstand all other forms of power that exist in rulers, authorities, cosmic forces of darkness, and spiritual forces of evil (see Eph 6:10–17). It is Pilate who is amazed and afraid, not Jesus.

N. T. Wright says that the Apostle Paul came to understand this form of power as it related to politics:

> Just as Paul has given, in his major theological expositions, the foundation for what later became known as Christian theology, so he has given, by clear implication, the foundation for what might be called a Christian political vision: neither Marxist nor neo-conservative, neither Constantinian nor Anabaptist, neither "left" nor "right" in our shallow modern categorization, but nuanced and differentiated in quite other (and still very Jewish) modes . . . In a world where many, not least many pious and zealous Jews, were eager for military revolution and rebellion against Rome, Paul insisted that the crucial victory had already been won, and that the victory in question was a victory won not *by* violence but *over* violence itself . . . The power and pretensions of Rome are downgraded, outflanked, subverted and rendered impotent by the power of love: the love of the one God revealed in the crucified and risen Jesus, Israel's Messiah and Caesar's lord.[40]

The kind of power that Christians would choose in the political marketplace was straightforward for a couple of hundred years. It became more complicated with the Edict of Milan in the year AD 313 when Christianity was given legal status in the Roman Empire and Christians were relieved of persecution, soon to be followed by another edict that would make Christianity the state religion of the Roman Empire. Prior to AD 313, it was "easy" to align with the "least of these" and to engage those who were suffering because Christians were the ones on the bottom of

---

39. Myers and Enns, *Ambassadors of Reconciliation*, 11.

40. Wright, *Paul*, 1319.

society, and they were the ones being persecuted. It was "easy" to choose another form of power as distinct from the power of the empire because they had almost no power in the empire.

But what happens when the church and state become intertwined? What happens in a country like the United States where there is a legal separation of church and state and, yet, a *de facto* entanglement of church and state to the degree that many refer to the state as a Christian nation and many refer to their religion as Christian nationalism? What happens when someone who identifies as a Christian is responsible as a citizen for participating in or sustaining the imperial *pax Americana*? What does it mean to have Jesus standing before Pilate now?

Without making a conscious choice, we will always default to the power of empire, just as we will always default to our ego-defenses if we do not make a conscious choice to change the core operating systems of our minds. Therefore, the choice we make about power when we enter the marketplace as a Christian citizen begins long before we enter that marketplace. Jesus' preparation for the moment in which he stood before Pilate started long before he was ever brought into the governor's court.

When asked about his victory over Napoleon at the battle of Waterloo, Britain's Duke of Wellington famously replied, "The Battle of Waterloo was won on the playing fields of Eton." Of course, Eton College is one of the most prestigious schools in the world, founded in 1440 by King Henry VI and providing the education for many well-known British leaders. Applying this statement by the Duke of Wellington to the study of Christian ethics, Samuel Wells says,

> The Duke of Wellington's famous reflection on the climax of the Napoleonic Wars was not a statement of personal modesty. It was a recognition that success in battle depends on the character of one's soldiers. It was a statement that Britain had institutions that formed people with the kind of virtues that could survive and even thrive in the demanding circumstances of war. The argument of this chapter is that the moral life is more about Eton than it is about Waterloo. Eton and Waterloo represent two distinct aspects of the moral life. Eton represents the long period of preparation. Waterloo represents the tiny episode of implementation—the moment of decision, or "situation."[41]

Although the analogy is strained because the training at Eton has a lot more to do with the training of those "at the top" in preparation for

41. Wells, *Improvisation*, 73.

wielding the powers of the empire, the point is the same—there is a long period of preparation that must undergird any moment in the marketplace when a Christian must decide about *process, power, and position.* There needs to be a long and consistent training that works to tip the balances in our core operating systems (from the ego-mind to the mind-of-Christ). This needs to happen *before* we "stand face-to-face with Pilate." Only then will we find ourselves so rooted and grounded in agape-love that we are non-defensive, not afraid, and nonviolent, and it is Pilate who becomes amazed and afraid.

Without this training, we will enter the marketplace bringing the forces of disruption and destruction but not the force of disequilibrium that fosters change. Without this training, we will not have the wisdom to discern between charismatic leaders who offer a veneer of Christianity to manipulate our passions and transformational leaders who seek to transform unhealthy systems. Without this training, we will have no core foundational story by which we judge the many conspiracy (and other) theories that compete in the marketplace to capture our every thought. Without this training, we will not have the humility to evaluate our own hypocrisy in giving loyalty to the "Prince of Peace" while clinging to a theology of sacrificial violence that bleeds over into the "official sanctioned violence"[42] of the state. Nor will we be able to own our hypocrisy at expecting the state to legislate morality or legally protect our rights when we have failed to build the family, religious, and civic structures where morality and fairness are modeled and embodied.

Again, we simply need to look at the evidence. If there are leaders who are inflaming our passions, creating enemies for us to hate, arousing fear about our future, or being unclear about the truth, do not follow them. If we are negative, defensive, hateful, violent, or reactive when we engage in marketplace politics as a Christian citizen, then we have not done our homework, and we have lots of data to take back with us for our own cruciform process of divinization.

However, once we have done our homework to the best of our ability (we will never be finished), the Christian citizen must be a continual witness in the marketplace to a power that is different than the power of the empire or state. Being a witness in this way will at times cause us to live into the full meaning of "martyr." We are not called to be martyrs in the "attention getting" sense, but in the sense of being willing to engage

42. Myers and Enns, *Ambassadors of Reconciliation*, 92.

suffering as we advocate for those with "no voice," direct resources to the "least of these," bring light to shine on the "invisible hands" operating in darkness to create "top" and "bottom" in society, name the relational evidence that no one wants to talk about, and constantly seek nonviolent solutions that are rooted and grounded in love. For this we will be accused of being unpatriotic, un-American, anti-business, nonrealistic, un-Christian, or worse. We will inevitably find ourselves "standing before Pilate."

Like the Apostle Paul, we will be in the precarious position of having to use the state, but not be used by the state, at times criticizing the very powers of the state that are protecting our freedom to speak out and our ability to move freely about the country. This is not the criticism of the anarchist who seeks to overthrow the state but the honest voice of a citizen who, as US Representative John Lewis famously said, at times is called to make "good trouble" and must always take the long view.

Our criticism is the honest voice of a citizen who brings to the marketplace dialogue a reminder that there are other kinds of power to consider before we ever consider violence. This is the honest voice of a citizen who can step back and see where the union is not perfect, constantly bringing to the marketplace a vision of a higher form of citizenship that we slowly move toward over hundreds of years. This is the honest voice of a citizen who can combine criticism of the "not-yet-there" with thanksgiving for "that-which-is," always humbly praying for those who govern and who, at least in a democracy, are tasked at times to make horrendously difficult decisions regarding how to protect the space where life, liberty, and the pursuit of happiness can flourish.

This continual witness to a different form of power means that the Christian citizen is called, thirdly, to occupy a unique *position* in society. It is the position of "betwixt and between." To some extent, this is what Alexis de Tocqueville found when he visited America in 1831 and wrote *Democracy in America*. He became curious about the significant influence of religion in this new democracy where there was a proscribed separation of church and state which gave no political power to the church. From interviewing clergymen, de Tocqueville discovered that their power in society came from never getting involved in party political disputes. Jonathan Sacks summarizes this discovery by saying,

> He writes in *Democracy in America*: "When I came to enquire into the prevailing spirit of the clergy, I found that most of its members seemed to retire of their own accord from the exercise of power and they made it the pride of their profession

to abstain from politics." When he asked clergymen why they stayed out of politics, they said, in essence, "Because all politics is intrinsically divisive. Therefore if we were involved in the political system we too would be divisive. Therefore we avoid politics." Instead, religious leaders in the 1830s were involved in strengthening families, building communities, and starting charities. They inspired people to a sense of the common good, educating them in "habits of the heart," and bequeathing them the "art of association" that de Tocqueville called "their apprenticeship in liberty."[43]

What de Tocqueville found gives some insight into the "betwixt and between" position exercised by Christians when it comes to politics. For instance, it illustrates that the form of power Christians are to have in society is different from the power of the state and, at the same time, is crucial to the functioning of the state. It also illustrates the nature of "between-ness" that wisely does not align with any political party. However, it is not a complete understanding of the Christian position because this avoidance strategy often fails to give voice to those who have no voice in society and can, by its silence, become complicit with the core operating systems of society that create inequality and injustice. For example, silence regarding slavery, Jim Crow, and white supremacy fails significantly at any "apprenticeship in liberty" and is significantly different from the silence of Jesus standing before Pilate.

Abraham Lincoln struggled to find this "betwixt and between" position from inside the political system. He faced horrendously difficult decisions as a Christian elected to political office. In September 1862, he wrote in his personal diary what he called "A Meditation on the Divine Will," saying,

> The will of God prevails. In great contests each party claims to act in accordance with the will of God. Both *may* be, and one *must* be wrong. God cannot be for and against the same thing at the same time. In the present Civil War it is quite possible that God's purpose is something different from the purpose of either party.[44]

In this case, Lincoln is in touch with the Christian position of "betwixt and between" where the will of God is not aligned with any political party. He did try to incorporate this position in his political decisions.

43. Sacks, *Morality*, 255.
44. Quoted in Sacks, *Morality*, 317.

These decisions cost him his life and, to some extent, illustrate the cruciform pattern of his life. Unlike the clergy of the 1830s, who did not align with any political party by avoiding politics altogether, Lincoln aligned with the Republican party and clearly was involved in transactional politics at times. However, he seemed to operate in significant transformational moments as if he were just over the threshold on the "edge of the inside"[45] of the party, which allowed him to see the whole without a blind party alignment or totalizing ideology. He may have even pivoted on the threshold in those times, moving from the inside edge to the outside edge of the party. On the outside edge of the party, he would have encountered the "betwixt and between" position.

The "betwixt and between" position, then, is cautious about any party alignment but not avoidant of politics. The purpose is to create enough distance through non-alignment so that the Christian has a unique leverage for transformation using a different kind of power. The Greek mathematician Archimedes (d. 212 BC) is reported to have said, "Give me a lever long enough and a fulcrum on which to place it, and I shall move the world." The fulcrum is that place where one is firmly rooted and grounded in agape-love, connected to Being itself, and the lever is the nonviolent power similar to Jesus standing before Pilate. But the lever needs some length, some distance, to have leverage. If Jesus had been too aligned with the Sadducees, the Pharisees, or the Roman overlords, he would have had no power. If he had simply taught people how to be nice without offering kingdom-of-God parables with political overtones or without taking political action (such as riding into Jerusalem during Passover on an ass to fulfill Zechariah's prophecy about the arrival of the king), he would not have moved the world. Similarly, Christians who become too closely aligned with a political party or a political identity position often lose their leverage and their moral authority. They may gain some transactional power but lose the power of transformation and often end up being used by politicians for political gain. But neither can they be avoidant without losing their soul, having heard the groans of the people and having found in the sighing/groaning of creation/spirit the power to push the lever that changes the world. Those Christians who feel called to political service will have to be comfortable on the threshold, operating sometimes on the inside edge and sometimes on the outside edge of

45. Rohr, "Mystics and the Margins."

political systems, but always with an understanding of the "betwixt and between" position.

This Christian (but not exclusively Christian) "betwixt and between" position, then, is something of a safe zone for re-creation or transformation. It is a position which lies outside the normal structures of society, outside the core operating systems and algorithms of custom, convention, ceremony, and law. It is a position with similarities to what anthropologist Victor Turner referred to as "liminality" (*limen* signifying "threshold" in Latin) and identified as a space "between" one phase and another in any transition of place, state, age, position, or society. He says,

> The attributes of liminality or of liminal *personae* ("threshold people") are necessarily ambiguous, since this condition and these persons elude or slip through the network of classifications that normally locate states and positions in cultural space. Liminal entities are neither here nor there; they are betwixt and between the positions assigned and arrayed by law, custom, convention, and ceremonial.[46]

He goes on to say that the liminal *personae*, while appearing to have no status or even "inferior" status in society, often held a certain kind of "power in weakness" or "ritual power" in the culture. They often developed their own *communitas*, or community, of equal individuals who submitted to a higher authority but were in a position outside of structured society which was defined as "a structured, differentiated, and often hierarchical system of politico-legal-economic positions with many types of evaluation, separating men in terms of 'more' or 'less.'"[47]

Being outside of structured society, liminal *personae* could form spontaneous communities where people could truly be *with* one another in *I-Thou* relationships (Turner draws on the work of Martin Buber here) and where the hierarchical systems that separated people into "more" and "less," "top" and "bottom" no longer existed. Turner observed that those liminal *personae* who formed their own *communitas* did not exhibit anarchy and were not characterized by unconstrained biological drives or herd instinct, but had characteristics of rationality, volition, and memory developed through lives acquainted with society and were "men in their wholeness wholly attending."[48] In *communitas*, the liminal *personae*

---

46. Turner, *Ritual Process*, 94.

47. Turner, *Ritual Process*, 95.

48. Turner, *Ritual Process*, 108.

("threshold people") played a vital role in structured society, continually providing society "with a set of templates or models which are, at one level, periodical reclassifications of reality and man's relationship to society, nature, and culture."[49] He says further,

> Communitas breaks in through the interstices of structure, in liminality, at the edges of structure, in marginality; and from beneath structure, in inferiority. It is almost everywhere held to be sacred or "holy," possibly because it transgresses or dissolves the norms that govern structured and institutionalized relationships and is accompanied by experiences of unprecedented potency.[50]

The position of power, then, is the position on the margins ("betwixt and between"), occupied by those who are often seen as inferior, but who play a vital role in keeping structured society from becoming too rigid and who continually are a reminder of the constant need for structured society to "reclassify" its understanding of reality, or (in the language of this book) to transform its core operating systems and the very grammar by which it develops its common stories.

Victor Turner thought that Christianity (and other religions) held many of the characteristics of *communitas*, especially when it retained the centrality of community members as strangers and sojourners in this world, as pilgrims, as travelers, as those with no place to lay their head, but lost those characteristics when it became a part of the institutionalized state or became an institutionalized state of its own. When that happens, in my opinion, the church itself becomes rigid. Rather than providing the wise visionary voice that calls for the periodic reclassification of reality and humankind's relationship to society, nature, and culture, it becomes anxious and attempts to assert itself within the structures of society by means of transactional politics. Ironically, the church, then, ends up closer to the position of Pilate than the position of Jesus and loses its unique power in society as liminal *personae* ("threshold people").

With further irony, it is interesting to someone like Linda Ceriello that some of you as Nones—especially the Spiritual But Not Religious— now represent the position of "betwixt and between" in society or of a *"heterotopic liminality"* where there is a real space lying beyond structured society.[51] Robert Putnam and David Campbell categorize some

---

49. Turner, *Ritual Process*, 108.

50. Turner, *Ritual Process*, 107.

51. Ceriello, "Toward a Metamodern Reading," 210.

of you as "liminal Nones" who are just over the "threshold" of religious affiliation.[52] Could it be that some of you as Nones are now occupying the position of the liminal *personae* or "threshold people" in society? At the very least, in our dialogue, your presence seems to be calling those of us who are Christian across the threshold of the church to see ourselves from the outside and, perhaps, to regain our position as liminal *personae* who have been called to a non-hierarchical *communitas* of agape-love, standing outside of structured society in alignment with the "least of these" and, inspired by a higher vision, continually advocating with the voice of non-violent power for the reclassification of reality and relationships in society.

An Upward Evolutionary Call

It does seem as if we are never finished. Just as the voice of creation never stops and the cries of the people never stop, so also the liminal *personae* are *continually* advocating for a new reality. Even when society heeds our call, it rarely goes far enough, or the success merely allows other imperfections in society to come to light. Suffering may be eliminated here, and it rebounds from unintended consequences over there. One form of government is replaced with another form of government, promising real change. But while the core operating systems/algorithms controlling society change physical hands, the functional "invisible hands" change very little. Even those who are continually advocating for a new reality find that their ability to form *communitas* and live in a "beloved community" is always a work in progress, running parallel with their own inner work to change the core operating systems of their minds—which is never finished! Unintended consequences, an unpredictable turn of events, accidents, storms, or new insights all contribute to the never-ending call to reclassify reality and relationships. Seen pessimistically, this reality can lead to despair. What is the point? Seen in a more favorable light, this unfinished nature of things is a sign of a system that is alive and continually on the move; a dynamic disequilibrium that is inherent to creation.

While change is guaranteed in this dynamic system, unlimited progress is not. Émile Coué's (1857–1926) famous phrase, "Every day in every way I am getting better and better," had relevance for the mental positivists, spiritualists, and science-of-mind practitioners of his day (and ours),

---

52. Putnam and Campbell, *American Grace*, 590–91n56.

but it only went so far in changing the personal core operating systems of the mind. Its application to the whole of society was nearly impossible after two World Wars and the steady downturn of almost all indicators of progress for fifty years after the turbulent 1960s.

But what is progress? Even in its dynamic disequilibrium, does creation have a direction to it or a core organizing principle revealing a fractal-like structure in seemingly chaotic events?[53] Is the continual reclassification of reality and relationships merely random, or is it guided by some higher vision or force? Christian teachings indicate that there is not only a purpose for the game of life but also a purpose and direction for creation itself. As it says in the Epistle to the Ephesians, God "has made known to us the mystery of his will, according to his good pleasure that he set forth in Christ, as a plan for the fullness of time, to gather up all things in him, things in heaven and things on earth" (Eph 1:9–10). Jesus taught about a "kingdom of God" and that one should pray for that kingdom to come "on earth as it is in heaven" (Matt 6:10). The Apostle Paul spoke of transformation "from one degree of glory to another" (2 Cor 3:18) and of an upward goal to which he was moving: "Not that I have already obtained this or have already reached the goal; but I press on to make it my own . . . Beloved, I do not consider that I have made it my own; but this one thing I do: forgetting what lies behind and straining forward to what lies ahead, I press on toward the goal for the prize of the upward call of God in Christ Jesus" (Phil 3:12–14). The writer of Revelation offered a vision of a new heaven and a new earth where all things are made new and God "will wipe every tear from their eyes. Death will be no more; mourning and crying and pain will be no more" (Rev 21:4).

Teachings such as these would indicate that Christians who find themselves in the position of the liminal *personae* have some idea of a higher vision and a progressive upward call when it comes to their continual advocacy for the reclassification of reality and relationships. Just like in a marriage, that higher vision allows them to engage in "conscious suffering"[54] for the benefit of society and creation. Choices made in alignment with that higher vision do not guarantee some predestined package of progress but, as C. S. Lewis said, allows for a "good infection"[55] in

---

53. Delio, *Emergent Christ*, 26.

54. Wellwood, *Love and Awakening*, 8.

55. Lewis, *Mere Christianity*, 183.

society which periodically leads to shifts in evolution itself that no one could have predicted by simply looking at the past.

Building on the work of the Jesuit priest and paleontologist Teilhard de Chardin, Ilia Delio speaks of evolution as a movement toward more complex forms of life. "The foundation of things is not so much a ground of being sustaining its existence from beneath as it is a power of attraction toward *what lies ahead.*"[56] Human beings are a part of a long "biological ascent" toward more complex life forms. "Hence, the human person is not a random event but the arrow of evolution,"[57] and that arrow points toward increasing complexity and consciousness. "It is this inner energy of evolving consciousness that gives evolution its qualitative direction"[58] and that inner energy Teilhard de Chardin defines as Omega—present at the Big Bang and, also, the *goal of evolution*—an Omega point. Delio goes on to say,

> David Bohm speaks of a quantum potential in nature that underscores unbroken wholeness of the entire universe despite quantum fluctuations. Omega is like the quantum potential in that it subsists throughout nature as the centrating principle or the principle of integrated wholeness. It is present from the beginning of the Big Bang and is the goal of evolution, according to Teilhard . . . [who] identified this deep personal presence of centrating energy—Omega—with the ultimate depth of love we name God.[59]

In the midst of all the fluctuations of creation and the unfinished nature of our human experience, then, there is a call to move "from glory to glory," a "straining forward to what lies ahead" in an alignment with the "inner energy of evolving consciousness" that has a "qualitative direction" revealed clearly in Christ as love, the God-Omega-Love, the beginning and the end, the "centrating energy" that is like the quantum potential in nature providing unbroken wholeness despite all apparent fluctuations.

That is to say, there is a clear "qualitative direction" brought by the liminal *personae* in the *continual* advocacy for the reclassification of reality and relationships, which is a *continual* attempt to bring their lives, the life of their community, the life of society, the life of all the world

56. Delio, *Unbearable Wholeness*, 18.

57. Delio, *Unbearable Wholeness*, 21.

58. Delio, *Unbearable Wholeness*, 39.

59. Delio, *Unbearable Wholeness*, 41.

into alignment with the centrating principle of all creation and the arrow of evolution. But while we as liminal *personae* may have some vision of a "plan for the fullness of time," it is still a "mystery" (Eph 1:9–10) at any given point in time. We know and we do not know at the same time. We know when something does not align with love and the fruit of the Spirit—whether personally, politically, or ecologically—but it may remain a mystery to be worked out how exactly alignment will take place. We know when our actions, or the underlying forces of society, produce anger, hatred, violence, or injustice. But it may remain a mystery how exactly those forces will be transformed. Like the artist, we may have some idea of where the painting or the sculpture or the novel is going, but creativity happens in the not knowing and in the evolving of the work of art guided by a sense of beauty, truth, or goodness—an underlying grammar that is applied moment-to-moment in the creative process.

The Christian teaching would say, in my opinion, that in any circumstance—whether personal, political, or ecological—we must learn to listen for a resonance with the centrating principle of creation, and this, more than any predetermined stage development or vision of an apocalyptic ending, guides our every thought and action, making us participatory co-creators in an ongoing creation.[60] By way of a parable, Jesus says that the sheep know the voice of the Shepherd, and it is the ones who know and hear that voice, whether they are sheep from our fold or from other unknown folds (John 10:4, 26), who are at-one with the Word that has been spoken since the beginning of creation and spoken again in the Christ (John 1:1–3). That voice is the voice of light and love. It is that voice we learn to hear and allow to reverberate through all our thoughts and actions, thus aligning our very Selves with the heart of the unfolding creation. We know that voice, and we know when other voices are not in alignment with that voice. Yet, we often do not know how that voice will be heard in all creation or in what way those of other unknown folds are hearing that voice better than we are.

This is the true "betwixt and between" position of the liminal *personae*: to be between knowing and humbly not knowing. On the one hand, we align ourselves with the centrating energy which is the very voice of creation, and we know that voice. On the other hand, in order to know that voice, we have to empty ourselves of most other things we have come to know as we wait in the wordless silence for what is about to

60. Ferrer and Vickery, "Transpersonal Psychology," 226.

emerge in creation around us and within us—and we really do not know what that will be. Again, somewhat like the creative sound that emerges between the vocal folds of our own voice box in vibration with each other, new creation comes into existence with a resonance that emerges between knowing and not knowing, between revealed and not yet revealed, between already and not yet, between inside and outside, between material and spiritual, between heaven and earth, between human and divine. Using another metaphor, N. T. Wright says that we become "tabernacle people" who carry within them the ancient temple where God would meet with humankind. He says that this is how the Apostle Paul saw his mission, having himself encountered the coming together of God and humankind in Christ. He says that Paul "saw his vocation in terms of bringing into being 'places'—humans, one by one and collectively—in which heaven and earth would come together and be, yes, *reconciled*."[61] We stand "betwixt and between" heaven and earth.

In the betweenness, there is a point where something opens beyond us. Perhaps this is a nexus point, or an Omega point, or a threshold point for threshold people. We make ourselves available to this by training ourselves to hear the sighs or groans too deep for words practiced in moment-to-moment awareness and the wordless silence of apophatic praying. In the betweenness (as we saw in chapter 5), there comes an arcing of light which is a new creation. It is always a gift. We know it, but we never know what to expect. In a similar way, Thomas Merton says,

> Again, that expression, *le point vierge* (I cannot translate it) comes in here. At the center of our being is a point of nothingness which is untouched by sin and by illusion, a point of pure truth, a point or spark which belongs entirely to God, which is never at our disposal from which God disposes of our lives, which is inaccessible to the fantasies of our own mind or the brutalities of our own will. This little point of nothingness and of *absolute poverty* is the pure glory of God in us. It is so to speak his name written in us, as our poverty, as our indigence, as our dependence, as our son-ship. It is like a pure diamond, blazing with the invisible light of heaven. It is in everybody, and if we could see it we would see these billions of points of light coming together in the face and blaze of a sun that would make all the darkness and cruelty of life vanish completely . . . I have no

61. Wright, *Paul*, 1493.

program for this seeing. It is only given. But the gate of heaven
is everywhere.[62]

Those who experience this "betwixt and between" point are truly
liminal *personae*—"threshold people." They continually stand on the
threshold of transformation in their own lives but also on the threshold
of reclassifying reality and relationships in society and on the threshold
of heaven and earth. They are continually "straining forward to what lies
ahead" in what Gregory of Nyssa (AD 335–95) called a "stretching out
ahead" to a limitless Good that continues even after this life to an ultimate reconciliation of all things.[63]

Some of those "threshold people" may be standing over the threshold
of the church door on the inside. Some may be standing over the threshold
of that same door on the outside. There may be some who hear the voice of
the Shepherd who "do not belong to this fold" (John 10:16), those whom
we consider to be on the outside. What seems most important is whether
one hears the voice of the Shepherd and is aligned with the voice of light
and love that is the "centrating principle" of creation. Ilia Delio sees a new
spirituality emerging today that is a deepening of consciousness,

> a consciousness of whole-making that invites greater unity,
> forgiveness, reconciliation, peace, charity, kindness, mercy, and
> compassion. It is a new *zeitgeist* of Christ in evolution, a new
> breath of the Spirit. The reign of God is coming into the world
> not only through the front doors of a church but increasingly
> through human hearts outside the doors of the church.[64]

Like strange attractors that, according to chaos theory, first appear
as signs of disorder (such as Nones leaving the church in large numbers),
what is really happening is an emerging new order with fractal-like resonance in "basins of attraction, transcending institutional religion" where
there are "patterns of sharing, community, cooperation, mutuality, healing,
justice, and peace"[65] that follow the pattern of Christ. Delio goes on to say,

> They are quietly hidden throughout the world; they do not make
> the headlines because they are simply fostering goodness in the
> world, helping the world to evolve toward greater unity in love.
> Those who seek to be part of these new basins of attraction are

---

62. Merton, *Conjectures*, 155–56.

63. Meredith, *Gregory of Nyssa*, 22.

64. Delio, *Emergent Christ*, 144.

65. Delio, *Emergent Christ*, 145.

open to new ways of being in the world; they are not threatened by new relationships, nor do they fear loss of their individuality. Rather, their oneness of being opens them up to dialogue and sharing with others different from themselves. They desire to be whole-makers, to live cooperatively and compassionately, to share the energies and resources of life.[66]

Perhaps Nones and Somes in dialogue can become those liminal *personae* who stand on the threshold of an emerging new order together as "strange attractors," advocating for the reclassification of reality and relationships. As we pass over and come back in dialogue, perhaps we can experience moments of deep listening without fear of silence. And in the silence, perhaps we can hear the "sighs too deep for words," which is the very grammar of the interdependent, interconnected, and interbeing system of creation whose story continues to unfold. And then, we can find ourselves standing on the threshold where new stories are created and where the ascent of humankind is nudged ever so slightly upward.

66. Delio, *Emergent Christ*, 145.

Epilogue
On the Threshold of Possibility

*I am an old man full of love. I am a man of faith. But faith
is not necessarily, or not soon, a resting place. Faith puts you
out on a wide river in a little boat, in the fog, in the dark.*

—JAYBER CROW[1]

Something's Happening

MY NINETY-FIVE-YEAR-OLD MENTOR IN Scotland used to say that the
best translation for the Tetragrammaton (YHWH), revealed as the name
of G-d in Exodus 3:14, was not "I am who I am" or "I will be who I will
be" but "*Something is happening!*" because it captured the dynamic, ongoing creative Being of G-d.[2] When I think about my dialogue with you as
a None, I must admit that I have been attracted to this dialogue because
your increased presence in our society is indicative of something important happening. Given the number of books already written about you as
a None, as well as research papers written, sociological surveys collected,
blogs sent, and sermons preached, it would seem that I am not the only
one who thinks something is happening.

The basic fact that something is happening is not all that unusual or
remarkable. If we ask *why* something is happening, the simple answer is
because things are always happening; it is part of a creative system that
is alive; it is inherent in the Being of creation. Even if we look at what

1. Berry, *Jayber Crow*, 356.
2. Rushforth, *Something Is Happening*, 3.

is happening by the numbers—namely, with the percentage increase of you as Nones in the general population—it is not particularly unusual or remarkable and may simply be a recalibration of what has always been. As Robert Putnam points out, "At the time of the Revolution fewer than one in five Americans were members of any religious body, and the figure had risen to only 34 percent by 1850."[3] He goes on to say that by the end of the nineteenth century most Americans in their daily lives were "unchurched" or "churchless." "Like contemporary religious 'Nones,' those who profess no religious identity, these secular Americans were not necessarily unbelievers, but they were unattached to religious institutions by membership, attendance, or contributions."[4] In 1910, it was reported by some that only 43 percent of the total population claimed any church affiliation, "and a *Washington Post* article in 1909 offered a very similar estimate that the unchurched population in America 'probably outnumbers our church members in the proportion of about three to two.'"[5] What may be remarkable in American history was the dramatic increase in religious affiliation that reached nearly 80 percent in the late 1950s. "The tsunami of religious involvement during the 1950s was massive, reaching levels probably unrivaled in American history."[6]

So why is the "something happening" attributed to you as a None being perceived as so important? Perhaps it is because as a religiously unaffiliated None you are—at least in the minds of the religiously affiliated Somes—representative of and connected to many other changes that are happening in our society and world at this time. In a graph that charts the well-being of America in terms of economics, politics, society, and culture, Robert Putnam demonstrates that all the hard measures over the last one hundred years show a progressive increase from the 1890s until the mid-1960s. Then, from the mid-1960s until now—even with increased material comfort for many—the major indicators of stability have declined. The graph appears as an "inverted U," and Putnam calls it the "I-We-I" chart because along with the progress and decline is a parallel movement from individualism to progressive community engagement—focused on what we can do together—and back to individual rights and focus on the Self. He says,

3. Putnam, *Upswing*, 128.
4. Putnam, *Upswing*, 129.
5. Putnam, *Upswing*, 129.
6. Putnam, *Upswing*, 134.

Over the first six decades of the twentieth century America had become demonstrably—indeed measurably—a more "we" society. But then, as the foregoing graph indicates, and those who lived through that period know too well, in the mid-1960s the decades-long upswing in our shared economic, political, social, and cultural life abruptly reversed direction. America suddenly found itself in the midst of a clear downturn. Between the mid-1960s and today—by scores of hard measures along multiple dimensions—we have been experiencing *declining* economic equality, the *deterioration* of compromise in the public square, a *fraying* social fabric, and a *descent* into cultural narcissism.[7]

Since the charting of religious affiliation in America follows this same "inverted U" over the last one hundred years, as a None you may be representing far greater trends in society—at least in the minds of those who evaluate life through the lens of spirituality. Putnam suggests that we may be poised for another "upswing," similar to what happened in the first half of the twentieth century. But, as he says, it will depend on how we choose to come together, and religious organizations have always been one of the major ways in which we have come together. Hence, the "something" that is "happening" with you as a None takes on a great degree of importance as we are poised for an upswing—or not.

And the upswing—or not—is happening in a far larger context. Something may always be happening in creation, but there are "pivotal points" when the "happening" is more intense. The universe is always expanding, but sometimes planets collide. The mountain is always eroding, but sometimes the volcano erupts. The glacier is always moving, but sometimes it does so at a dramatic rate. Our physical bodies are always changing, but sometimes things unexpectantly grow or break. Society is always fluctuating, but at times there are revolutions. Relationships are always changing, but at times there are breakthroughs or breakdowns. Our minds are constantly processing sensory data, but sometimes there is sensory overload or radical shifts in how we organize the material in our minds.

When these changes happen to us as individuals, it is hard enough. When they happen to us collectively, the anxiety in society is palpable. Throw in a pandemic and videos of police brutality along with the hard measures of decline, and the anxiety goes "through the roof." Whether we are poised for a societal upswing, or for a change in cosmic consciousness

7. Putnam, *Upswing*, 11.

and the coming of the Second Axial Age, or for the "shattering of our carapaces" in a five-hundred-year cycle of change, or at a tipping point in evolution, *something is happening.* Which way will the society and the creation pivot? Somehow your increased presence as a None at this time seems to be connected to this question—at least in the minds of the religiously affiliated—and, hence, what is happening with you as a None seems far more important than a simple recalibration to previous levels of religiosity in America. In the minds of some who are religiously affiliated, your increased presence may be associated with other hard measures of decline in society and with an anxious trajectory of further decline, pivoting further down and not swinging up. And even if we are poised for an upswing (whatever that means!), your presence represents the uncertain period of waiting when nothing seems to be happening and we are in the great unknown—like being "on a wide river in a little boat, in the fog, in the dark."[8]

Beyond that, your increased presence as a religiously unaffiliated None calls into question the primary coping strategy that humanity uses in times of social upheaval and pivotal points of change. In times of such significant change, people usually turn to religion to make meaning of what is happening and to help in the regulation of anxiety. What happens if an increasing number of people do not turn to religion in a time when something is happening, and anxiety is high? For instance, the Black church, in times of social unrest, has always provided the strength and leadership necessary for African Americans to meet the challenges of injustice. What happens now when the #BlackLivesMatter movement is as much about voices coming from outside the Black church as it is about forces coming from inside the church? Or, as another example, since the 1700s, in times of social unrest White America has almost always turned to a pietistic form of Protestant Christianity not only for solace but also as a *de facto* state church giving power and a cohesive identity to the nation, complete with mythological stories about the faith of past and present leaders. What happens if White Evangelical Christianity loses its control of the national narrative in a time of great personal and social anxiety?

And that is also *why* your increased presence as a None in a time of "something is happening" takes on far more importance than a simple recalibration of the numbers of the religiously affiliated in America: your existence and the doubts to which you give voice call into question the

---

8. Berry, *Jayber Crow*, 356.

core meaning-making narratives that we have believed about our Selves, about our nation, about our religion, and about our God. This is *what* is happening, and it contributes to *why* your increased presence as a None is given such importance. You are helping to make the invisible stories become visible. You are exposing the contradictions in those stories. You are giving us the opportunity to evaluate the stories we tell ourselves about our Selves, often accompanied by the pain of seeing that these stories, associated with our core identity, may not be completely true or may be shockingly true in ways we did not realize.

For instance, the Black church now must look more closely at the level of diversity it will accept within its walls and with the nature of patriarchal leadership that has often held tight control.[9] The White church must examine its entangled church-state narratives about power, inclusive of deconstructing narratives about the Founding Fathers as pious evangelicals instead of the deists most were[10] and whose religion has borne fruit in the moral therapeutic deism[11] so prevalent today. Or perhaps Christians need to come to grips with how the unprecedented rise in the numbers of the religiously affiliated in the 1950s is less a story about transformational religion and more a story about expressing one's civic duty in the joining of any club, such as the Rotary, Kiwanis, Lions, Elks, Moose, or Odd Fellows, which so many did at that time. Robert Putnam says,

> It was not simply religious fervor that brought people to church in postwar America. For many of the families packing the pews, religious attendance was less an act of piety than an act of civic duty, like joining the PTA or Rotary, whose membership rolls, as we just saw, were also exploding in these same years. Religion represented the unifying theme of national purpose or what sociologist Robert Bellah would later term "civil religion."[12]

As Sydney Ahlstrom points out, this civil religion was a unique blend of general religiosity and self-satisfied patriotic moralism symbolized in the deistic statement of President Dwight D. Eisenhower when he said in

9. Gates, *Black Church.*
10. Mapp, *Faiths of Our Fathers.*
11. Dean, *Almost Christian.*
12. Putnam, *Upswing,* 135.

1954, "Our government makes no sense unless it is founded on a deeply felt religious faith—*and I don't care what it is.*"[13]

The point here is not to deny the reality of significant personal stories of religious transformation in the 1950s or the importance that people of faith can bring to government, but that the narratives underlying the way we think about religion in America may need to be reevaluated. This is part of the "something" that is "happening." This is *why* the increased presence of the Nones at this pivotal point in history is important.

For Christians, this actually increases the anxiety of the present moment, to which we can respond in several ways. We can play the victim and lament that the secularists combined with big government are trying to take away our faith. We can go on the defensive and double down on the narratives we have constructed about our religion and its role in society, running the risk of authoritarian solutions and rigid reinforcement of highly selective beliefs supported by theologies that sacralize violence and predict apocalyptic futures (more of a "backswing" than an "upswing"). Or we can do the spiritual work necessary to tolerate the anxiety of the pivotal moment, allow the stories we have told ourselves about our Selves, our religion, and our society to come to light for evaluation, and position ourselves as co-creators in an exciting time of "something is happening" as we wait for the revealing of still hidden truths necessary to revise our stories.

What's the Story Going to Be

Of course, in the heightened anxiety of pivotal moments we would like some futurist—or, even better, God or end-time stories written in the name of God—to tell us what the story is going to be. In ancient Israel, if one wanted to get a word from God about what to do or what to expect at a pivotal moment, one would go to a "seer." As the society developed, the "seers" became known as "prophets" (a speaker or spokesperson), as we see in the Hebrew Scriptures where it says, "Formerly in Israel, anyone who went to inquire of God would say, 'Come, let us go to the seer'; for the one who is now called a prophet was formerly called a seer" (1 Sam 9:9). As my seminary professor repeatedly reminded those of us in class, the prophets were more *forthtellers* than *foretellers*, helping people to make meaning of their current circumstances in the context

---

13. Ahlstrom, *Religious History*, 954, italics added.

of a far bigger picture about human life and purpose. To some extent, in the history of Israel, the focus shifted from what the prophet could "see" to how the prophet could "speak" in such a way that the *people* could "see and hear." For example, the prophet Isaiah was given a paradoxical message to proclaim to the people, saying, "Keep listening, but do not comprehend; keep looking, but do not understand" (Isa 6:9), meaning that if the people's lack of hearing and seeing persisted long enough, it would produce dire consequences that actually engendered a readiness to see and hear. Jesus quotes this passage from Isaiah when he explains why he must speak to the people in parables. He says, "The reason I speak to them in parables is that 'seeing they do not perceive, and hearing they do not listen, nor do they understand'" (Matt 13:13). But his ultimate goal was to produce disciples who could see and hear, as he goes on to say to his followers, "Blessed are your eyes, for they see, and your ears, for they hear" (Matt 13:16).

All of this indicates that our goal in the current pivotal moment is not so much to find the right futurist or prophet to follow, but *how* to be disciples of seeing and hearing, and *how* to develop places of seeing and hearing for all. What is the *process* by which we learn to see, hear, and understand in new ways? Maybe the question about "What's the story going to be?" is more importantly connected to "*How's* the story going to change?" and *how* at this pivotal point in history we can be fully present at the very "point" where our eyes and ears have the possibility of being opened and where hidden truths emerge for our eyes to see and our ears to hear.

The story is told that when the indigenous people on the Caribbean islands first encountered the ships of Christopher Columbus anchored offshore at a distance, they were unable to see the ships because there was no knowledge in their brain that would allow for a mental association. What existed on the horizon simply did not compute in their brains. One person from the tribe, who held the role of a shaman, first saw strange ripples on the water but no ships. Using his gifts as a spiritual seer, he continued to focus on the ripples in the water until a new reality emerged before his very eyes and he saw the ships. He then brought others to the shore and led them in the process of seeing. Because they trusted him, they, too, eventually were able to see the ships on the horizon. And in that seeing, their entire world changed.[14]

14. *What the Bleep.*

Christopher Columbus's westward voyage across the Atlantic Ocean was a great exercise in changing the way people see. Not only did the Caribbean people have their eyes opened to a new world, so did the European people who moved from a "flat-earth" understanding of the world to something more concentric. Now all of their stories about falling off the edge of the earth or what was under the earth had to change. And even though Christopher Columbus had already come to see the earth as round even before he made his voyage, when he looked out from his boat toward the Caribbean islands, he was not able to completely see either. He thought that he was seeing East Asia and mistakenly called the natives "Indians." Neither did he see the Caribbean natives as complete people, retaining his own flat-earth way of seeing the land of others as something to be conquered in pursuit of the ultimate vision of finding gold and spices and the concomitant fame and fortune.

I wonder how all of our stories would be different if Christopher Columbus had brought with him a shaman, a prophet, or a seer, and, as he looked out from the deck of the *Pinta*, allowed the seer to teach him to see what he could not see. What if the seer could have taught him to focus his attention long enough and deep enough to see the riches of a people who had something to teach him? What if the seer could have taught him a process of seeing and hearing in which those with new seeing on the Caribbean island and those with new seeing on the decks of the *Niña, Pinta,* and *Santa Maria* created together new stories of concentric wholeness that would supersede flat-earth stories of division and domination? And what if the *process* of seeing and hearing had a spiritual resonance to it commensurate with discoveries made by explorers of faith and following the "pioneer and perfector of faith," instead of the spiritual dissonance created by a religion in collusion with the explorers of empire whose imposed stories of faith at times resonated more with conquest than with agape-love?

Perhaps now, five-hundred-plus years later, we are being asked to leave behind our flat-earth theories in a way that Christopher Columbus never could; to see what he could not see; to engage in a *process* of seeing and hearing for which his culture and his religion did not prepare him. Could it be that this "something is happening" moment in which we find ourselves is about *how* we see and *how* we come to change the position from which we see? Or could it be about *how* we change the narrative filters by which we sort the two thousand bits of information that our brains are processing every minute?

Like Christopher Columbus and the explorers who came after him, we have been able to physically change the way we see the earth through redrawn maps of the world and through technological advances that have allowed us to see under the earth, under the oceans, and into the heavens. We can now step back and see how the systems of the earth work, such as weather patterns that are global and not just local. We can now step back and see the earth from the perspective of someone on the moon looking back at a beautiful whole, or from the eye of a telescope that gives us the perspective of being on a very small planet in the midst of an unimaginably large universe that continues to expand.

But also like Christopher Columbus, we have done very little to change our narrative filters of conquest, fame, and glory, driven by our ego-defenses and evidenced very clearly in the way we treat others, the way we see others, or the way we fail to see others—especially those whom we perceive as different. We have been slow to develop and adopt spiritual technologies that would free us from our basic ancestral passions and change the way we relationally see others, God, the creation, and our very Selves as fully human. Religion has often been complicit here—when it is in collusion with conquest, defers to domination, transmits transactional theologies of violence, and dangles the keys of hell in our face while withholding the keys of heaven. This is the kind of religion that you have walked away from as a None, while many Somes hold on to something just over the threshold barely inside the church door. And in your walking away, you are helping to expose the pivotal moment and the "something is happening" for the church (I can only speak from my unique perspective as a Christian)—namely, a moment in which the church steps back and sees itself and its task from a different perspective in such a way that it is freed from its transactional captivity and cultural collusion; freed to offer a path of transformation; and freed to lead in the co-creation of new stories that resonate with the "centrating energy"[15] of creation itself.

For instance, could the church step back and see itself not solely as the defender of dogma but as the pedagogue of interior process? Could it be that our understanding of faith as a doctrinal confession of "faith *in* Jesus Christ" needs to be balanced with our *process* understanding of what was the "faith *of* Jesus Christ" (especially since the translation of a key passage like Rom 3:22 can be translated either way)? How would it

---

15. Delio, *Unbearable Wholeness*, 41.

affect our "seeing" if we balanced our doctrinal understanding of Jesus' definition of himself as "the way, the truth, and the life" (John 14:6) with a *process* understanding of Jesus as a teacher of a particular path that can be followed, leading to a particular way of life that resonates with irreducible transcendentals such as truth?

Are we being called in this pivotal moment to shift the way in which we understand "the Way"? And would this not be in the spiritual sense tantamount to what Christopher Columbus did in the physical sense of moving us from a flat-earth view of the world, but now seeing what he could not see? It is as if we are being called to shift our attention from the maps that serve as parameters and signposts along the Way (i.e., the doctrines and confessions) to the way in which we walk along the Way, which, when it is the Way of Jesus, requires a certain cadence to the step, a certain attitude toward walking in the Way, and a certain qualitative desire that provides a particular energy for walking in the Way. It is not that the doctrines and confessions are unimportant, but when we focus too much on the parameters and the signposts, we can end up shifting our energy to debate what the signposts mean, or even setting up our tent and driving in our tent stakes at the signpost we see as most important. This creates a certain immobility along the Way. Ironically, when we do this, we can be on the path but not on the Way—i.e., not moving on the Way, which is intended to be a way of walking in life that has a certain cadence, energy, or resonance to it.

Evidence for how we are walking—if we are walking—in the Way comes from our relationships. It comes from all our relationships—with ourselves, with others, with God, with the creation. It requires a major shift of our attention to move from focusing on the signposts to becoming aware of how we are relating to everything around us and within us. This would be like Christopher Columbus thinking about having a compassionate dialogue with the native islanders of the Caribbean rather than focusing his attention on indicators of where the physical gold and spices might be. In the Christian Scriptures, Jesus is often encouraging the disciples to pay attention, to be awake, to be watchful (for example, Matt 24:42, 25:13). The Apostle Paul often exhorts the early Christian communities to be awake and sober (for example, 1 Thess 5:6). In every case, the call to be awake, to pay attention, and to be watchful has to do with focusing their awareness on how they are walking in their lives with reference to their relationship to God, to others in their community, to the least of these, and to their inner hearts and minds. Similarly, in our relationships we are called to pay attention, and like the shaman looking out from the Caribbean island and noticing ripples on the water, we, too, are called to notice the ripples in our relationships—the cracks, the inconsistencies, the ambivalence, the pain, the nonsense, or the joy, the love, the harmony—until we begin to see things that we have never seen before.

Jacob Needleman suggests that this ability to shift our attention and to pay attention has been lost in Christianity and is a necessary intermediate step before we can ever hope to walk in the Way of Jesus. He says, "And the bridge, the intermediate work, has to do with this factor of attention, awareness, presence."[16] And, like Jesus and the Apostle Paul, he says that this attention comes from a way of praying that, on the one hand, opens one to a deep inner stillness, but, on the other hand, opens one to the deep suffering of the world. It is a prayer of the heart with "sighs too deep for words." In his words:

> This attention of the heart, this quietness within movement is actually another, intimate movement that spontaneously arises in the moment between life and death, when the ego is wounded and God is still distant; this attention *is* prayer in the sense of the Psalmist who asks, and asks, and asks; it is that which watches and waits in the night.[17]

This prayer becomes prayer "without ceasing" (1 Thess 5:17) in that it brings a constant shift of attention to the way we are walking in the Way with a particular focus on our relationships and with a particular awareness of themes like agape-love and suffering, which have repeatedly been revealed as resonating with the very core of creation. As Daniel Siegel says, "Where attention goes, neural firing flows and neural connection grows"[18] to the point that the brain changes, the instinctual ancestral passions are rewired, and there is freedom from the ego-mind. And since the mind is a narrating mind, it now brings a grammar to all of the stories we create; stories that resonate with the core of creation and influence our way of interacting and understanding moment-by-moment on the Way.

I think that what has happened increasingly since the 1960s when the "inverted U" began its downturn—at least from a spiritual perspective—is that those of you who identify as Nones have noticed when religion has lost its resonance with the core centrating energies of creation. You have

16. Needleman, *Lost Christianity*, 158.
17. Needleman, *Lost Christianity*, 165.
18. Siegel, *Mind*, 179.

noticed when religious practitioners have failed to attend to the ripples on the water of their relationships—all their relationships—and failed to advocate for a *process* of change. And your very presence is calling those of us who identify as Somes to pay attention, to revise our stories, and to shift our understanding of what is at the heart of the story about the Way. If this is true, it is not unlike what happened when the Apostle Paul made significant revisions to the Jewish story of covenantal theology in light of his experience of a risen Christ. In so doing, he indicated at one point that those *outside* of the Jewish faith—that is, the "uncircumcised" or the "gentile"—might be keeping the spiritual commandments better than those *inside* the faith, or that the outsiders may be the true people of circumcision because their hearts are circumcised "and real circumcision is a matter of the heart—it is spiritual and not literal" (Rom 2:29). Coming, as you do, from a position "outside the faith," I wonder if your presence as a None is calling us to revise our covenantal theology again in ways that incorporate new twenty-first-century understanding with eternal resonances of the heart.

In our dialogue, perhaps we can work together in applying this resonating grammar to the new stories we are creating. Building on the work of Stephen Pinker, Jonathan Sacks relays the story about professional linguists who studied pidgin English, originally used by slaves:

> A pidgin has words but not grammar, vocabulary but no syntax. What the linguists had discovered, to their amazement, is that the children of pidgin speakers had created their own new language, called a creole, which is pidgin plus grammar. Their parents had been robbed of a language, but they, without even knowing what they were doing, had simply invented one.[19]

Whether we identify as Somes or Nones, we often come to a way of life with words, concepts, or ideas, but no grammar that brings a resonance and harmony to the inner and outer language by which we make meaning of the world. If we are willing to enter a state of childlike humility, perhaps we, too, might invent a new language for new stories, coming from a place of unknowing where there is a revealing of still hidden truths.

19. Sacks, *Morality*, 19.

On the Threshold of Possibility

On a recent visit to Charleston, South Carolina, I went to explore the marketplace in Old Charleston. Walking along North Market Street, I saw an interesting church that warranted further investigation. But as I got closer to the church, I could see that it was no longer a church. It was a peculiar experience when I opened the door of the church, crossed over the threshold, and found myself standing simultaneously on the inside of a beautiful old church and on the inside of what was now a restaurant that goes by the name of "5Church Charleston." I noticed a large five-dollar bill painted on one wall of the church under the stained glass window where the sacristy once was. Looking up to the scissor-trussed ceiling, I could see where all thirteen chapters of the fifth-century manuscript by Sun Tzu entitled *The Art of War* were transcribed by the artist Jon Norris. Why? Because, according to the owners, it serves as the company's mission statement and holds within it inspiration and theory that can be applied to everyday life.

As I sat down to eat, I wondered about the possible meaning of this church-cum-restaurant from the perspective of those of you who are Nones. At least from the perspective of those of you who identify as Spiritual But Not Religious, this seems to be the perfect "church"; something of a Nones' paradise. It is the perfect place for a spirituality that prioritizes what Elizabeth Drescher found among American Nones to be "The Four F's of Contemporary American Spirituality: Family, Fido, Friends, and Food"[20] (yes, Fido can wait outside with water). It seems to be a great spiritual meeting house, imbued with the spirit of an arcane Eastern spirituality on its ceiling which is operationalized in the business model of those who welcome and serve you. But also, it is a place providing art, humor, and intellectual challenge coming from the inspiration of Jon Norris, who has cleverly woven into the ancient Eastern manuscript on the ceiling lyrics from Pink Floyd's "Dogs of War" as well as quotes from Allen Ginsberg's "Howl" and the Simpsons. In addition, he painted his own philosophy, "War is the coward's excuse to escape from the responsibility of peace," into the roots of a tree that rises to the ceiling.

Even further are the unwritten challenges in this spiritual meeting house that seem to speak accurately to the growing edges that Nones might bring to the table. For instance, the artist's intention of having the manuscript written on the ceiling is to get people to look up from their

20. Drescher, *Choosing Our Religion*, 44.

iPhones and to instigate meaningful conversations around the table. Behind the placement of the work of art is an invisible story that speaks to the need for those in a technological culture to change the way they relate to each other and to the world around them. Those of you who identify as Nones are strong advocates for a spirituality of relationships with family and friends, but there is an appropriate challenge hidden in this spiritual meeting house to look more closely at the nature of those relationships. What would it be like to put down one's iPhone and have a conversation about the way technology helps or hinders our relationships? Or what would it be like to go deeper with relational questions such as, "How do relationships change, how precisely does one define a healthy relationship toward which one might grow, or how close do we want our relationships to be?"

Still further, around the tables Nones might want to ask about other invisible stories that reside in the spiritual atmosphere of this church-cum-restaurant, such as how the Eastern philosophy written on the ceiling has been Americanized to inform a business model in a consumer culture, and how Sun Tzu himself missed much of what the Taoist philosopher Lao Tzu had meant to convey when he turned Lao Tzu's philosophy into a strategy for war. Could the conversation move beyond a casual interest in Eastern spiritualities that have been woven into an anti-religious sentiment? Could there be an investigation of the deeper meaning of those spiritualities and ways in which they might interact with deeper aspects of many religions? How might those deeper investigations bring to light the most fundamental meaning-making stories of our lives and the grammar that holds those stories together, inclusive of the dangers inherent in removing angry religious gods and unwittingly replacing them with far more oppressive cultural and personal gods residing in the shadows of our automatic beliefs or in the power of whatever is trending now in the culture?

But also, as I sat down to eat, I wondered about the possible meaning of this church-cum-restaurant from the perspective of those of us who are Somes, especially Christian Somes. There are plenty of reminders in this spiritual meeting house of the importance of a sacred meal at the heart of Christian worship, of fellowship around a table that builds a new community, and of beauty that incorporates the transcendent. But there are also challenges to Christians sitting in a church that is now a restaurant. I wondered what led to the closure of the Church of the Redeemer, which previously occupied this space. What happened to the Harriet

Pinckney Home for Seamen, which at one time was a thriving mission of this church? What are the invisible stories that reside in the walls of this church building? Perhaps the five-dollar bill painted on the wall behind the former sacristy is a haunting symbol of dwindling income and failed budgets that led to the sale of the church property. Did the spirituality of true connection around a sacred meal evaporate in quarrels over dogma or anxious conversations about their survival as a church? Did they fail to look up or look out? Did they fail to shift their mission when demographics changed or when the dock location changed and the seamen were further away? Did they not know how to engage in dialogue with those in the marketplace just outside their door in the way that the Apostle Paul engaged the religions, philosophies, and cultures of his day in the ancient marketplaces? (I later learned that the Charleston Port and Seafarers Society now carries out the mission of the Harriet Pinckney Home for Seamen in various terminal locations.)

It is a strange experience to be on the threshold while standing in the doorway of a church-cum-restaurant at 32b North Market Street in Charleston, South Carolina. If I look into the building, I see a church *and* I see a restaurant. Inside is a restaurant and not a church operationally, but it is *not* not-a-church. Looking outside I see a marketplace, but I wonder if that is the church. It is technically not a church, but it *not* not-a-church. It is technically not a marketplace for true dialogue, but it is *not* not-a-marketplace for true dialogue. Which then leads me to wonder what is the threshold on which I am standing. Physically I am standing on the threshold of a building, but spiritually it is something more. It is *not* not-the-threshold of a physical doorway. But, also, it is *not* not-a-spiritual-threshold that opens to infinite creative possibilities. This is not the "gate of heaven" experienced by Jacob at Bethel when he said, "'Surely the Lord is in this place—and I did not know it!' And he was afraid, and said, 'How awesome is this place! This is none other than the house of God, and this is the gate of heaven'" (Gen 28:16b–17). But it is *not* not-the-gate of heaven.

This physical threshold produces for me a threshold moment which follows the "apophatic logic of double negation."[21] Building on the theology of Nicholas of Cusa (1401–61), William Franke says it is "a logic of double negation that admits a third term besides A and not-A, namely,

---

21. Franke, *Universality of What Is Not*, 117.

not-not-A, emerges and replaces, or at least displaces binary logic."[22] This is, then, an apophatic threshold that opens to something that is universal. It is where "the universal opens up from within divisions and annuls their discriminatory and exclusionary limits."[23] It is a threshold that cuts across differences—like the Apostle Paul did when he said there is no male or female, slave or free, Gentile or Jew (see Gal 3:28)—"so as to cut them open: they are no longer dichotomies of mutually exclusive terms. Instead, each term is broken open to *another* difference that is absolute and not relative to its opposite, not the counterpart of a binary."[24] It is a threshold of double negation that opens to a "*positive* modality of freedom."[25] It is a threshold of freedom from limited language and from constructed stories of difference and defense which opens us to an infinite possibility beyond words.

To some extent, in the dialogue we have been having between you as a None and me as a Christian Some (and which others have been overhearing), we have been operating as if we are standing on either side of a church doorway. It is as if we are standing on either side of a threshold with Nones culturally defined as outside and Somes culturally defined as inside. But perhaps what the current pivotal moment requires of us is to dialogue in such a way that both of us end up standing on the threshold together until the binary logic disappears and we find ourselves standing on a threshold that is much greater than a church door. On that threshold, Somes are not Nones, but they are often *not* not-Nones in their own inner questioning and doubts necessary for transformation. And on that threshold Nones are not Somes, but they are often *not* not-Somes in their prioritizing of relationships or their desire for truth. And if we can stand on that threshold—a threshold where we need each other to create this "not-not" experience—maybe we will find an opening to a "betwixt and between" place where we often must "sigh" because it is too deep for words. And in the sighing, we find ourselves resonating with *something* that is unspeakable yet *happens* to hold all things together and is pregnant with the possibility of revealing still hidden truths.

Perhaps we are already standing on that threshold and, like the prophet or seer, can see "ripples on the water" indicative of new possibilities that are emerging. As Nones, you are in the position of being able to

22. Franke, *Universality of What Is Not*, 116.
23. Franke, *Universality of What is Not*, 117.
24. Franke, *Universality of What Is Not*, 117–18.
25. Franke, *Universality of What is Not*, 117.

see what the church cannot see and to shed light upon uncomfortable hidden realities lying in the shadows of its policies and proclamations. In this, you are *not* not-the-church because this is something that is required of a healthy church. Perhaps the growing edge for you as a None is to apply this same questioning curiosity to the culture, to your relationships, to your inner Self in a way that takes you beyond any position that is defined simply by being against something or that so values free choice to the point of being unable to choose. As G. K. Chesterton allegedly said, "Merely having an open mind is nothing. The object of opening the mind, as of opening the mouth, is to shut it again on something solid."

For Christian Somes to see the "ripples on the water," we may need to empty ourselves of what we think we see already and embrace something of the "nothingness" that Nones are bringing to the threshold experience. In this we are not Nones, but we are *not* not-Nones. We also may need to recognize when we are church but *not* behaving as church, perhaps starting with an apology for helping to create hard categories of religious affiliation in which we see others as "nothing" until they have been conquered and formed in our own image. At least we need to ask, "When are we church, when are we not church, and when are we *not* not-church?" We also need to ask whether the "ripples on the water" are the result of our own hidden stories that have cracks, inconsistencies, and intentional obfuscations in them, and that often lack a grammar that resonates with agape-love.

Beyond this, as Christians we might see the "ripples on the water" as the place where our flat-earth stories are about to change. Instead of responding anxiously and doubling down on dogma, we might consider how churches could become places of *narrative incubation* where there is an atmosphere of "come and see" (John 1:39) that allows for new stories to emerge. As Ryan Burge reminds us, behind every data point in the analysis of the religiously unaffiliated is a human being with a story to tell. "Whatever their motives, we should be seeking out people willing to tell their stories, inviting them to tell us, and listening—really listening—to them."[26] How might we become safe houses for the revealing of spiritual stories—almost like a spiritually-focused StoryCorps or spoken word—with an emphasis on deep listening, critical self-reflection with pedagogical tools of interiority, and an experiential and energizing resonance with agape-love? And, of course, this would require becoming

26. Burge, *The Nones*, 129.

places of *narrative experimentation* as we develop prototypes of thinking and acting where we work out how to apply the energy of agape-love to all of our relationships.

To become safe houses of *narrative incubation* and *narrative experimentation*, we may need to revise our understanding of the roles played in the body of Christ. While not denying or diminishing the roles defined for the body of Christ as found in Rom 12: 3–8, 1 Cor 12:4–26, or Eph 4:4–7, other creative roles to consider would be: (1) *evidence collectors*—those who are gifted in seeing the real evidence that emerges from the data of our relationships; (2) *alignment educators*—those gifted with discerning when we are in or out of harmony with the centrating energy of creation; (3) *depth practitioners*—those gifted with awareness of the differences between the ego-mind and the mind of Christ; (4) *process pedagogues*—those gifted with the process for changing the inner mind and changing the invisible stories in individuals, organizations, and society; (5) *prototype developers*—those gifted with bringing visions of what can be, or what is coming, into the reality of what can be done now; (6) *narrative incubators*—those gifted with evoking and safely holding the stories that emerge from the place of unknowing and unsaying; (7) *marketplace evaluators*—those gifted with discerning where marketplace dialogue and story incubation is happening or can happen, whether inside a church building or not; (8) *perscrutators*—those who are "seekers of pearls"[27] who embody a wisdom that comes when knowledge is deepened with love, and who have an intuition about the "pearl of great value" (Matt 13:46) and the "twelve pearls" (Rev 21:21) that represent the gates to the heavenly Jerusalem. These roles could be exercised without regard for race, gender, nationality, sexuality, and, at times, religion. The one requirement would be a commitment to the health and wholeness of the one body in the spirit of love as ambassadors of reconciliation (see 2 Cor 5:18–20) who seek the reconciliation of all things.[28]

Perhaps an *apology* is in order when we see the threshold as simply the threshold of a church door with you as a None on the outside and Christian Somes on the inside. The real threshold is far bigger than that and involves transformational matters of the heart, mind, and soul where we are challenged to see what we cannot see and hear what we cannot

27. Delio, *Unbearable Wholeness*, 140.

28. See Acts 3:21 and the various translations of *'apokatastáseos pántov*.

hear. Perhaps the *appeal* is to discover that other threshold together with its infinite possibilities.

But it is undeniably for all of us, whether we identify as Nones or Somes, a place of "threshing" where the husks of our defenses must be removed, the carapaces of our meaning-making must be shattered, and the coconut shells of our cultural encapsulation must be broken open. Again and again and again. Until we find ourselves in the place outside of, beyond, or "betwixt and between" the husks, the carapaces, or the coconut shells. And we become aware that we are not only standing on a threshold, but we are also becoming *at one* with the *threshold* and *at one* with the *process* of the revealing of still hidden truths.

Bibliography

Ahlstrom, Sydney E. *A Religious History of the American People*. New Haven: Yale University Press, 1972.

Ammerman, Nancy T. "Spiritual but Not Religious? Beyond Binary Choices in the Study of Religion." *Journal for the Scientific Study of Religion* 52.2 (2013) 258–78.

Asquith, Glenn H. Jr., ed. *Vision from a Little Known Country*. Decatur, GA: Journal of Pastoral Care, 1992.

Atwood, Margaret. *The Handmaid's Tale*. New York: Anchor, 1998.

———. *The Testaments*. New York: Doubleday, 2019.

Augsburger, David. "Interpathy Re-Envisioned: Reflecting on Observed Practice of Mutuality by Counselors Who Muddle Along Cultural Boundaries or Are Thrown into a Wholly Strange Location." *Reflective Practice: Formation and Supervision in Ministry* 34.1 (2014) 11–22.

———. *Pastoral Counseling Across Cultures*. Philadelphia: Westminster, 1986.

Barnhart, Robert K., ed. *Chambers Dictionary of Etymology*. New York: H. W. Wilson, 1988.

Bass, Diana B. "The Future of Faith as the Way of Salvation." *Oneing* 7.2 (2019) 49–55.

Baumeister, Roy F. *Meanings of Life*. New York: Guilford, 1991.

Bender, Cortney. *The New Metaphysicals: Spirituality and the American Religious Imagination*. Chicago: Chicago University Press, 2010.

Berry, Wendell. *Jayber Crow*. New York: Counterpoint, 2000.

Bonhoeffer, Dietrich. *Letters and Papers from Prison: The Enlarged Edition*. London: SCM, 1971.

Bourgeault, Cynthia. *The Heart of Centering Prayer: Nondual Christianity in Theory and Practice*. Boulder, CO: Shambala, 2016.

Bowen, Murray. *Family Therapy in Clinical Practice*. Northvale, NJ: Jason Aronson, 1988.

Brenner, Charles. *An Elementary Textbook of Psychoanalysis*. Revised edition. Garden City, NY: Anchor, 1974.

Bright, Bill. "Four Spiritual Laws." 2007. https://campusministry.org/docs/tools/FourSpiritualLaws.pdf.

Browning, Donald S. *Religious Thought and the Modern Psychologies*. Philadelphia: Fortress, 1987.

Bruteau, Beatrice. *The Holy Thursday Revolution*. New York: Orbis, 2005.

Burge, Ryan P. *The Nones: Where They Came From, Who They Are, and Where They Are Going*. Minneapolis: Fortress, 2021.

Burton, Tara I. "Our Civil Religion Is Business. The Virus Response Proves It." *The Washington Post*, March 29, 2020.

―――. *Strange Rites: New Religions for a Godless World*. New York: Public Affairs, 2020.

Cannon, Dale. *Six Ways of Being Religious*. Belmont, CA: Wadsworth, 1996.

Carrette, Jeremy, and Richard King. *Selling Spirituality: The Silent Takeover of Religion*. New York: Routledge, 2005.

Cashwell, Craig S., Philip B. Clark, and Elizabeth G. Graves. "Step by Step: Avoiding Spiritual Bypass in 12-Step Work." *Journal of Addictions & Offender Counseling* 30.1 (2009) 37–48.

Cashwell, Craig S., Jane E. Myers, and W. Matthew Shurts. "Using the Developmental Counseling and Therapy Model to Work with a Client in Spiritual Bypass: Some Preliminary Considerations." *Journal of Counseling & Development* 82.4 (2004) 403–09.

Catechism of the Catholic Church. Second edition. New York: Doubleday, 1995.

Cawley, Luke. *The Myth of the Non-Christians: Engaging Atheists, Nominal Christians, and the Spiritual but Not Religious*. Downers Grove, IL: Intervarsity, 2016.

The Century of the Self. TV program. Directed by Adam Curtis. Aired 2002. London: RDF Television BBC.

Ceriello, Linda C. "Toward a Metamodern Reading of Spiritual but Not Religious." In *Being Spiritual but Not Religious: Past, Present, Future(s)*, edited by William B. Parsons, 200–218. New York: Routledge, 2018.

Coakley, Sarah, and Charles M. Stang, eds. *Rethinking Dionysius the Areopagite*. Chichester, UK: Wiley-Blackwell, 2009.

Conley, Garrard. *Boy Erased: A Memoir of Identity, Faith, and Family*. New York: Riverhead, 2016.

―――. "Land of Plenty." In *Empty the Pews: Stories of Leaving the Church*, edited by Chrissy Stroop and Lauren O'Neal, 29–38. Indianapolis: Epiphany, 2019.

Craddock, Fred B. *Overhearing the Gospel: Preaching and Teaching the Faith to Persons Who Have Already Heard*. Nashville: Abingdon, 1978.

Daniel, Lillian. *When "Spiritual but Not Religious" Is Not Enough: Seeing God in Surprising Places, Even the Church*. New York: Jericho, 2013.

Davidson, Richard J., and Sharon Begley. *The Emotional Life of Your Brain*. New York: Plume, 2013.

Dean, Kenda Creasy. *Almost Christian: What the Faith of Our Teenagers Is Telling the American Church*. New York: Oxford University Press, 2010.

de Catanzaro, C. J., trans. *Symeon the New Theologian: The Discourses*. Mahwah, NJ: Paulist, 1980.

Delio, Ilia. *The Emergent Christ: Exploring the Meaning of Catholic in an Evolutionary Universe*. Maryknoll, NY: Orbis, 2011.

―――. *The Unbearable Wholeness of Being: God, Evolution, and the Power of Love*. Maryknoll, NY: Orbis, 2013.

Diagnostic and Statistical Manual of Mental Disorders: DSM-5. Arlington, VA: American Psychiatric Association, 2013.

Dickinson, Emily. *The Complete Poems of Emily Dickinson*. Edited by T. H. Johnson. Boston: Little, Brown, & Company, 1960.

Doehring, Carrie. *The Practice of Pastoral Care: A Postmodern Approach*. Revised edition. Louisville: Westminster John Knox, 2015.

Drescher, Elizabeth. *Choosing Our Religion: The Spiritual Lives of America's Nones*. New York: Oxford University Press, 2016.

Ecklund, Elaine H., and Di Di. "Global Spirituality Among Scientists." In *Being Spiritual but Not Religious: Past, Present, Future(s)*, edited by William B. Parsons, 163–78. New York: Routledge, 2018.

Fairless, Caroline S. *The Space between Church and Not-Church: A Sacramental Vision for the Healing of Our Planet*. Lanham, MD: Hamilton, 2011.

Ferrer, Jorge N., and William Z. Vickery. "Transpersonal Psychology and the Spiritual but Not Religious Movement." In *Being Spiritual but Not Religious: Past, Present, Future(s)*, edited by William B. Parsons, 219–35. New York: Routledge, 2018.

Fitzpatrick, Sean, and William B. Parsons. "The Triumph of the Therapeutic and Being Spiritual but Not Religious." In *Being Spiritual but Not Religious: Past, Present, Future(s)*, edited by William B. Parsons, 30–44. New York: Routledge, 2018.

Foley, Edward. "Reflective Believing: Reimagining Theological Reflection in an Age of Diversity." *Reflective Practice: Formation and Supervision in Ministry* 34.1 (2014) 60–75.

———. *Theological Reflection across Religious Traditions: The Turn to Reflective Believing*. Lanham, MD: Rowman & Littlefield, 2015.

Fox, Jesse, Craig S. Cashwell, and Gabriela Picciotto. "The Opiate of the Masses: Measuring Spiritual Bypass and its Relationship to Spirituality, Religion, Mindfulness, Psychological Distress, and Personality." *Spirituality in Clinical Practice* 4.4 (2017) 274–87.

Francis, Pope. *Laudato si'*. 2015. https://www.vatican.va/content/dam/francesco/pdf/encyclicals/documents/papa-francesco_20150524_enciclica-laudato-si_en.pdf.

Franke, William. *On the Universality of What Is Not: The Apophatic Turn in Critical Thinking*. Notre Dame, IN: University of Notre Dame Press, 2020.

Freire, Paulo. *Pedagogy of the Oppressed*. New York: Seabury, 1970.

Friedman, Edwin H. *A Failure of Nerve: Leadership in an Age of the Quick Fix*. New York: Church Publishing, 2007.

Fuller, Robert C. "Minds of Their Own: Psychological Substrates of the Spiritual but Not Religious Sensibility." In *Being Spiritual but Not Religious: Past, Present, Future(s)*, edited by William B. Parsons, 89–109. New York: Routledge, 2018.

Fuller, Robert C., and William B. Parsons. "Spiritual but Not Religious: A Brief Introduction." In *Being Spiritual but Not Religious: Past, Present, Future(s)*, edited by William B. Parsons, 15–29. New York: Routledge, 2018.

Gadamer, Hans-Georg. *Truth and Method*. Second revised edition. New York: Continuum, 1994.

Gassin, Elizabeth A., and Stephen J. Muse. "Beloved of God: An Eastern Orthodox Anthology." In *The Psychologies in Religion: Working With the Religious Client*, edited by E. Thomas Dowd and Steven L. Nielsen, 51–68. New York: Springer, 2006.

Gates, Henry L. Jr. *The Black Church: This Is Our Story, This Is Our Song*. New York: Penguin, 2021.

Gates, James. "Symbols of Power: Adinkras and the Nature of Reality." *Physics World* 23.6 (2010) 34–39.

Gault, Matthew. "Climate Change Is Breaking Open America's Nuclear Tomb." *Vice*, November 11, 2019. https://www.vice.com/en_us/article/3kxmav/climate-change-is-breaking-open-americas-nuclear-tomb.

God in America. A Nation Reborn: Of God and Caesar. DVD. Directed by Sarah Colt. 2010. Arlington County, VA: Public Broadcasting Service.

Graham, Elaine, Heather Walton, and Frances Ward. *Theological Reflection: Methods.* London: SCM, 2005.

Griffith, James L. *Religion that Heals, Religion that Harms: A Guide for Clinical Practice.* New York: Guilford, 2010.

Gunderson, Gary. *Boundary Leaders: Leadership Skills for People of Faith.* Minneapolis: Fortress, 2004.

Hall, G. Stanley. *Jesus, the Christ, in Light of Psychology.* New York: Doubleday, 1917.

Hanh, Thich Nhat. *The Heart of Understanding: Commentaries on the Prajnaparamita Heart Sutra.* Berkeley, CA: Parallax, 2009.

————. *Living Buddha, Living Christ.* New York: Riverhead, 1995.

Hart, David B. *The Experience of God: Being, Consciousness, Bliss.* New Haven: Yale University Press, 2013.

————. *That All Shall Be Saved: Heaven, Hell, & Universal Salvation.* New Haven: Yale University Press, 2019.

Hedstrom, Matthew S. "Buddhist Fulfillment of a Protestant Dream: Mindfulness as Scientific Spirituality." In *Being Spiritual but Not Religious: Past, Present, Future(s),* edited by William B. Parsons, 57–71. New York: Routledge, 2018.

Howells, Edward. "Apophatic Spirituality." In *The New Westminster Dictionary of Christian Spirituality,* edited by Philip Sheldrake, 117–19. Louisville: Westminster John Knox, 2005.

Jain, Andrea R. "Yogi Superman, Master Capitalist: Bikram Choudhury and the Religion of Commercial Spirituality." In *Being Spiritual but Not Religious: Past, Present, Future(s),* edited by William B. Parsons, 146–62. New York: Routledge, 2018.

Jeffery, Steve, Michael Ovey, and Andrew Sach. *Pierced for Our Transgressions: Rediscovering the Glory of Penal Substitution.* Wheaton, IL: Crossway, 2007.

Jung, C. G. *Aion: Researches into the Phenomenology of the Self.* Edited by H. Read, M. Fordham, G. Adler, and W. McGuire. The Collected Works of C. G. Jung, Volume 9, Part II. Princeton: Princeton University Press, 1959.

————. *The Undiscovered Self.* The New American Library. New York: Mentor Books, 1957.

Kabat-Zinn, Jon. *Full Catastrophe Living.* Revised edition. New York: Bantam, 2013.

Kadloubovsky, E., and G. E. H. Palmer, trans. *Writings from the Philokalia on Prayer of the Heart.* London: Faber and Faber, 1951.

Kavanaugh, Kieran, ed. *John of the Cross: Selected Writings.* Mahwah, NJ: Paulist, 1987.

Keating, Thomas. *Intimacy with God.* New York: Crossroad, 1994.

Kegan, Robert. *The Evolving Self: Problem and Process in Human Development.* Cambridge: Harvard University Press, 1982.

Kelly, Jason J. "Rogue Mystics: The Ecology of Cosmic Consciousness." In *Being Spiritual but Not Religious: Past, Present, Future(s),* edited by William B. Parsons, 181–99. New York: Routledge, 2018.

Kielsmeier-Cook, Stina. *Blessed Are the Nones: Mixed-Faith Marriage and My Search for Spiritual Community.* Downers Grove, IL: Intervarsity, 2020.

Kierkegaard, Søren. *Concluding Unscientific Postscript.* Translated by D. Swenson and W. Lowrie. Princeton: Princeton University Press, 1941.

Kingsolver, Barbara. *The Poisonwood Bible.* New York: HarperCollins, 1998.

Kohut, Heinz. *The Analysis of the Self.* Madison, CT: International Universities Press, 1987.

Laird, Martin. *An Ocean of Light: Contemplation, Transformation, and Liberation.* New York: Oxford University Press, 2019.

———. *A Sunlit Absence: Silence, Awareness, and Contemplation.* New York: Oxford University Press, 2011.

Lasch, Christopher. *The Culture of Narcissism.* New York: Warner, 1979.

Levinovitz, Alan. "Goop Teaches Us We Can Be Pure—If We Spend Enough Money." *The Washington Post,* January 19, 2020.

Lewis, C. S. *Mere Christianity.* Revised edition. London: Fontana, 1955.

Lewis, H. D. "Self, Philosophy of." In *Dictionary of Pastoral Care and Counseling,* edited by R. J. Hunter, 1125–26. Nashville: Abingdon, 1990.

Lim, Chaeyoon, Carol A. MacGregor, and Robert D. Putnam. "Secular and Liminal: Discovering Heterogeneity among Religious Nones." *Journal for the Scientific Study of Religion* 49.4 (2010) 596–618.

Manning, Cristel. *Losing Our Religion: How Unaffiliated Parents Are Raising their Children.* New York: New York University Press, 2015.

Mapp, Alf J. Jr. *The Faiths of Our Fathers: What American Founders Really Believed.* Lanham, MD: Rowman and Littlefield, 2005.

Marion, Jim. *Putting on the Mind of Christ: The Inner Work of Christian Spirituality.* Charlottesvile, VA: Hampton Roads, 2011.

Marz, Megan. "There's an Exodus from Christianity. These Onetime Believers Explain Why." *The Washington Post,* January 19, 2020.

McArthur, Shirin. "The Future of Christianity in a Global Context: A Conversation with Wesley Granberg-Michaelson." *Oneing* 7.2 (2019) 83–90.

McEntee, Rory, and Adam Bucko. *The New Monasticism: An Interspiritual Manifesto for Contemplative Living.* Maryknoll, NY: Orbis, 2015.

McLaren, Brian D. *The Great Spiritual Migration: How the World's Largest Religion Is Seeking a Better Way to Be Christian.* New York: Convergent, 2016.

Mercadante, Linda A. *Belief without Borders: Inside the Minds of the Spiritual but Not Religious.* New York: Oxford University Press, 2014.

Meredith, Anthony. *Gregory of Nyssa.* New York: Routledge, 1999.

Merton, Thomas. *Conjectures of a Guilty Bystander.* New York: Image, 2014.

Mitchell, Mark T. *The Limits of Liberalism: Tradition, Individualism, and the Crisis of Freedom.* Notre Dame, IN: University of Notre Dame Press, 2019.

Mozley, J. K. *The Doctrine of Atonement.* London, England: Gerald Duckworth, 1915.

Myers, Ched, and Elaine Enns. *Ambassadors of Reconciliation, Volume 1: New Testament Reflections on Restorative Justice and Peacemaking.* Maryknoll, NY: Orbis, 2009.

Needleman, Jacob. *Lost Christianity: A Journey of Rediscovery.* New York: Penguin, 2003.

Nelson, Anne. *Shadow Network: Media, Money, and the Secret Hub of the Radical Right.* New York: Bloomsbury, 2020.

Newberg, Andrew, and Mark R. Waldman. *How God Changes Your Brain.* New York: Ballantine, 2009.

Nicolaou, Corinna. *A None's Story: Searching for Meaning Inside Christianity, Judaism, Buddhism, and Islam.* New York: Columbia University Press, 2016.

Niebuhr, H. Richard. *Christ and Culture.* New York: Harper and Row, 1951.

Oakes, Kaya. *The Nones Are Alright: A New Generation of Believers, Seekers, and Those in Between.* Maryknoll, NY: Orbis, 2015.

O'Donohue, John. *To Bless the Space between Us: A Book of Blessings.* New York: Doubleday, 2008.

Panksepp, Jaak, and Lucy Biven. *The Archaeology of Mind: Neuroevolutionary Origins of Human Emotions.* New York: W. W. Norton, 2012.

Parsons, William B., ed. *Being Spiritual but Not Religious: Past, Present, Future(s).* New York: Routledge, 2018.

Peck, M. Scott. *People of the Lie: The Hope for Healing Human Evil.* New York: Simon and Schuster, 1983.

Peterson, Christopher. *A Primer in Positive Psychology.* New York: Oxford University Press, 2006.

Pevateaux, Chad J. "Being Spiritual but Not Hierarchical." In *Being Spiritual but Not Religious: Past, Present, Future(s),* edited by William B. Parsons, 236–52. New York: Routledge, 2018.

Pew Forum. "In US, Decline of Christianity Continues at Rapid Pace." October 17, 2019. http://pewforum.org/2019/10/17/in-u-s-decline-of-christianity-continues-at-rapid-pace/.

———. "'Nones' on the Rise." October 9, 2012. https://www.pewforum.org/2012/10/09/nones-on-the-rise/

Polanyi, Michael. *Personal Knowledge: Towards a Post-Critical Philosophy.* Chicago: University of Chicago Press, 1962.

———. *Science, Faith, and Society.* Chicago: University of Chicago Press, 1946.

———. *The Tacit Dimension.* Gloucester, MA: Peter Smith, 1983.

Putnam, Robert D. *The Upswing: How America Came Together a Century Ago and How We Can Do It Again.* New York: Simon and Schuster, 2020.

Putnam, Robert D., and David E. Campbell. *American Grace: How Religion Divides and Unites Us.* New York: Simon and Schuster, 2010.

Rao, D. C. "Understanding Hinduism: Basic Concepts Explained." The American Foundation. https://www.hinduamerican.org/wp-content/uploads/2020/03/Understanding-Hinduism-Basic-Questions-Answered-DC-Rao.pdf.

Rieff, Philip. *The Triumph of the Therapeutic.* New York: Harper, 1966.

Rinpoche, Yongey Mingyur. *The Joy of Living: Unlocking the Secret & Science of Happiness.* New York: Three Rivers, 2007.

Roberts, Alexander, and James Donaldson. *The Ante-Nicene Fathers: The Writings of the Fathers Down to AD 325. Vol. 1: The Apostolic Fathers, Justin Martyr, Irenaeus.* Peabody, MA: Hendrickson, 1994.

Roberts, Rachel. *Confessions of an American None: A Credo of Sorts.* United States: American None, 2020.

Rodgerson, Thomas E. "Attending to Hidden Realities: Contributions from the Work of Michael Polanyi to Supervision in Pastoral Care and Counseling." *Journal of Pastoral Care and Counseling* 62.3 (2008) 195–206.

———. "Clergy Self-Renewal Themes in Clinical Practice." In *Clinician's Guide to Self-Renewal: Essential Advice from the Field,* edited by Robert J. Wicks and Elizabeth A. Maynard, 397–419. Hoboken, NJ: John Wiley & Sons, 2014.

———. "To Diagnose or Not to Diagnose: Pastoral Counseling Distinctives in Conceptualizing and Engaging Human Distress." In *Understanding Pastoral Counseling,* edited by Elizabeth A. Maynard and Jill L. Snodgrass, 101–13. New York: Springer 2015.

Rogers, Carl R. *On Becoming a Person*. Boston: Houghton Mifflin, 1961.

———. *A Way of Being*. Boston: Houghton Mifflin, 1980.

Rogers-Vaughn, Bruce. "Pastoral Counseling in the Neoliberal Age: Hello Best Practices, Goodbye Theology." *Sacred Spaces: The E-Journal of the American Association of Pastoral Counselors* 5 (2013) 5–45. http://www.aapc.org/media/127298/2_rogers_vaughn.

Rohr, Richard. "Contemplative Consciousness: Action and Contemplation." January 19, 2020. https://cac.org/contemplative-consciousness-2020-01-19/.

———. "Contemplative Consciousness: Wounded Healers." September 18, 2020. https://cac.org/transforming-our-pain-2020-09-18/.

———. *The Divine Dance: The Trinity and Your Transformation*. New Kensington, PA: Whitaker House, 2016.

———. "Mystics and the Margins: Margins Create Liminal Space." September 27, 2020. https://cac.org/margins-create-liminal-space-2020-09-27/.

———. *The Universal Christ*. New York: Convergent, 2019.

Rushforth. Winifred. *Something Is Happening: Spiritual Awareness and Depth Psychology in the New Age*. Wellingborough, Northamptonshire, UK: Turnstone, 1981.

Sacks, Jonathan. *The Dignity of Difference*. New York: Continuum International, 2002.

———. *Morality: Restoring the Common Good in Divided Times*. New York: Basic Books, 2020.

Scharmer, C. Otto. *Theory U: Leading from the Future as It Emerges*. San Francisco, CA: Berrett-Koehler, 2009.

Scheidt, Michelle A. "Out of the Closet and Out of the Church: The Spiritual Lives of Queer People Who Are Spiritual but Not Religious." PhD diss., Chicago Theological Seminary, 2017.

Schliermacher, Friedrich. *On Religion: Speeches to Its Cultured Despisers*. Translated by J. Oman. New York: Frederick Ungar, 1955.

Schmidt, Leigh E. "The Death-of-God Theology and the Birth of the SBNR Sensibility." In *Being Spiritual but Not Religious: Past, Present, Future(s)*, edited by William B. Parsons, 45–56. New York: Routledge, 2019.

Senge, Peter M. *The Fifth Dimension: The Art and Practice of the Learning Organization*. Revised edition. New York: Doubleday, 2006.

Shakespeare, William. *Love's Labour's Lost*. Edited by William A. Wright. New York: Doubleday, 1936.

———. *A Midsummer-Night's Dream*. Edited by William A. Wright. New York: Doubleday, 1936.

Siegel, Dan J. *Mind: A Journey to the Heart of Being Human*. New York: W. W. Norton, 2017.

Singh, Kathleen D. *The Grace in Dying: A Message of Hope, Comfort, and Spiritual Transformation*. New York: HarperCollins, 2000.

Smith, Paul R. *Integral Christianity: The Spirit's Call to Evolve*. St. Paul, MN: Paragon House, 2011.

Stearn, Jess. *Yoga, Youth, and Reincarnation*. New York: Doubleday, 1965.

Stein, Edward. "Reactions to Dr. Oden's 'Recovering Lost Identity.'" *Journal of Pastoral Care* 34.1 (1980) 20–23.

Strawn, Kelley D. "What's Behind the 'Nones-Sense'? Change over Time in Factors Predicting Likelihood of Religious Nonaffiliation in the United States." *Journal for the Scientific Study of Religion* 58.3 (2019) 707–24.

Stroop, Chrissy, and Lauren O'Neal, eds. *Empty the Pews: Stories of Leaving Church.* Indianapolis: Epiphany, 2019.

Sugiuchi, Diedre. "Fundamentalist." In *Empty the Pews: Stories of Leaving Church,* edited by Chrissy Stroop and Lauren O'Neal, 119–28. Indianapolis: Epiphany, 2019.

Tamir, Christine, Aidan Connaughton, and Ariana Monique Salazar. "The Global God Divide." July 20, 2020. https://www.pewresearch.org/global/2020/07/20/the-global-god-divide/.

Tan, Chade-Meng. *Search inside Yourself: The Unexpected Path to Achieving Success, Happiness, (and World Peace).* New York: HarperCollins, 2012.

Thiessen, Joel, and Sarah Wilkins-Laflamme. *None of the Above: Non-Religious Identity in the US and Canada.* New York: New York University Press, 2020.

Tickle, Phyllis. *The Great Emergence: How Christianity Is Changing and Why.* Grand Rapids, MI: Baker, 2008.

Tippett, Krista. *Becoming Wise: An Inquiry into the Mystery and Art of Living.* New York: Penguin, 2016.

Torrey, R. A., and A. C. Dixon, eds. *The Fundamentals: A Testimony to the Truth.* Grand Rapids, MI: Baker, 2003.

Turkle, Sherry. *Reclaiming Conversation: The Power of Talk in a Digital Age.* New York: Penguin, 2015.

Turner, Victor. *The Ritual Process: Structure and Anti-Structure (Foundations of Human Behavior). 1969.* Reprint, New York: Routledge, 2017.

Van Gelder, Craig, and Dwight J. Zscheile. *Participating in God's Mission: A Theological Missiology for the Church in America.* Grand Rapids, MI: Eerdmans, 2018.

Vick, Karl. "Trial by Fury: Scandal Sentenced Ted Haggard to a New Life." *The Washington Post,* January 25, 2009.

The Way of a Pilgrim. Middletown, DE: Magdalene, 2015.

What the Bleep Do We Know? DVD. Directed by Mark Vicente, Betsy Chasse, and William Arntz. *2004.* Beverly Hills: Twentieth Century Fox.

Weber, Max. *The Protestant Ethic and the Spirit of Capitalism.* Oxford, UK: Backwell, 2002.

Webster's New Twentieth Century Dictionary, Unabridged. Edited by Jean L. McKechnie. Second edition. New York: Collings & World, 1975.

Wells, Mel. "Burden of Proof." In *Empty the Pews: Stories of Leaving Church,* edited by Chrissy Stroop and Lauren O'Neal, 155–63. Indianapolis: Epiphany, 2019.

Wells, Samuel. *Improvisation: The Drama of Christian Ethics.* Grand Rapids, MI: Brazos, 2004.

Wellwood, John. *Love and Awakening; Discovering the Sacred Path of Intimate Relationship.* New York: Harper Collins, 1996.

Wheatley, Margaret J. *Leadership and the New Science: Discovering Order in a Chaotic World.* Third edition. San Francisco: Berrett-Koehler, 2006.

White, James E. *The Rise of the Nones: Understanding and Reaching the Religiously Unaffiliated.* Grand Rapids, MI: Baker, 2014.

Wicks, Robert J. *Prayerfulness: Awakening to the Fullness of Life.* Notre Dame, IN: Sorin, 2009.

———, ed. *Prayer in the Catholic Tradition: A Handbook of Practical Approaches.* Cincinnati: Franciscan Media, 2016.

Wiggins-Frame, Marsha. "Spirituality and Religion: Similarities and Differences." In *Integrating Spirituality and Religion into Counseling,* edited by Craig S. Cashwell and J. Scott Young, 11–25. Alexandria, VA: American Counseling Association, 2005.

Wikipedia. "Transcendentalism." https://en.wikipedia.org/wiki/Transcendentalism.

Wilber, Ken. *Integral Spirituality.* Boston: Integral, 2006.

———. *The Religion of Tomorrow: A Vision for the Future of the Great Traditions.* Boulder, CO: Shambhala, 2017.

Wilcox, Melissa M. "Consuming Spirituality: SBNR and Neoliberal Logic in Queer Communities." In *Being Spiritual but Not Religious: Past, Present, Future(s),* edited by William B. Parsons, 128–45. New York: Routledge, 2018.

Williams, Peter W. *America's Religions: Traditions and Cultures.* Chicago: University of Illinois Press, 1998.

Wittgenstein, Ludwig. *Philosophical Investigations.* Fourth revised edition. Edited by Gertrude Anscombe, Peter Hacker, and Joachim Schulte. Chichester, West Sussex, UK: Wiley-Blackwell, 2009.

Wright, N. T. *Paul and the Faithfulness of God.* Minneapolis: Fortress, 2013.

Wuthnow, Robert. *After the Baby Boomers: How Twenty- and Thirty-Somethings Are Shaping the Future of American Religion.* Princeton: Princeton University Press, 2007.

———. *After Heaven: Spirituality in America Since the 1950s.* Berkeley, CA: University of California Press, 1998.

Index

9 781666 716191